Th
Nov

CW00868046

by

David Meah

Copyright © 2019 by David Meah

All rights reserved. This book or any portion thereof may not be reproduced or used in any manner whatsoever without the express written permission of the publisher except for the use of brief quotations in a book review or scholarly journal.

Published by David Meah

Cover illustration by Angela Johnson

First Printing: 2019

ISBN: 978-0-244-76100-4

CONTENTS

Acknowledgements

I would like to thank my family, without whose understanding of my madness; this book would never have been completed.

Thank you for your patience.

Thank you to my work colleges who were pained in the writing of this book. Zara, Sandra, John, and Gareth for taking the time to check it and point out the little-detailed facts. For having taken the time to assure and encourage me to continue.

A special thank you to Angela Johnson for her creative art, producing the cover.

Andy Hall again for the endless conversations and his fearful bus journeys to and from work, while reading an entire chapter after chapter to guide me for a continuance.
Much appreciated.

Most of all, to all the readers who have taken the time to acknowledge and read my work.

Thank you.

David.

INTRODUCTION

The landscape has lost its colour, the green of the grass disappearing under the whiteness of snow. The trees now bare from the autumn season, allowing no shelter from the sharp, cold, and intense north-east winds. The bleak harshness of the freezing winter is settling in fast, the temperature dropping below zero for the first time in many a year.

The year is 1963; the winter months are unforgiving, the severe weather taking its toll on this tiny island of ours.

With the lakes and rivers frozen, even parts of the sea. Ice patches stretching miles, leaving fishing boats motionless, trapped in an eerie lifeless harbour, with mountainous snow drifts some thirty feet high. The murderous winter leaving lines of frozen, dead sea life indented and fossilized into the thick ice, far across the horizon.

The countryside also not escaping the blight and torment of this winter season, displaying fantastic bizarre, and unusual scenes. Waterfalls iced over, solid like decorative garden centrepieces, the rivers solid like glaciers dividing the land.

Livestock separated from their farms, searching, foraging for food from the little shrubbery and foliage left behind. The local wildlife suffering, frozen in glassy icy cages.

The arctic conditions bringing the nation to its knees, almost at a standstill. Thousands of schools closed, with thousands more telephone lines down disrupting communications. Industries, halted with the transport network almost non-existent, the endless miles of empty snow-covered motorways, along with the railway lines submerged under three feet of snow. Coal mines deserted, too dangerous to work, due to the risk of flooding, leaving no fuel for the power stations, triggering the blackouts. Darkness enveloping this small Island of ours in twilight, after the short daylight hours of winter close in.

To most, this was a time of fun, skating, sledging, and snowman making.

To others misery and illness, even death.

Chapter 1

ALONE

The sun edges out from behind the clouds, high against the white sky, sending glimmers of light in all directions, as it reflects on the icy road.

The glare from the road penetrates the car window, splaying a multitude of colour dazzling through. The driver squints distorting his view from the path ahead. Carefully he steers his vehicle, heading onwards to his destination.

The pale blue VW Beetle jitters down the icy isolated cobbled streets, exhaust fumes churning out, exaggerated by the chilly air.

Charcoal coloured smoke plumes rise out above from the chimneys on the rows of snow-covered terraced houses on either side. The red-brick jungle, the housing of the working classes.

Cliff Richard's Bachelor boy's playing on the car radio. Inside, the two occupants are joyfully singing along.

The unlikely pair, a tall 5ft 7 inches' fair-faced brunette, seated in the passenger seat, her hazel eyes, sparkle as she gazes across at her husband. A tall, dark, handsome, well-dressed man from Bangladesh. Hair neatly combed over, his bright blue suit and high collared pale shirt, with his pencil-thin black tie, complimenting his dark complexion, reminiscent of the pop stars of the day, while he's driving and singing, his accent not quite matching the radio.

Feeling her stare, attentively he turns to his wife, "Jane, are you happy?" his face kind and genuinely in love. Without a thought, and without notice, Jane leans over and pecks him on his cheek.

"Of course, Khalil, my handsome husband ...I'll love you to the end of my days," her radiant smile beaming as she touches his hand. Her soft light touches comforting; she squeezes a little tighter. Khalil pulls up by the kerb. They kiss, a lingering kiss on the lips, time stops momentarily. She smiles another smile at him as he returns his attention directly to the road. Khalil pleased, happy, and content continues their journey. Jane relaxes, her back fitting snugly into her seat; fond memories play again in her mind.

It was the second Friday of June 1955, 12:30 PM in LEEDS at the Roundhay Park lake; the hot sun warming the lush green fields stretching out as far as the eye could see, the hills smothered in yellow buttercups shimmering in the bright sun light, the lake a deep blue, rippling along with the light summer breeze.

Jane strolls along with her friends, walking down the path running by the side of the lake, enjoying the slightly cool breeze refreshing her body, their escape during their dinner hour, away from the daily factory life, and the blistering heat from the machines and the warmth from the outdoor heat penetrating through the glassed roof windows.

4

It's a glorious day; the suns' rays beating down hard. The temperature soaring into the mid-twenties. Jane and her friends rest by the ice-cream stand, accepting the cool refreshing taste of the vanilla cones, soothing their parched throats.

Khalil makes his way along the cobbled path, taking his usual afternoon walk. He passes the group at the ice cream stand to his right. Jane blushes for no reason, other than Khalil had caught her eye. Milly Tafferton observing this, asked, "Hey Jane, what you are looking at" her own eyes spotting him too. "He's gorgeous isn't he" Jane questions, not taking her eyes away from him, his tall but masculine slender figure topped off with the darkest wavy pompadour hairstyle, and had his complexion been fair you would have sworn you had just seen the famous actor, Montgomery Cliffe. "Oh, he's so dreamy" Jane continued. "He is, but he's a Paki, so even if I wanted to go with him, I couldn't, Dad would skelp me hard, so I guess I won't interfere" nodded Milly, a little malice in her voice yet somewhat a little disappointed. Milly was one of those girls who had the looks, a typical 36 – 24 - 36 figure the type of girl who knew if she wanted you, you would. She was a beauty beyond beauty, trouble was her parents were the ones who took charge of the matters of her heart, and no way would she dare to disappoint.

Jane was quite the opposite of Milly, and Jane being Jane, took things as she saw them, and having a mind of her own, she did pretty much what she liked, getting into trouble more times than it was worth. Once she got an idea in her head, she was pretty much determined to see it through.

Jane had moved out from her parents' home some six years earlier when she was nineteen; her father had used his belt on her after a drunken row over the boy she was seeing.

This was the last straw, the last time he would ever strike or raise his hand to her, no longer being his punch bag, no longer being the one he took his frustration out of.

She did sympathise with him on losing his wife, her mum, to illness when she was fourteen years old, and him struggling to bring up his only daughter, on his own, but after so many years of his beatings, she vowed never to step foot in his home again and never had.

Now living on her own and very independent, she did pretty much what and when she wanted.

Khalil continued to amble down the path, taking in the cool breeze, taking advantage of the beautiful surroundings. The lakeside to his right was going berserk, the horde of ducks was frantic, eating the offerings from the many afternoon strollers, tossing breadcrumbs into the lake. Taking time to watch the chaos, he stood close to the edge of the path, amazed at how much the birds fought over the bread, even though there was more than enough to feed three times as many. The feeders playing their part in toying with the ducks, tossing it towards just a few, all for a reaction. Khalil observed the crowd with such disapproval.

"Hello" her voice was sweet but confident. Disturbing Khalil's concentration as he watched the ducks feed, Khalil turned his head, a little startled to see an attractive young woman stood in front of him. "Hello" he replied, his Bangladeshi accent strong. "What you doing here?" she said, innocently, her head tilted to the right, Khalil straightened, his body rigid, "What you mean little girl, you come to see a Bengali, face to face so that you can mock me?" his reply a little defensive. Jane pauses and looks at him again, thinking, should I bother? Yes, he looks good, different, even charming, but seems to have a chip on his shoulder. "Just wanted to say hello and find out your name." They both stand there, facing each other. Janes appearance pleases Khalil; she is very easy on the eye. Her slender figure, added with all the right curves in all the right places, and her face, beautiful against her dark black hair. His gaze speaks volumes; she could see he was interested, Jane knew she was. There was something about him she instantly liked; she was mesmerised, almost trance-like.

Is this what was meant by love at first sight? Her heart beating vigorously, dryness of the throat, a little giddy inside, but can't stop smiling.

Apologetic and kind of nervous, Khalil speaks slowly, not wanting to make a mistake "So very sorry madam, my name is Khalil Khan, I am from Bangladesh." His voice is soft and calm "I decided to stay here after serving in the war, I now work night shifts at the spring factory on Kirkstall road as a joiner." His smouldering gaze has Jane captured.

7

His place of work is a factory hot spot in the engineering field; many grey slate-roofed buildings run the length of this road, housing anything from textiles to sheet metal, to precision CNC work, supplying the motor and clothing industries. A major employer for a vast majority of the Leeds native population.

Jane finds his accent a little amusing but doesn't want to offend him, so she offers out her hand. His hand responds quickly, and they shake. "Nice to meet you, Khalil, my name is Jane," her voice mellow and sincere, "Likewise, Jane, it's nice to meet you too."

Both eyes meeting, neither one of them wanting to break away. Time stands still. Just the two of them stood face to face, the rest of the world and sounds disappear out of reality. "Jane, Jane" Milly's voice interrupts, breaking their moment, urging Jane to return to work. "See you tomorrow Khalil?" Jane asked, her eyes still staring at his, "Hopefully Miss Jane, I would like that, see you at the ice-cream stall?" he replies. Jane nods full of hope, as she and her college's head off up the path, making their way back to the clothes factory on Harehills road.

Khalil smiles, happy in the knowledge; he is to meet Jane once more.

The song fades into silence; the voice of the radio DJ breaks Jane from her thoughts and transports her thoughts back to the present.

His warm tones emit from the car radio. "It's another chilly winter's morning. The time now is half-past eight on this bitterly cold Monday, the 14th January 1963, the weather tragically claiming more casualties as the temperatures continue to plummet well below freezing"

He takes a pause before he continues, his voice giving more urgency. "The emergency services and the armed forces are working around the clock to get to the many cut off villages, throughout the Uk, and with the roads and waterways almost at a standstill, this is proving a difficult task, but more about that in 30 minutes" After another pause he shouts out. "Now let's get some tunes on, beat boppers, here's one from that lovely young lass from Bethnal Green, Helen Shapiro, with, you don't know." The radio belts out the song, while the Volkswagen beetle continues its journey. The two occupants singing along with the radio.

A dozen streets up the road, Jim Clegg, and his old friend Carrot top, (an old grey Shire stallion) are delivering the coal to the many residents of Armley, a sizeable industrial suburb of back to back terraced houses in Leeds, where the proud lower paid working class reside. These streets normally teeming with screaming, shouting and laughing children of all ages, but for now the streets are quiet and empty.

Jim clears the snow and lifts the cellar trap doors, one by one releasing sack after sack down the chutes, the next harder, more exhausting than the one before, the day is long and tiresome, his early start taking him through to midmorning.

The cold north-easterly winds are blowing hard, spiralling the loose-lying snow, adding to the drifts, climbing the walls some nine-foot-high, making the treacherous roads narrower than usual, the washing lines that run across the streets resembling thin metal tubing, now frozen solid. The wooden window frames

9

expanded, unable to open. Condensation freezing, leaving icy droplets like teardrops on the glass windows.

The residents not daring to venture out, keeping close to the warmth from the comfort of their coal fires.

Jim chooses to walk by the side of Carrot top, rather than sit on the cart as he usually would.

Carrot Top's balance waivers; his muscular legs buckle, shaking under the slippery road surface, each menacing step causing him pains. The trail of coal dust from the sacks as they manoeuvre from one street to the next is exaggerated in contrast, in the white snow, falling from between the gaps in the plank cart floor, leaving its tell-tale signs of their journey.

Covered in the black soot from head to foot, the burly mammoth six foot seven large muscular framed man carries out his task. Wrapped up in layers. His thick cotton shirt, underneath a black polo neck jumper that had seen better days, his worn-out sleeveless leather jacket and backing hat protecting his back from the hard rubbing of the sacks. Still, Jim continues his deliveries while supporting his companion, keeping him upright. "Won't be long now Carrot top, will have you back in't stables soon … Just a few more deliveries and we'll be finished?" he says in his broad Yorkshire accent, reassuringly. "Everything will be fine mi friend" giving a comforting pat on Carrot tops neck. The horse responds with a neigh and a nod of his head, understanding every word of his masters' voice.

The heavens open, as the snow floods, settling fast, the weather taking a turn for the worst, harsh winds' blow, lifting the loose snow like a mist, hindering their vision, and covering the treacherous glassy cobbled roads, hiding the dangers from view. The drop-in temperature allowing the icy cold to bite at their faces, burning hard on their lungs with every breath. Each step drawing on their resolve.

Jim takes a looks at his pocket watch, "Five-to Nine, Carrot top my old friend, last drop, then home," grinning at the thought of home, turning his cart into Greenhill Road; both tired and wet, their last port of call for the day, an end in sight. They head towards the large Victorian building. The courtyard resembling an ice rink. Uniformed nurses wrapped in their heavy overcoats and head scarfs, along with the white-coated doctors, walking gingerly towards the main entrance, careful not to slip.

Young Nurse Gladys Hartles, her beautiful bobbed hair and made up face, all done to impress Dr. Carter, the Doctor she has a crush on, the one she dares not directly look at. Nervously she takes her careful steps, one at a time, with her arms outstretched for balance; she wobbles, becoming unstable underfoot. Like a magnet, the ice clings to the heel of her shoe, jerking her foot, unable to free her shoe; frustration getting the better of her, she falls rapidly to the ground, accidentally kicking Carrot top's front right leg as they enter through the gateway.

The horse startled, panics. Carrot top tries to bolt, his head nodding and swaying from side to side, kicking his hooves hard on the ground unable to keep a grip on the icy surface, his legs kicking out anxiously. Jim drops

11

the reins in the commotion, even with his strength he can't hold on; the horses' front legs give way as he's wavering around trying to grasp, clinching at any chance of staying upright. Gladys screams in horror as the horse blunders and begins to fall, the onlooker's watching, horrified by the scene. Carrot top buckles under his own weight and begins to topple over, his head hits the ground with a cruel crushing blow on the frozen cobbled yard, breaking his jaw, as his head rebounds off the courtyard floor. His rear twisting awkwardly, back legs frantically lashing out, striking the cart hard. Giant Jim Clegg is forced to the left, collapsing as the wagon spins, snapping the wooden harness. The cart now soared into the air, releasing the sacks of coal as they hurtle down toward where Jim lay, the first sack striking him hard in his face, forcing his head back, hitting the cobbled surface, snapping his neck. Jim's head splits open, the damaged skin tissue revealing the skull. The warm blood freezing as it streams onto the solid iced floor, changing the white of the snow to claret bloody red.

His body lays limp on the frozen, snow-covered cobbles. Jim dies instantly, not knowing his fate. Several sacks hit his torso as they continue to rain down from the cart, breaking his limbs as they hit his lifeless body.

The cart now rotating a full 360 degrees, rains down on both the horse and the nurse, snapping her left leg as the rear 28-inch iron wheel impacts. Her scream deafening, the pain soars like a runaway train through every inch of her being. Gladys falls into a panicked shock and loses consciousness, her body's self-mechanism, protecting her.

Carrot top twisted torso lays there not moving, the poor horse dying from his wounds. His front legs twisted among the cart wreckage, the wooden strut protruding from the horse's back. His beautiful grey coat now a glistening red. Still, the crowd watch bewildered.

Unknowing, the Volkswagen enters the gateway. Without warning; Khalil instantly sees the danger and instinctively applies his break, right foot slamming down hard on to the peddle hard. The car swerves to the left, Khalil's eyes open wide, recognising the threat facing them, heightening his senses. Nothing can stop the vehicle and its occupants from colliding. The wet, icy road invites the car to swerve in all directions as Khalil attempts to navigate around the carnage in front of him, his hands gripping, fighting the steering wheel hard.

Jane hysterically screaming as the vehicle hits the horse at speed. The heavy jolt impacts, and Khalil fails to hold on to the steering wheel, loses his grip; thrown hard into the back of his seat, unable to control the vehicle.

They skid, circling, then another jolt as the front drivers' wheel buckles, driving over the unconscious body of Nurse Hartles, rolling the car over and over repeatedly, leaving the nurse crushed, and her bruised body silent in a pool of her own blood.

Janes deafening screams fill the courtyard as she is launched out of the front window, glistening icy glass shards exploding, flying across the yard. Jane lays there motionless, the onlookers, like transfixed statuettes, are dazed in bafflement, not believing what they are witnessing in front of them. None able to speak, lost in their own shock.

The VW now turned on its crumpled roof skids across the courtyard before it comes to a screeching halt, hitting the boundary wall. Smoke billowing out from the rear engine compartment, screeching loud, metal to metal, sparks, spitting out into the air every few seconds. Khalil scuttles through the broken window screen. His shiny blue silk suit and pale shirt ruined, now torn and dark red; stained with blood.

Khalil shivering and exhausted places his back up against the side of the vehicle for support. His neatly combed hair matted, the razor-like cuts covering his distorted face, making him unrecognisable, the swelling covering his eyes and mouth, blood layering his face, his arms twisted and broken dangle from his torso, motionless unable to support him. Breathing laboriously as the ice-cold air burns deep into his lungs. He coughs, and splutters, dark red blood spots spill out through his teeth, dripping onto his chest.

Doctor Jones is the first to react; reality taking hold from his trance-like state; his tall, slender frame sliding across, he takes in the carnage, fearing the worst, racing towards Khalil. Kneeling down he begins to aid him. Visualising the injuries and how and what he needs to treat him, he knows this isn't good, just one look told him that, and where to start? Two of the nurses follow and assist the doctor.

The courtyard burst into a frenzy of scream, the realisation of the chaos becoming a reality to the onlookers. Khalil strains to look over the doctor's right shoulder searching for his wife, fear installed, racing through his mind, is my beautiful wife alive? Dreading the worst and unable to focus through the tiny slits of his swollen eyes. He fights the pain; pushing his body forward, unaided by his damaged arms, stretching to search a better view, his wife his primary concern. Hoping and praying she has survived the crash. "Please doctor ...My wife, you need to help my wife," his sobbing voice desperate, tears forming from the small slits. "We are expecting our first child today." His weak body slumps back onto the side of the vehicle, sapped of all his strength he looks out blankly into nothingness tears stream down his face.

Doctor Jones turns his head; he sees Jane lying in the snow, holding her stomach. A sudden feeling of sickness overwhelms him, he takes a few gulps of air to compose himself.

A new urgency grips Dr. Jones, taking command, he yells at the nursing staff still stood there, most screaming. He awakens their senses and begins delegating the crowd to assist.

The courtyard breaks into a hive of activity as the nursing staff, like robots turn off their shock, like a flick of a switch and rush towards the injured, some slipping as they make desperate haste.

Away from the chaos, inside the hospital, Mike the head porter is watching the carnage through the main door window. Without a moment's notice, he orders other Orderlies to assist in getting the injured inside.

With the precision of a military operation, the massive doors of St. Mary's hospital entrance open, eight porters explode into action. Two to a bed trolley race towards the injured casualties.

Jane, nine months pregnant, her injured body is found lying face down in the snow, cradling her stomach, weak, shallow moans emit from her mouth, Mike crouches next to the doctor trying to treat her, "Can we take her in?" he asks. The doctor turns and nods, between them, the doctor and the two porters lift her critically injured, blood-soaked body and place her gently onto the trolley; they waste no time in rushing her straight to the labour ward.

Sirens sounding. The patrol car halts outside the gate, eagerly two young policemen race towards Dr. Jones. They assist the porters with Khalil onto the trolley bed. Khalil is rushed to the emergency ward, with Dr. Jones following closely.

The clean-up of the horse takes time; while Jim's body is recovered from the pile of coal sacks, both Jim and Nurse Hartles are transferred to the mortuary.

Inside the tiny white-painted cubicle, there is a rush of activity, the strip lighting flickering, the sound of the hospital generator echoing through the walls, another power cut, during another cold blighted winter day.

Dr. Jones carefully removes the glass shards from Khalil's face and neck, one of the nurses hectically mopping up the blood, trying to minimise the flow, the second nurse following with the stitching striving to keep Khalil alive.

Jones examines Khalil's body for more injuries after stemming the blood flow; after some twenty minutes of stitching Khalil's body, he finds a sizable dent in Khalil's chest, where the steering wheel must have impacted.

He shakes his head; the three nurses look on, all-knowing this could be futile.

Khalil's breathing increases as panic plagues his body, going into shock, his whole physique now shaking; blood appears in the corner of his mouth. Khalil lunges forward rapidly, taking the three nurses by surprise, hurling a bloody vomit over his torso, splattering on to the medics helping. The spewed out blood taints the excellent clean white doctor's jacket. Dr. Jones shows no reaction, just coolly continues with the job at hand.

Khalil's face turns pale, colour draining from him, and his lips turning blue, falling back onto the bed noisily.

His eyes are staring into the unknown, the shine diminished, just dull empty dark eyes staring into nothingness. His chest ceases to heave as his head slumps to the left. Doctor Jones knows the all too familiar sight; he looks at his watch, the three nurses aware of what's coming, stand in silence.

"Time of death is 09:46 am 14th January 1963...do we all agree?" The words from the doctor are deliberate but not without empathy, the nurse's nod as the senior nurse moves closer, she places her hand on Khalil's

17

face; stroking his forehead, allowing her hand to travel down closing his eyes. The cubicle is silent as they bow their heads.

Meanwhile, in the labour ward, Jane lays there unresponsive, her stomach opened as the doctor performs a caesarean delivery, the midwife assisting.

With Jane's injuries severe, two other doctors tend to her wounds, avoiding the delivery of the child.

Struggling with her injuries and the intense pain, Jane's body rises, almost sat upright, responding to her pains, her heartbeat intensifies, her pulse climbing, repelling, going into shock. Unable to control her body, she begins to shake forcefully, screeching out to an ear piercing deafness, the pain overwhelming, soaring through, her erratic breathing subsides, becoming more laboured, her scream sinks into a gasping whisper, the doctors step backward momentarily. Janes body slumps back, thumping the trolley mattress hard. She ceases to move, rigid like a stone carving, leaving only the oxygen mask to aid her, keeping her alive. The doctors show more haste; time is not on their side.

The child must be delivered quickly if it is to survive.

A few minutes later Midwife Pearce accepts the newborn; the doctor separates the cord.

The cries of a child fill the room. Midwife Pearce holds the baby close to her; heartfelt tears roll down her face as she walks over to the scales, 09:44 Am, at 7 pounds and 2 ounces, a young healthy boy is born.

Jane is pronounced dead two minutes later.

Jane never got to hold her child or feel his heartbeat next to hers.
Her child never saw his mommy's smile.

CHAPTER 2

THE NAME

St Mary's hospital maternity block is buzzing; a real excitement is flowing through the wards. The nurses and doctors looking up boy's names for the newborn. The media playing a significant part exposing the child to all the world, explaining he had no living relatives, both his mother and father being the last of the line in their families. It was up to society to name and care for the child.

The long pale blue corridor is silent, the footsteps of Midwife Pearce echo, sending out a warning she is on her rounds. She looks in on the boy, peering through the half-opened door, Nurse Brown, a mature, more experienced nurse is feeding him, the warm milk in the bottle disappearing fast, the child suckles hard on the teat. Nurse Brown's kind brown eyes and her sweet smile omit a caring nurturing towards the child. Holding him close, she looks up to face the midwife, "Would love to keep him ...Don't think Harold would be too keen though" she says chuckling. Her mellow voice sincere.

Midwife Pearce, a tall, stout woman, yellow blonde curly shoulder length hair, hiding under her nurse's cap, her freckled face smiling back, "Why not ask him? ...Someone has to look after the beloved little one." Replies the midwife, entering the room, closing the door behind her, Nurse Brown looks quizzingly at Midwife

Pearce asking, "Do you think they would allow us to have him?". Nurse Brown and her husband both now in their early forties, regrettably, have never been able to have children, due to Harold's accident when he was a boy. He had fallen out of the tallest tree in their village and landed badly, causing him to be sterile in later life, giving them a childless marriage. Nurse Brown had never blamed Harold for the childless marriage, she never saw this as a fault, yes, she would love a child in her life, but she had accepted this many years ago. She loved her husband, he was her world, and she was his, they married young, at nineteen and had never been apart since. Nurse Brown loves her Harold as much today as she always had.

Midwife Pearce places her right hand on Brown's shoulder pressing lightly, "Why not, nothing would be nicer than you and Harold having a child in your lives ...anyway that would be better than putting the poor little darling into an orphanage, it would suit you both if you did adopt him." With that, and no other word said, Midwife Pearce leaves the room and returns to her duties. Her footsteps disappearing down the corridors.

Nurse Brown, a Welsh woman originally from Swansea, notices the word spoken by the midwife (beloved), with this word planted in her mind she considers the chance of being a mother, this appeals to Nurse Brown, here is an opportunity that could change her life, how will Harold react when she places this idea of hers into his lap. Potentially turning his world upside down.

With the baby now back in his crib in the hospital nursery, all settled and fed, Nurse Brown, with a mixture of fear and excitement, ponders on the thought of adopting the child. She hurriedly makes her way to the ward, repeatedly whispering to herself "The beloved one," almost singing it, humming a tune.

The sister and a group of nurses are standing in the centre of the ward, engrossed in the debate, shouting out what name we should call the child? Ringo, Paul, John, and George being the most common.

"Hello girls," shouts Nurse Brown looking very pleased with herself, almost skipping towards them. "Hello, Margaret" replies the Sister still jotting names on the pad in her hand.

The room is filled with conversations, the sound of the visitors next to the beds distorts as they all speak simultaneously to the mums with their newborn lying next to them, the room containing a dozen beds each side, with the spacious aisle running down the centre. The nurses stood in the middle engrossed in their own conversation.

Margaret joins in with the nurses. "I have been talking to Annie Pearce, and she thinks me and Harold should adopt the little one. What do you all think?" she asks the group excitedly, the women look at each other wide-eyed, all replying a giddy yes, the excitement showing on their faces. "What will you call him," shrieks Julie, the tiny four foot six young nurse giggling at the same time. "Well I thought David would be a good name for him as Annie called him the beloved child, and in Welsh beloved is the meaning for David" Margaret replies calmly. The nurses jig a giddy dance with excitement, with Margaret joining in, "That would suit him just fine" replies the Sister, very assured.

CHAPTER 3

THE ADOPTION

The hype from the national daily morning papers keeps the public wanting more on this child, wanting to know all the tiny details, the ins, and outs of the little child's life. The media continuing to play on the nation's feelings of sympathy, selling their story. The miracle of life, from death.

Nurse Margaret Brown is no longer allowed to care for the newborn, Julie is given the task of watching over him now. Margaret not being too upset, in the knowledge of the adoption now in full flow.

Margaret still misses him desperately, his little face staring up at hers, his small familiar sounds, and even his cry, informing he needs a feeding or a changed. His round little face with the dark curly mop of hair on his head, his little hands clutching her fingers. Margaret has grown fond of this child, her attachment becoming intense, enough to believe she could care for him forever. Margaret had fallen in love with this little boy, to most this could be an awkward thing to do, after all, he was not a blood relative, in fact, he wasn't a relative at all. He was just a child, and all alone, Margaret never felt sorry for him, she just genuinely cared.

Harold had never seen the boy, he just knew this would make Margaret's life complete, and this made him happy, knowing he could finally give her a child, the only thing that could complete their family.

The snow-covered back to back houses, still evident of the harsh winter, the temperature just below freezing. Smoke ascends from every chimney pot, black soot spots blending in with the white snowy rooftops, the heavy snowfall laying thickly over the streets, stirring a swirling mist of snow as the hard winds elevate it from the ground. The parks, shops, and streets deserted, the residents staying indoors, evading the cold.

At number twenty-two, the local social worker and her manager are seated on the Brown's sofa, sifting through the lives of Harold and Margaret in detail. The small room heated from the glowing coal fire, emitting a cosy warmth. The apprehension from the questioning, causing an uneasiness in an otherwise pleasant surroundings.

Harold and Margaret feel as if they are being interrogated, sitting hand in hand, answering the questions nervously. Margaret, up and down making the many pots of tea, keeping herself from going mad. Being a feeder, she keeps the guest nourished and calm. The uncertainty clawing at her confidence.

Jenny sits upright and straight on the Danish Teak sofa, scribbling her notes on the pad, resting on her wooden clipboard. Jenny, an average five-feet three young women, her long black hair flowing down from beneath her floral headscarf, her pale, bespectacled wiry, long face with her dark painted red lips displaying a perfect set of white teeth.

Looking directly at the couple, her posture upright, and very deliberate. "Now we have completed the forms and our ... For a better word interrogation of you is all over," she pauses, side glances at her manager, who nods in agreement, then continues "It's all up to the courts now" she says in her perfect teacher voice, showing no sentiment or emotional state. Margaret smiles, a nervous smile, unsure of herself, clutching at Harold's hand. He squeezes back in response.

Raising from their seats, they all stand face to face; no one speaking a word between them; after a minutes pause, which seems like an eternity to the Browns, wondering if they should say something? The silence is broken, the manager offers his hand "Good luck and hope to see you with the boy in a few days," Harold returns the offer and politely shakes his hand "Thank you for your time." He walks them to the door.

The social workers stride out into a noisy crowd of locals who have gathered at their doorway. All are waiting to hear the good news. The national morning newspaper reporters are stood pen and notebooks in hand, shivering from the long wait in the frozen winter afternoon chill. Without a word or any form of response to the barrage of questions thrown at him, the manager opens the passenger car door, allowing Jenny to take her seat. He scurries around the bonnet, forcing his way through the crowd, almost slipping, looking down his nose at the sniggering crowd, and hurriedly drives away in their 1962 Hillman Minx, the car skidding slightly on the snow-covered road.

Mrs. Connor from number 30, (the young little miss busy body of the street), hobbles over gingerly to the door almost slipping numerous times, "Well Margaret what they say? Are you getting him or not" the sound more of a shrill than talking. Margaret being a polite, responsible person replies in a calm voice "We don't know yet ...Have to go to court first" Mrs. Connor's face screws up and bleats out "Bloody silly beggars ...You and Harold would be great parents. Folk eh." her heart in the right place, knowing Harold and Margaret deserve something good in their lives, having three young children of her own and the knowledge of the joy they bring.

Harold and Margaret thank their neighbours for their kind words. They wave goodbye to each other wishing them luck as the door closes, and the couple retreat to the warm glow of the coal fire burning brightly, dancing flames, flickering, a comforting warmth, easing their minds, not quite sure on how they should be feeling, with the daunting unsurety ahead of them.

The reporters left a little bewildered, stood outside in the snow, still none the wiser of what just happened, parting with very little to report.

The big day at the Leeds magistrate's court arrives, the sun is smiling down, sending out a good omen, breaking through the cotton wool clouds, sending warm currents of fresh flowing air around the streets.

The town centre is a burst of activity, people wrapped up in layers, braving the last of the winter snow. The shops are enjoying a late but new surge in the winter sales. The first signs of normality, the return of the hustle and bustle, the sound of the streets coming alive.

The old Victorian building with all its splendour hides the true nature of its business behind the weighty broad oak doors. With the cells looming below. Today is going to be different, no prison sentences to be given out from room six, no, quite the opposite, a chance of a new beginning, a chance of a normal upbringing, the opportunity to have a complete family with a child.

Harold and Margret walk up the stairs to courtroom six, both a little nervous, they kiss lightly on the lips before the corporate security uniformed guard beckons the couple into the courtroom.

The room is set. The large embossed City of Leeds coat of arms looms high above the large chair with seats on either side, behind the extra wide, well-polished mahogany table. Two suited gentlemen occupying the chairs, all spit and polished up, looking very formidable with the air of competence. Their highly pressed blue suites matching.

In front of the mahogany table, stand four rows of four tables, each with four chairs behind them. The front left tables are occupied by Doctor Jones and Midwife Pearce, and the two from the social services behind them. Margaret and Harold take the vacant seats next to Doctor Jones. He stands as Margaret take her place, sitting down, smiling nervously. Midwife Pearce hugs Maggie, who now is pale and looks drawn from the occasion, reassuringly Midwife Pearce whispers some kind words into her ear, this seems to have helped settle Margret. Harold looks on contently.

The man to the right of the bench stands "all rise for the honourable Judge Nelson" his voice loud and imposing. The clattering of chairs as the room stands for Judge Nelson to take his place.

Judge Nelson looks out across the room, and smiles, "Please be seated," the calm voice of the Judge, helping to soothe the mood, removing some of the anxiety the couples still feeling.

The room now seated. The silence piercing the air, waiting for the Judge to speak. It's as if time had stood still; the silence unbearable, the ticking of the wall clock deafening.

A few minutes pass, the Judge leans forward, dressed immaculately in his court gowns, and his wig placed neatly upon his head, looking the very part of authority. Scanning the room, he takes a deep intake of air, releasing it with a huge sigh, breaking the silence. His arms outstretched in front of him, "Welcome to my court on this a joyous occasion, with the legal bonding of new parents with the child." Sitting upright and placing both hands on the table, he looks like he has the winning hand in a game of poker, his voice fills the room. "It gives me great pleasure today, as this is a auspicious occasion, and not the usual drone of the bad, unpleasant matters I usually deal with, day after day."

His face brightens as he displays a broad grin across his wrinkled face. He continues his speech on the topic of the day; this goes on for a further fifteen minutes.

Margaret exhales a deep breath, now at ease, tension released knowing this is all but complete and soon she will have a little child in her arms to finally call her own. Margaret regains the colour back in her face, instead of dread, now replaced with ease and calmness, in anticipation of receiving the boy.

The Judge turns to the left and whispers into the attendant ear next to him; the attendant nods, then quietly removes himself from the room. Casual conversation fills the room, Judge Nelson telling a few but corny jokes, a breakout of laughter takes over. Suddenly this is broken to the sound of the door opening, and replaced by the sound of a baby crying. Margaret turns eagerly towards the door, feelings of yearning and wonderment fill her every pore, after not seeing or been allowed to care for him over the last two weeks during their assessment, Margaret craves to have him in her arms.

She has so missed him, and how he has grown. Margaret turns and grabs Harold's arm, squeezing it tight, tears rolling from her happy smiling eyes, she tightens her grip on his arm, without a word, and ignoring the pain Harold turns to his wife and kisses her lightly on the cheek, she returns a blushing affectionate look, to his relief, loosening her grip on him.

Her heart pounding, ready to explode, her body shaking, the tears now flowing freely. Harold leans into her whispering "It's all but done now, relax my darling, you'll have him in your arms soon enough" handing over his clean white handkerchief. Silently she wipes away the tears.

The attendant strides over to Margaret and places the child in her arms; he winks as she cradles the child, holding him close to her as if she would never dare to let him go. Harold sheds a tear, quickly wiping them away, and clearing his throat, this being the first time he had laid eyes on him. "He's beautiful isn't he Harold" whispers Margaret, Harold nods in agreement, wiping away a newly formed stream of tears. Harold gives into his feelings, who's he trying to kid, this is a colossal emotional time.

Judge Nelson, applauds Margret as she takes hold of the child, expressing his happiness and pleasure of the occasion, wiping a tear from his eye, pronouncing to the room "Thank you to everyone who has taken the time to see this day come. It gives me extreme pleasure to announce the bonding of Harold and Margaret Brown with their now legal son David, born on the fourteenth of January 1963 to the late Mr. and Mrs. Khan. Now to be known as David Brown from today Tuesday 26th February 1963," with his eyes set on Margaret he continues, "May I be the first to take the pleasure of congratulating you all, three cheers for the Browns hip hip" the room respond "hurray."

With everyone now taking to the floor, Judge Nelson passes over a large brown envelope to Harold explaining, "This contains David's new birth certificate and a birthday card signed by all who attended today." Once again, he congratulates Harold; they shake hands,

Margaret clutching at the child, moves closer to Judge Nelson, and kisses him gently on his left cheek, full of joy, his face reddens as he blushes. "I don't normally have people give me a hug," he says sniggering like a silly schoolboy looking down on Margaret's face beaming with gladness. "Good luck Mr. and Mrs. Brown, and may your days be full of the wonders this child will bring you." With that said Judge Nelson departs, leaving the room to chat amongst themselves.

With all the talking done, the room evacuates as they all make their way out. Doctor Jones walks with the Browns to the main exit; he once again congratulates them, pecks Margaret on her cheek, wishing them all the luck in the world, then takes his leave.

Outside the wind blows a light breeze on the snow-covered pavement, the sun sends beams of warm sunlight through the cloudy skies, the sunbeams fall over Margaret and her baby. The newspaper reporter snaps a picture of the Brown family stood on the steps of the court buildings, capturing the sun's rays, like a guiding light from the heavens. The evening tabloids front page story. "Adoption approved by the Gods."

Harold opens the taxi door as Margaret lowers herself, cradling David all the while, wrapped up in his warm woollen blanket. Margaret ambles across the seat as Harold follows, shutting the door behind him. The taxi drives away, heading for home.

CHAPTER 4

HOMECOMING

The afternoon sun continues to shine down on to the snow-covered landscape, pockets of waterlogged puddles emerge where the snow has melted, the green of the grass spanning out sporadically, allowing the normality of life to strive once again.

The wheels of the taxi come to a halt, pulling up outside number twenty-two, the engine idles. Minutes pass before the occupant's exit.

The driver hobbles around to hold the rear left side door open, Harold shuffles out first; inhaling a large gulp of winter air, coughing loudly to clear his throat. His arm stretched out with his hand in Margaret's, still clutching the child close as she follows. The driver wishes them well, takes his fare and drives away, turning right at the junction, back towards the city centre. Harold and Margaret left standing in silence.

The weather, now changing for the better, sees the sun break through the winter sky, sending out a warm glow, as the wind blows a gentle warmth around the street. The trickle of water flows down the roads, as the snow melts, slowly disappearing, entering the drain system like mini waterfalls. The cold of winter changing into the warmth of spring, allowing the new year its rite of passage.

The neighbours anxiously waiting to get their first glimpse of David, peering out from behind their twitching curtains. Harold and Margaret, unsure of the welcome, wait outside their door. The front doors to the two rows of houses are flung open, and a rush of mums along with the whole female population of the street congregate over, surrounding Margaret, just to steal a glimpse of the newborn. The excitement of the coos and aahs are ear-splitting, continuing for unlimited minutes, each of them, in turn, brushing the thick dark locks on his head with their fingers. Margaret elated, happy her neighbours are pleased, looking down on her child adoringly. It would seem nothing could take this moment away from her.

Mrs. Connor breaks through the crowd of women excited, pushing through to take her turn to peek at the newborn. Smiling she lowers her head, "Who's a pretty" cutting short mid-sentence, her eyes stare down at the child, her face turns pale with shock, the horror sweeps over her, how dare they? She takes a step back, fighting to find her words, then no holding back. She stammers out her vile cold words, full of malice and hate, aloud and tormented for all the world to hear. "How dare you bring a coloured into this street, he's not even our kind," the crowd of women gasp in total surprise, offended by her words as she continues, "Shouldn't be allowed a Pakistani, dirty people" her words and body displaying disgust. "You should be ashamed," standing there, pointing her finger at Margaret. Margaret who is now almost torn to tears, her world shattered in an instant, never considering it mattered what ethnicity a baby had to be, to be loved.

"Not as if there aren't enough white kids out there who need looking after, don't think I will be helping you if you need it" Her revolting tone shouts. Her face red, burning with anger as she spits on the pavement in front of them. "You're disgusting, the pair of you," she continues, turning and starting to head back to number 30, chuntering offensive words as she goes, Harold stands tall, regaining his thoughts, and composure, his body shape defensive. He retaliates back, shouting "How dare you, to call yourself a Christian woman." His face ablaze full of rage, he continues. "And as far as you been on our Christmas list, my wife and I will not miss you" his words stumbling out through his anger, "if anyone should be ashamed it's you," his arm aloft pointing his finger. Their neighbours repulsed by her actions.

Mrs. Connor retreats entering her home, disappearing behind the closed door.

Harold cowers down and apologises to the gathering, explaining he's not an aggressive man. The crowd reassures him all is fine and that they understand his frustration at her wrongdoing, and that no apology needed to be said.

The women reassuringly smile at Margaret, promising her all is good, and her baby is a beautiful boy, all at the same time toying with David's hair, pulling funny faces, and making silly noises, none of which the infant can understand.

Ann Carter from 26 asked "can I hold him, Maggie?" Maggie happily agrees, passing the child over as Ann cradles him in her arms, affectionately, tenderly, and truly delighted as she holds him closer, "He's beautiful Maggie, he'll have all the girls chasing him when he's older, you'll see." She passes him back, beaming, her affection sincere. Margaret takes David in her arms, holding him close, "Thank you all for your kindness," Maggie replies, wiping away her tears.

Margaret rubs Ann's tummy, "How long now before your due Ann?" Ann heavily pregnant replies "Just four days to go, and I should be in labour." Her stomach rounded showing off her large bump. "Hope my baby will be as beautiful as yours," Ann adds looking directly at Margaret, "Of course your child will, look at you and Johnny, you two handsome young kids, any child you have will be an utterly gorgeous child," Margaret replies kissing Ann on the cheek. All coy, Ann blushes.

The child begins to whimper, the hunger pangs nibbling at him, time for his feed, told only how an infant can.

Harold calmly places his arms around Margaret, pulling her close, "Well ladies we need to get him inside, keep him warm" ushering Margaret as they retreat through the door, back into the warmth of the cosy brightly lit coal fire.

The women say their goodbyes and head off to their homes, waving and looking back as they go.

CHAPTER 5

THE MOVE

Four years have passed since the adoption. It's February 1967. The year our government signed the outer space treaty, alongside the Soviet Union and the United States. All sides agreeing to keep the weapons of mass destruction out of earth's orbit. The world sent into sci-fi terror, feeling vulnerable, and Hollywood cashing in on it, with their version of terror sci-fi movies.

The winter season had been long, the misery had it caused was unbearable. The dark nights and short days disappearing, turning warm; but mainly rain these days, with the snow almost melted, replaced with muddy fields and puddles. Primarily a dreary month with grey skies and torrential rain to match. No fun playing out days, with most of the nation's youths stuck indoors, and still miserable.

Harold left the house at seven O'clock promptly. His vast strides, almost marching his way to the office, taking in great gulps of fresh air with each stride, filling his lungs, never breaking into a sweat, the same as he did every Monday to Friday, ready for whatever the day had to offer, repeating the same walk home at five in the evening, no matter the weather. His daily walks to and from work keeping him trim and healthy.

He stood a tall five feet eleven, his slim frame giving the appearance of someone taller. He never suffered illness, and never had, nor had he ever had a day off to sickness. He was a role model for all.

Margaret considered herself lucky, having a good provider, and a man who doted on her, she loved him without question, he was her world. Saying all that, he was no James Bond look alike but had an interesting face, which many women found attractive. Margaret was still a beautiful woman; her slender frame, a perfect size ten, also keeping her hair short, the bob style with a feathered fringe, this suited her oval shaped face. Harold considered himself lucky, always said he was punching above his weight, having Margaret by his side. Margaret would just tell him to stop been daft and blushed for hours. If ever there was such a thing as a perfect couple, these two weren't far from it.

With the house free of dad for the next eight or so hours, mum got on with her daily routine of house cleaning and washing, also mainly keeping a watchful eye on me, as I tore through the house, playing with my imaginary friends and my Poo bear.

Margaret had given up her job at the hospital weeks after I had come into their lives. She doted on this child; nothing could take this away from her, this is what she lived for. Margaret and Harold had never been so happy. David had changed their lives, made them richer and more fulfilling. Life was good in the Brown household.

Working away at her daily task, mum threw caution to the wind and danced as she laboured with the hover, keeping the carpets spic and span, almost new looking, even though they had been laid for years. Completing her cleaning routine for the day, with the kettle boiled and the teapot filled, and the pouring of a china cup of tea topped up with a drop of milk, Mum placed herself comfortably in her chair, glancing over at the settee where I lay sleeping.

Taking the Mills and Boon from the table and settling down in her chair, she escaped into a world of romance and fantasy.

Startled by the loud knock on the door, breaking the silence of her day, Margaret lifts herself from the comfort of the fireside chair, setting her Mills and Boon on the arm. The impatient rap on the door repeated. "Wait please I'm coming" yelled mum at whoever was on the street side of the door, walking through to the hallway to answer the door. She opens the door, in front of her stands two grey suited gentlemen.

The taller of the two removes his grey coloured trilby hat displaying his excellent groomed head of hair, combed to the right, his slender frame covered in grey jacket and trousers, his white collared shirt gleaming. The man next to him a short man dressed similar but not able to carry the effect looks untidy.

"Good morning Mrs. Brown how are you today" trilby in hand and nodding his head, greets the taller of the two.

"I am fine sir and how can I help you" replies Margaret looking wary of them and feeling somewhat at a disadvantage.

I am stood between her legs, my tiny hands clinging to the hem of her dress. A little wobbly from being disturbed from my sleep. The tall man reintroduces them. "We are from the Council Mrs. Brown, and as you know this is one of the streets under the new-build re-housing program," sensing mums reaction, he feels a little nervous and a bit unsure of what to say next, the shorter man chirps in. "We need to give you notice, that by March, Monday 20th you need to be rehoused, these are due to be demolished." Pointing at the surrounding area. He pauses for a breath before continuing his spiel. "The area of relocation is going to be Seacroft, most of your neighbours have already been relocated." his small chubby face smiling, his little eyes penetrating hers, making Margaret uneasy.

"You are aware that we own this house?" scolds mum, unaware of the program, only evident from the neighbours leaving. The taller man cuts in quickly "Sorry Mrs. Brown, please let me introduce myself ...I am Mr. Stuart Vincent head of reformed council housing" his tone light and friendly, "We will, of course, be compensating you and your husband for the cost of moving and the loss of your premises, we did meet up last month after we sent out the letters, ...Your husband never got back to us, so I'm afraid the government has placed a compulsory purchase order on your home".

Mum takes a few steps backwards, not allowing them to see her disappointment, and invites them in. They talk some more, going over the more delicate details, then depart, leaving mum with the task of telling dad.

Mum was upset for most of the day, she even brushed me off, I was at a loss not knowing why I was being scolded, mum didn't shout, ever, never raised her voice at me, always the sweet, and pleasant mum, this news had taken her aback a bit, she was disappointed in dad. Dad had not told her; he was evading the matter, deluding himself of the inevitable.

Margaret had simmered down by the time dad arrived home. His dinner set out on the table as usual. That evening mum informed dad of the visit. With the look of a reprimanded child he apologised to mum for his stupidity, thinking this would just disappear into nothingness, mum hugged him, assuring him all was well. She kissed him tenderly on the lips; he looked up, his face brightened, breaking into a smile. They sat in their chairs talking through to the early hours about the move. "Harold this is bricks and mortar, our memories are in our hearts" mum whispered, "I know love" dad replies, standing up, "Come on lass, let's go to bed, got a few busy days ahead of us now." Without a word, mum turns out the light, and they both climb the stairs and disappear into their bedroom.

March 16th, and what a stressful few weeks they were leading up to today. A dull wet grey Thursday morning, setting the melancholy mood for the day.

The taxi arrives promptly at ten O'clock as requested, and with the removal van loaded, and on its journey to our new home, leaving mum and dad standing in the empty living room. Whispery images of times gone past float around, the echoes of many years vibrate through the walls.

"So many memories Maggie, feels like our whole lives have been ripped away," he says holding mum close, Mum smiles back at him, looking up, her expression, pleasant and kind, showing no regret and ready for the move ahead. "Harold, as I said before, all the love you have had and the memories, they will stay in our hearts, but for now, we have to move on and start some new ones." Both stand in the middle of the room, face to face, they embrace, saying goodbye to their yesteryears; the smiles, the tear and laughter, the good and the bad, leaving them behind, ready to start a new chapter.

The taxi still idles by the kerb. I sit there waiting, alone on the rear seat. The driver honks his horn, his patience wearing thin, mum appears through the doorway, followed by dad.

Harold locks the front door for the final time, emotionally distraught, he fights back his tears.

They enter the taxi, and we embark on our journey across Leeds to Seacroft, mum and dad weep as we leave our street, the strain finally winning over, as we say our last goodbyes; it is the last time we saw the house. The street was demolished just three weeks later.

Our new three bedroomed semi-detached brick-built house is a beautiful spacious home; the lounge has a bay window looking out to a small lawned front garden, with a privet boundary, beyond that is an oval-shaped grassed area, just large enough to have a decent game of football. The rear kitchen is housing the new fitted red worktops and stainless-steel sink. The clean, fresh black and white tiled patterned linoleum lay on the floor. Mum says she feels like a queen, so much room to serve and cook. She twirls around the spacious floor, Harold clapping, he steps up and takes her hand, they being to waltz around the floor to an imaginary tune, gaiety and laughter fill the room.

The large rear and side garden, both house a small lawn, a bit overgrown, but nothing dad couldn't put right. The garden boundaries edged with tall, thick green privet. Dad loves the idea of a garden. "Somewhere for David to play," he says. I'm all the while running around, up, and down the stairs and exploring each room, screaming at the top of my voice. My parents stand and watch, laughing as I jump and skip, my eyes almost popping out in awe.

Natural light floods through the large windows in the spacious bedrooms, making them bright and airy. The sight of the indoor toilet and bathroom sends my parents wild, something we never had in the old house, having to walk down the garden path to the outhouse to do our business. Dad over giddy flushes the toilet repeatedly, mum stands there laughing, as for me I just look at them both bewildered, not really knowing what all the fuss is about.

Gone is the coal fire, replaced with state of the art silver boxed gas fire. No more cursing from dad, attempting to get the coal fire lit.

The suburb of Seacroft is one of the largest in Yorkshire, with some ten to twelve thousand council residents, yet there is so much space and greenery.

We thought Armley was a large estate, even crowded, quite claustrophobic. The terraced back to back houses cramped together, with no greenery to be seen. The improvements here were evident to see. No factory buildings looming in the background churning out smoke, no cobbled roads, and high raised pavements. The streets were tarmacked and low kerbs, making it easy to manage for both young and old alike. The foliage evident, the grass verges neatly cut, with trees lines running the length of the avenues, displaying a modern scenic street view.

The street we live on is called Alston Lane; ours was number twenty-five, the newly painted blue door with the large black numbers painted on a white background square. Most of the buildings built during the nineteen forties.

Mum and dad were out shopping most weekends buying new furniture. They had the house carpeted thought-out. It was like living in a palace compared to our little back to back terraced home. Mum wondered how we ever survived in our old back to back. But in her heart she missed it.

My parents had fallen in love with our new home; both were so pleased, you could see it in their faces. Dad would tend to the garden, growing brightly coloured flowers and keeping the lawns trimmed, maintaining the garden, looking clean and colourful, always complimented by our neighbours. Mum would tend to the housekeeping, always spotless, just in case we had visitors, my parents were both very proud and expressed this in everything they did. We were nicknamed the posh house of the estate, mum delighted in this, dad thought nothing of it, but sometimes had to remind mum we were all the same, just we were better off than most in our street.

At only four years old and not quite ready for school life, I spend most of my time in the backyard playing with my toys; my favourite is the Winnie the Pooh bear, he never leaves my side. Dad had bought this for me on my first birthday; Pooh bear had become my best friend. We went on many fantastic adventures, under the watchful eye of mum through the kitchen window.

Elizabeth Stuart, the four-year-old girl from next door often came to play, her mum Janet, a single parent, struggling to cope on her own, with the loss of her husband. Janet had told mum he had drowned two years earlier, in an accident while serving in the Royal Navy, he was in some faraway land, the other side of the world, his body was never retrieved. Janet wasn't able to gain any closure from her grief and had never desired a new relationship; she immersed all her energy into bringing up their daughter Elizabeth.

Elizabeth was a cute little girl, her long brown hair set in pigtails, her sparkly green eyes and her button nose covered in freckles, she was friendly and quite spritely, always jumping about, her vocabulary outshone mine by far, and could she talk, well she just never stopped. We played together for hours, often shared our lunches, she was a sweet kid who was innocent to the world of racism, Janet too had no thoughts about skin colour making a difference to who lives where. To be truthful few did on our estate, most homes didn't have much in luxuries or care, as the hand me downs were a common thing and passed from house to house. If you had no one in your family who could wear them, they were passed onto the next family. We all, well almost all just got on with it.

Mrs. Connor and her family had also moved on to the estate just three houses away on Hawkshead Crescent; the street ran from the top of the hill and some six hundred meters down to the left of ours. She still resented me as some lower-class human, spoiling the gene pool of life. Mum and dad always avoided her. She always had something nasty to say about us. Mum told me Mrs. Connor was jealous, we were better off than her family, her husband Grant, an ex-marine, was unemployed and at the age of forty-four and some twelve years older than Mrs. Connor, had arthritis in his legs and could hardly walk. He was nothing like Mrs. Connor; he was a gentleman, Grant was always polite to everyone he met, he had even sneaked me some penny sweets when she wasn't looking. I like Grant.

Harold's world had gotten a little more chaotic; now he had to use the public transport system to get to work. He was used to walking to the post office building, in the Leeds city centre. It was about four miles from our old home, he loved the stroll, greeting the regular fellow walkers on his route.

Now he hates the crowded mornings, the rush for the first bus, the unwashed, the half drunks and the smokers polluting his space. Dad was always a clean-shaven, well-groomed man, nothing less than a clean shirt and tie every working day.

He does, however, enjoy his new life with Maggie and David. He is happy to have this little boy causing havoc in his home; he feels there is more purpose in his life, now he has a son. Harold looks forward to playing games and his favourite time, to read bedtime stories, observing the amazement on my face, as he takes me off on an adventure in a faraway land.

With the compensation money acquired from the house, both mum and dad decided it was the time dad had learned to drive. So, for the next few weeks, that's what he would do, he would take driving lessons twice a week. Mr. Jakes was his instructor, an old sixty-one-year-old, dad always described him as the walking dead, mainly due to the paleness of his face. Dad said this man was waiting for God, I could hear mum and dad laughing while he told his stories to mum, of the days driving practice.

As for Margaret, she was in seventh heaven, David, her child, her pride, and her joy. She adores watching him play and grow, teaching him all the things in life grown-ups take for granted. Life was good in the Brown household.

CHAPTER 6

MISS POINTER

September 1967, seven O'clock, Tuesday morning, Dad had passed his driving test some months past, He had enjoyed his lessons, it only took him ten to pass his test, and it had him hooked. The following day he went to the showroom and purchased a Morris Traveller for £620 brand new. Became his pride and joy, he loved driving it and any excuse, he would be in it, driving to some shop or other.

He was up and gone by the time mum had my breakfast on the go. Mum's was busy in the kitchen, making porridge, also pouring me a small glass of milk. She added two spoons of sugar, sprinkled over the hot porridge, now smelling extra sweet.

I could smell it from the bedroom, I leapt out of bed, a rush of blood hitting my head, almost tripping over my blanket. I rushed down the fourteen stairs, bouncing about like Zebedee from the Magic Roundabout, giddy as anything.

Mum looked at me with those smiling eyes, just as she did every day before. "Come on, you lazy little sleepy head, or you will miss your first day at school," arms stretched waiting to lift me on my chair. It didn't take me long to demolish the milk and porridge, and soon after I found myself washing my hands and face followed by brushing my teeth. Mums regime, "got to have healthy gums, they look after your teeth" she would often recite to me, especially when I was in one of those toddler moods. Mum always fussed over me, constantly having me brush my teeth, smelly breath was one of mums' pet hates, she could not stand the stench from some of the people she had met, always saying there was no need not have clean smelling breath, also adding, a beautiful smile could transform a day.

I stood there in my new grey blazer, short pants, and my pale blue shirt all buttoned up. My grey knee-length socks with my feet tucked into my new black lace-up shoes. There I was dressed up to the nines, mum with her Polaroid 210 land automatic camera pointing at me, "smile" she said followed by the click and me blinded by the flash. Mum placed the camera down on the table, knowing it would take a while for the photo to develop. With the time now 08:45 am mum signalled me towards the door, pointing her finger. "Time to go now David," said mum already passing me, and halfway out the door. Suddenly, a surge of dread shrouded me, giving me that sick tingle feeling in my tummy. Mum placed her gentle warm hand in mine and winked at me as we left the house and started the dreaded walk up Hawkshead crescent towards the school. We had travelled this road many times, but today the hill seemed like a mountain. The street was empty, most of the kids would be in class now, just the odd straggler racing up towards the school gates.

The sun shone brightly, breaking through as the clouds began to disappear into blue skies. It was a perfect weather day for the onset of a new chapter in my life, but my poor little heart didn't feel this way. It was beating frantically; I was finding it hard to breathe, fear racing through my body. I didn't want to go to school; I wanted to stay at home with mum as I had always done. Tears were forming, soon rolling down my face. Mums' sideways glance knew I was hurting, she knelt and kissed my forehead, followed by the wiping away of my tears, with the handkerchief she had pulled from her right coat pocket.

"Nothing to worry about David, it's going to be a lovely day, and you will make some new friends too," she said, her reassuring smile and tender words comforting me. I looked up into her face, my bright baby dog eyes accepting her words, pulling me closer, feeling her warmth as she hugged me tightly, and ruffling my hair, before we set off again, heading towards the school gates.

We passed through the large iron school gates, following the concrete path towards the main door. My stomach still churned, but no longer the sickness churn, a nervous, anxious churning, a let's just piss myself kinda churn, needless to say, I didn't.

There loomed the school, an old grey looking building with a small annex forming from the main building at the top right-hand corner. The main build was a square with a small garden situated in the centre of the building, a courtyard full of plants and flowers. This was to become our environmental studies area in later years.

Inside, it had an appearance of an endless structure, dark battleship grey coloured corridors travelling on forever, with doors, so many doors, thought I would never remember which one was my classroom. Through the large metal window framed windows, spanned the concrete square schoolyard edged by the school sports fields, the housing estate loomed beyond.

Escorted by Mrs. Haigh, the headmaster's Secretary, heading down the long corridor towards my class. Mum and me almost running, struggling to keep up with her. Her long legs outstretched with every step as if she was marching, and her clothes making her look older than her thirty-three years, resembled more of a uniform. Her white blouse and grey jacket and knee-length skirt. She had mousy brown hair tied up in a bun, clean face, naked of makeup apart from a bit of blusher and lipstick, but even that was minimal. She wasn't unattractive, just very average looking, but looked quite intimidating, had that look of authority about her. In my later years and with my odd run ins with her, I often wondered if there was a Mr. Haigh, and if he felt as intimidated by her as much as I did. She was quite a frightful woman. No matter right or wrong, if you had the displeasure of being sent to her office for detention during your break times, you were always wrong.

We enter room sixteen; the class is well underway, the kids shouting out the two times table, the twenty-three children sat on little wooden chairs behind a small wooden desk. Silence breaks all conversations as we enter. The teacher, a beautiful young woman (not that I knew of that kind of things then, but in later years I learned well.) but even as a child you could see how beautiful she was. She resembled a young Ann-Margret from the movies. Her shiny red shoulder length hair

51

with her symmetrical face. Her perfect nose and full-lipped mouth.

Mrs. Haigh introduced us to Miss Pointer, and then without another word left the room, leaving mum, and I stood in front of the class. Miss Pointer asked Mum a few questions and then asked mum to leave me with her. Mum began her departure out of the room. Instantly I began to cry and started to run, heading straight for my mum, Miss Pointer was too quick and like a flash of lightning, intervened, scooping me up in her arms; you could smell the fresh flowery scented perfume on her. This fragrance had a calming effect on me, and I was soon subdued.

Mum wept as she left the room and out of the schoolyard for home, mum had never allowed me to leave her side over the last four and a half years. Suddenly she felt very lonely, her day now empty, at a loss with herself, no longer needed to watch over me. This was a heart-breaking moment for the both of us.

Mum closed the front door behind her, walking into a house of silence, only the sound of her footsteps making her way to the kitchen.

Margaret seized the camera and removed the photo from the Polaroid 210; her face breaking into a smile as she looked down proud, and lovingly at the picture, then placing it on the mantelpiece. Dad would be very proud of his little boy, all smart and grown up in his new school clothes.

Pouring herself a fresh cup of tea in her favourite china cup, Margaret retreats to her Mills and Boon, to escape the trauma of me starting school, transporting herself into a world of love and romance.

Miss Pointer held my hand as she returned her attention to the class, mixed with boys and girls from four and a half to five years old. Speaking in a soft, mellow tone, she glances over her class, "Let's all say hello to David, our newest member of the class." The room erupts into a frenzy, all the pupils clapping and screaming, giving me an enthusiastic welcome. Miss Pointer with her hands on her hips and shaking her head, sternly tells the class to settle down, then summons me to find an empty desk.

Exploring the room, I find space on the second row of the six, each housing five writing desk. The familiar face of Elizabeth sat in the one to the right of mine; she smiles her gorgeous smile as I sit in my chair for the first time.

Over the next few hours, we sing nursery rhymes and display our skills at painting. I join in, painting a picture of a red fireman stood next to his engine. It was my love of watching the Trumpton towns firemen, Pugh, Pugh, Barney, Magrew, Cuthbert, Dibble, and Grubb, on children's afternoon TV that inspired me, singing the song in my head as I continue to splash red paint with every stroke of my brush. Unlike most of the kids who drew their homes and family, like any average kid that age would.

Elizabeth had drawn a sad picture of her mum crying; Miss pointer stares at the picture feeling a little distressed and uncomfortable, asking her "why is she crying in the picture," Elizabeth only knowing the truth, answers, "because she had lost my daddy, and mummy always cries in her bed at night." Miss Pointer gives out a caring look, holding Elizabeth's hands explaining to Elizabeth, that in time things would change. Even though Miss Pointers words were kind and sincere, Elizabeth's mum still cries herself to sleep most nights.

As the weeks passed, me and Elizabeth were accepted into the fold of kids in our class, Ryan Backhouse, the oldest at five years was a tall, plump kid, round freckled faced, blonde haired, with rosy cheeks and always dirty, his clothes were second hand, his dad was unemployed like most on our street. The economy had hit a low causing many to be unemployed, most of the factories were laying off workers now automation had settled in, the new age of mass production.

Ryan took it upon himself to look after me. He had taken quite a shine to me, had never seen a mixed race kid before, vowing we would be friends forever. I have to admit he's good to have on your side, keeps the other kids at bay.

His carefree attitude making him the comedian of the group, always making faces and making us all laugh, yet also the hardest kid in my year and someone to fear.

Ryan learned how to fight at such a young age; his older brothers saw to that, Phil and Carl. Two big twelve-year-old twins who were always on the wrong side of the law with their petty stealing, mainly from the local store, I wouldn't mind, but they weren't that good at it, they were caught more often than not. Sent home with a size eleven kick up the backside from the owner Mr. Green, a tall mountain of a man, at six feet five and muscles on top of muscles, not someone you really want to trifle with.

Mr. Green was a pleasant man in general, but had, had his share of bad luck, lost his wife to Yellow fever just over three years ago, after a trip to Africa. A holiday that should have been a holiday of a lifetime, now at twenty-eight, he found himself alone. He never showed his feelings to the outside world, but like Janet, often cried before he escaped into slumber.

During the first school term, nothing much changed, I had learned how to count to 20, write our names and sing a lot; in fact, all we did was sing. Miss Pointer was a delightful teacher, kind and thoughtful. She was patient and gentle, and always had time for all of us. Every morning we drank from our small bottles of milk before starting our lessons; this would calm us down, ready to listen.

She would bake cakes and buns at home and share them with us on Friday afternoons as a treat for our good behaviour. Her influence flowed smoothly through the class; her teaching methods were simple. It was her genuine compassion and affection towards her children that made it a pleasure to be at school. School was fun. I had settled into school life well, no hang-ups about my skin colour, I was the only kid from an ethnic background, not that you would have known, the infant's school kids never thought of anything different between us, it was an age of innocence before a child learns the realities of life, and the cruel torment it can bring.

As we got older, I moved along with my class, further up the education path, learning and accepting the rules of school life, discipline, and gaining new friendships.

Most mornings me, Elizabeth and Ryan would meet outside my gate and walk to school together; our school was only at the top of our street, so we were allowed to go on our own, unaided by a grown up. Life seemed simple those days. Minimal traffic, possibly no more than four car owners on my street.

The media wasn't the world contracting onto a little box you watched 24/7, no, TV finished about midnight most nights, and the world was still innocent to many eyes, unexplored. We had three channels, ITV, BBC 1 and 2, and no mobile phones or personal computers with internet. The world still had a lot to offer, many adventures with unknown people and unknown places yet to explore.

We were known as the terrible threesome, mainly because Ryan beat up the other kids and made them give Elizabeth and me their sweets, Ryan hardly ever kept them for himself, he had some kind of allergic reaction to sweets, and sugar based foods, the doctors couldn't say what it was. Ryan's taste buds rejected the taste for some reason. Was told it was some kind of a rare condition, not commonly found in Britain, so he managed on a strict diet, cutting out sweets and keeping to the more savoury food types, this wasn't an easy task as we hadn't explored the variety you see in supermarkets these days, food in the UK was still rather bland. With all that said, Ryan would sooner eat a stick of celery than a chocolate bar, at least it didn't make him sick. He had missed three weeks of schooling this last few months, while the doctors scratched their heads wondering why and what made him suffer like this. We had missed his jovial antics, some of the school kids relived, not being bullied, but our class had really missed him, he was a popular, fun and sporty kid, Miss Pointer had us make get well cards, I delivered them with mum on one of our many hospital visits. Ryan's family would be there visiting him too, the boys scoffing down candy bars, (no doubt stolen from the local sweet shop), always offering me one. I would thank them and tuck into the one of many they had helped themselves to. Phil and Carl took me under their wing, just like Ryan, always looking out for me, just in case.

With time passing by, Ryan was turning into a real figure of a lad, shooting up, he was the tallest kid in our year, even some of the girls had noticed, and alerted their attention towards him. Ryan blushed quite quickly and was always avoiding them; they would tease and chase him around the playground, screaming after him.

Watching Ryan evade the interest of the girls was highly hilarious, most of us kids, mocking him, in truth, we were a little jealous of all the attention he was getting.

CHAPTER 7

GOODBYE MISS POINTER

It was the last term at school before Christmas 1970, with three years of schooling under our belts. We were more than happy, in fact, I found it a pleasure to go to school, hang out with my friends, listen to their gossip, and playing together. The most significant bonus was, I was doing very well in all my lessons.

The school was in a vibrant mood. It would seem everyone was on a high; even the cold, wet winter weather couldn't dissuade us from this feeling. The smell of chocolate, the aroma of cinnamon, and the overall Christmas seasonal festivities had taken over. The school ceilings were loaded with streamers and paper lanterns, plus many other colourful handmade decorations splashed in every room. Not one kid refused to help, this was a child's ideal school lesson, messing up with paints and glue. Peeling the dried-up glue from our hands like peeling skin, chasing the girls, revoltingly blowing glue snot from our noses, and watching them scream. Miss Pointer waving her finger and shaking her head in disapproval, but leniently allowing this, due to the time of year and the fact there was no malice intended, Just boisterous fun.

Back home, mum and dad were out shopping most Saturdays, enjoying the singing, the Salvation army choirs on every corner, the smell of chestnuts roasting, the street vendors selling them by the bag full, the hot chocolate piping hot, steam rising from the cardboard cups, and the in-store Christmas music, the bright lights shimmering on the precinct Christmas tree.

It was the time of the hustle and bustle of getting presents, being knocked, and pushed, the rush to buy the most wanted got to have toys, and the stocking up of extra food and drink ready for the Christmas shut down.

I don't think the larder could have taken anymore, the fridge was full, even the cupboard under the stairs.

It seemed unfair that most of the families in our street and surrounding areas on the estate, couldn't afford what mum and dad could. Christmas could be hard for some of our neighbours, I never realised, just like most kids, what you see in your home is pretty much the norm, and we would carry on our lives entirely oblivious to needs of others.

My parents were very charitable this time of year, always giving to the Salvation Army. A donation of food, with a few wrapped-up presents for the less fortunate. These were gladly received, and a special pray was given to mum and dad with their blessings. My parents didn't practice any religion; they always told me it's not who or what you believe in, it was always about doing the right thing.

Chris Parker and his sister Jenny were from such a family; their parents always struggled to make ends meet. It wasn't that they couldn't afford pleasant things, quite the opposite, their father Barry was in good employment; he was the foreman at the ice cream factory in Crossgates, about four miles from where we lived. The trouble with Barry and Joan was that they were very sociable, this was to be their downfall. They were regulars in the local pub most days of the week, drinking away their housekeeping, leaving their children living on scraps and hand me downs from others in the street. It wasn't that they didn't love their children, but from an early age before Chris was born, Barry and Joan had lived the high life, trouble was they live a champagne life on a beer money existence.

Chris hung around with us on the street, a popular kid who didn't mind being the quiet one, the one who just got on with it, the kid who never took charge or imposed his ideas on others.

Chris was a quiet kid, but smart. He excelled well above the rest of us in class, we never picked on him for being a swat, mainly because he didn't flaunt it.

Half the kids from our street loved playing in their yard, especially every Friday evening; this was mostly due to Barry's satchel full of ice lollies and choc ices. Our faces were covered in ice cream and chocolate as we made our way home at the end of play. For some of the gang, it was the best day; it was the only day in the week they got treats unless they managed to grab some from over the newsagents counter when he wasn't looking. I'm sure he knew but never said anything. Mr. Roberts was an elderly gent, probably about sixty years old. We thought he must have been the oldest man ever, his weathered, wrinkled face and his thin head of wiry grey hair. He was never cross with us if he caught us, just asking us to return them, then gave us a few back in our hand and told us to get lost before he forgot his manners. It was comical; we always said thank you to him as we left his shop. This would amuse him. To this day, I will never know how he kept that shop going.

Chris was the same age as me, was in my class too, Jenny was younger at five years old; she followed Chris as if they were joined at the hip, she was petite and shy, Chris had many scuffles, trying to protect her from the bullies on the street. On one such occasion, Karen Simonds, a twelve-year-old, twice Jenny's age and size, started hitting Jenny and calling her names, all because she could, knowing Jenny was too small and frightened to fight back. Chris did what any older brother would; he had gone up against her, receiving a black eye for his troubles. The unfortunate thing for Karen was, her mum had seen the whole saga. Karen was made to apologise and couldn't sit down for a few days after that. Poetic justice was such a good thing, not that we knew of or understood it back then.

Even though the clothes they wore were hand-me-downs from the street, they were spotless and pressed, never tatty or torn, both always polite, smart too; no one could ever say a wrong word about these two, probably the best-behaved kids in the street. Even at this youthful age Chris and Jenny could read from big books with small writing, and their vocabulary and written work were far advanced for their age, it was the one thing Joan did for her children, she believed that education was the only way to get out of this poverty-stricken estate.

Class five C, with the thirty-two, seven to eight-year-olds, all sat behind their little wooden desk. The racket was quite deafening, all of us trying to speak over the next kid, laughter erupting at the silliest of jokes. Miss Pointer sat watching, relaxed, pondering over the magazine she was reading, allowing us to get it out of our system before the start of lessons.

Ryan sat there; his audience captivated, all us kids crouched around his desk daring not to speak or move just in case we missed the punch line, his face a light, glowing, eyes wide, knowing he had us all transfixed, he blurts out his joke "This man walks into a bar … Ouch". Well, he fell off his seat erupting into a fit of giggles, rolling all over the floor laughing and kicking his legs, the rest of us sat there on our chairs gobsmacked, not one of us got it, Miss Pointer gave a quiet titter. I'm not entirely sure if it was at us or the joke she found funny.

Ryan's brother Phil had told it to him two days earlier. Phil had spent a further ten minutes explaining it to Ryan, who now spent the rest of the morning explaining it to us. Miss Pointer used the joke for her lesson. How we interpret words with more than one meaning.

The dining hall was overcome with noise, the dinner ladies were baffled at the laughter and gaiety in the dinner line. "Ouch" the word rang out from the queue of children. Miss Pointer looked on as the dinner ladies tried to stop and control us, she continued to walk to her table smiling, informing the Headteacher why we were all excitable, he gave out a huge belly laugh, which made us laugh all the more. Ryan was king for a day in our eyes.

The dinner time break ended, and we returned to the class, double filed marching towards the classroom door. Outside the class window we could see the older children still playing, they had another ten minutes before their break time ended. We watched them, envious, wishing we were still out there too, running, screaming, and making a nuisance of our selves.

Miss Pointer called for our attention, wanting to tell us something important. We sat there in front of her on the large floor mat, waiting for her to speak. Then came the crushing blow, the announcement she was leaving teaching and wouldn't be returning after Christmas, the room fell into a deathly silence, we sat there dumbfounded, not wanting to believe the words that transmitted from her mouth. A cloud of misery engulfed the room; you could have cut through the atmosphere with a knife. Miss Pointer explains she's getting married to someone called Eric Platt, an engineer in Saudi Arabia; she had us all look it up on the big map of the world pinned on the back wall.

"This is where I will be living after I get married," she said pointing at some unpronounceable name on the map, a trembling in her voice, her face no longer displaying her natural beautiful cheery smile, and the sparkle in her eyes seemed to diminish. Not wanting her to leave us, I shouted out, she could stay and marry me in five years when I'm older; she stands and makes her way over to me, and kisses me on the forehead, her smile now broad across her face, amused from my words. "David as sweet as you are, I think you need to be older than twelve to get married, and anyway I will be old and wrinkly by then" came her reply, toying with my thick loose curly dark mop with her fingers. Elizabeth chirps in "Miss you will never be wrinkly … you're too beautiful" the class agree. "If only that were true," thought Miss Pointer making her way back to her desk.

The mood changed from the mornings fun and joviality; we sat there sobbing for most of the afternoon, tears rolling, weeping unable to do any work. Miss Pointer had played a big part in our lives, and we were very fond of her. She had guided us over the last three or so years, taught us how to read and write, and how to be polite and use our manners, and how to be acceptable in today's society, Miss Pointer was going to missed, and whoever was to replace her, had a large gap to fill.

Miss Pointer plucked at her guitar strings and began to sing, lightening the mood, by the end of the day, we were all back smiling, joining in and playing games. Afterwards had a special tea party before we left that afternoon, and Miss Pointer gave us all a special present as we left for home. My gift was the new Batman annual. This book stayed on my bookshelf for the rest of my life; this was a lifelong treasure, one of my treasured possessions.

The short journey home took longer than usual; we didn't run excitedly, jumping, and screaming at the top of our voices, we were sad and gloomy, far too upset to join in any games. "I hate her" said Ryan weeping, wiping his runny nose on his sleeve, "No you don't Ryan, your just upset the same as me" chirped Elizabeth (the sensible one) looking just as moody, as for me, well, I too had lost the appetite for fun as we all moped home, heads down and shoulders crumpled over.

Mum could see how upset I was, to me, it was like losing a friend, Miss. Pointer was someone who I had grown close to and trusted above all in the school. Miss. Pointer was the next best thing to being my mum. I was left to sulk in my room that evening. Mum explained to dad why I was not my cheery self and not to antagonize me, due to not being in a playful mood. Mum underestimated dad; he knew how to bring me back out of the gloom, he was a sensitive man at heart.

Dad knocked on my door before he entered. I laid there on my bed, my head tucked under my pillow, his firm hands cradled my shoulders. "It's all ok to be upset son, you'll see, you will be ok tomorrow, not great son; but ok," then I felt the light pat of his hand on my back. I shuffled out from beneath my pillow; Dads reassuring face shone down at me, I could sense the hurt draining away, knowing he was right. "I love you dad" I yelled, jumping into his arms, he hugged me tightly. His arms folded around me. "Go on son, go call for Ryan and Elizabeth, I think you kids need some fun time," came dads reply, then placing a fifty pence piece in my hand. "Go on then, get to the sweet shop before he closes." He watched me jump off the bed and race out of the house to Ryan's, shouting back at him, "Thanks dad, love you." Mum linked arms with dad, as they watched me running up the hill. "You softy old fart" chuckled mum, his response, was a kiss on her cheek.

The following mornings school assembly, Mr. James the head teacher was droning on, who had achieved what and what he was expecting after the Christmas break, then came the crunch, the announcement of our new teacher for class six C as we will be known then. He stood there in his regular worn out tweed jacket, arms behind his back. His strong Irish accent filling the hall. "I would like to introduce you all to the teacher replacing Miss Pointer," followed by a cough to clear his throat before continuing. "Who we will all miss terribly, however, I would like us all to congratulate Miss Pointer on her impending wedding, and to thank Miss Pointer for her years of valuable service and for the kindness she has given and shown her children." The whole of the school assembly stood and applauded continuously for five to seven minutes, sounding like a thunderous ear-splitting boom. Mr. James raising his arms urging us all to settle, before continuing his speech again as the hall fell silent, "ladies and gentlemen, boys and girls this is Mr. Preston" the hall erupted into applause welcoming the new teacher, all apart from our class. We stood there with our heads down, not one of us took a peak, curiosity not getting the better of us.

The young, tall stranger stood, a well-groomed athletic man, his long strides across to the podium seemed effortless as he passed the congregation of staff and pupils. "Hello all, my name is Darren Preston, I am honoured to be teaching here after the school holidays, and I will give my all to ensure that class six C are a credit to this school … Thank you" he sat down as quickly as he had risen.

It was several minutes before the assembly finished, single file by single file the large hall emptied.

We had our usual Christmas dinner at lunch, instead of the typical stodgy school dinner. The afternoon carol service from the senior classes rang out across the hall, and finally, Mr. James stood seizing all the attention from the hall, wishing everyone a wonderful Christmas and a happy new year.

The school had finished for the holidays, emptying the school in record time.

Outside the school gate, we heard the war cry, "Snowball fight" bellowed by some older kid. That was it, the start of over one hundred kids hurling snowballs at each other. The parents who had taken the time to collect their children from school got caught up in it too. At first yelling abuse at us all, and realising this was futile and getting them nowhere, so they too picked up handfuls of snow and rolled them up and joined in the fun.

By the time I got home I was soaked through, mum just giggled at me, exploding into fits of laughter, finding it amusing as I entered the house covered in snow.

CHAPTER 8

CHRISTMAS 1970

Our street looked a picture postcard, a true white Christmas. Snow dropping from the skies on Christmas day, the snow-capped roofs flowing down to the even layer of snow across the roads, the family cars resembling marshmallow man vehicles, all fluffed, fully covered, not a glimpse of metal to be seen. Snowdrifts rising over the footpaths like royal icing, perfectly layered on top of a cake, not one blade of grass escaping, covering the whole of the central grassed area in front of our house.

Even the solitary tall oak at the right of the green had a snowy top, draping down from its branches like a willow.

The fine snow dancing, and swirling like the morning mist, a ballet of colourless shapes.

The chill from the pane of glass, my face pressed against the cold glass window, taking in the beautiful sight, watching the snow glide down from the white skies covering all in its path. The enchanting patterns swirling, dancing in the light chilly air, kissing the window as it settled, sliding down the pane, retaining its snowflake shape.

Christmas day had finally arrived, the smell of the fat bird cooking in the oven, mixed with an array of sweet Christmassy scents, Christmas pudding, cinnamon, sage, and chestnut stuffing, the unmistakable aroma of chocolate and dad's aftershave, mums Chanel perfume and the clean-cut flowers set out in the vase on the table.

The five-foot spruce-pine Christmas tree aglow with hundreds of fairy lights, with the neatly wrapped presents concealed underneath. The stress of the build-up and anticipation of the coming of the day no more, no longer scurrying around searching the house for the hidden presents, and not finding any, no more rushing, in, and out from one shop to the next, no longer trying to stay awake just to get a glimpse of Santa.

It wasn't long before the ritual of Christmas day started, with the sound of paper rustling, torn from the presents. Me overjoyed, the excitement beaming, my broad smile displayed on my face, mum watching, her delight evident as I played with the new batman car, firing red torpedoes from out of the top, and my commando action men, with all their accessories. I got two, what a lucky kid I was, jumping up and down; full of the joys of Christmas, dad capturing the image on the Polaroid camera. Mum buoyant with the look of amazement on my face, with every scream of delight as I open present after present.

Music filled the house, Dave Edmunds', I hear you knocking, playing on the radio, the Christmas chart number one, Dad stomping about while mum twirled until she was dizzy. Mum and dad singing to every word, a celebratory drink in hand. This was going to be the best Christmas ever.

09:20 am, we found it quite unusual to have someone knock on our door, so early on a Christmas morning. Most families would be going through the same ritual as us. The sharp rap at the door is repeated.

Horror and dread shroud mum's face as she opens the door. Looking down to witness Chris and Jenny stood there shivering, frozen through to the bone, their dark-rimmed eyes, evident of their constant weeping, dressed in oversized pyjamas, Wellington boots and hand me down overcoats covered in snow.

The sound of a scared child's voice trembling as he spoke. "Mum and dad are not home Mrs. Brown, and we can't find them in the house". Huddled up together close, they stood blue with cold, shivering, and constantly weeping, overwhelmed with worry, not knowing their fate.

Had their parents left them? or just too drunk to make their way home? Mum grabbed them instantly, whisking them up in her arms, at the same time, bursting into tears, overwhelmed with pity, hurriedly she got them near the fire, to get them warm. Dad rushed into the kitchen and made two fresh hot chocolates and some toast; they look famished. Who knew when they last ate.

Chris and Jenny were now sat at the dining table guzzling down the offerings. Mum was on the phone, contacting the police; she was quite calm now, her tears subsided not letting the situation get the better of her.

I joined dad to check the house, only to find it deserted. The scene was unbelievable; a deep sadness veiled me, the house was bare from anything to do with

Christmas, not a card or decoration could be seen, not even a Christmas tree. The unhappiest thing I noticed was that there were no presents, anywhere.

The house was clean but shown minimal offerings, most surprising was no television. How did these two kids survive? We searched every room, the stairs had no carpet, the wooden treads were clean, varnished to show off the grain. Inside the children's rooms, we found no evidence of toys, a bare wooden floor with a rug next to the single bed. Both rooms were identical, only the cloths in the cupboards gave tell whose room was whose.

Dad and I returned home, Dad said I was to tell no one what I had seen, or should I say the lack of what I saw, responding I gave him a nod.

Mum, who was still on the phone with the police passed the phone to dad. Dad took another four minutes speaking to the police before hanging up.

I sat watching the two children; I could see the distress in their eyes, the swollen dark baggy eyes, the tear stains embedded onto their faces, the look of fear seeping out from every pore. I felt sorrow creeping over me; I wanted to let them have some of my sweets to try and cheer them up, dad told me even though that was a kind gesture, it wasn't what was needed now and ushered me back into the living room. Sulking I meander back into the room.

The two of them looked as if they had not slept for days, both heads nodding, as they tried to fight it, fighting to stay awake. Dad took one look at them, noticing these children struggle to keep from sleep yet needing it, he scoops them up in his arms, and makes his way to his and mum's bedroom, laying them on the large king-sized bed, covering them up as sheer exhaustion wins over, and the two lay, sleeping heavily, looking very tiny and lost on this large bed.

It took no longer than seven minutes for the police to arrive at our door. The three men led by Detective Inspector Collins, a tall, wiry fellow, balding on top, evident when he removed his grey trilby, his ageing face looking like a wounded animal, displaying a pain that could not be seen, "Good morning Mr. Brown ...My name is Detective Inspector Collins; these are my colleagues DC Fletcher and DS Shackleton." His arm outstretched as his gravelly voice introduced his colleagues.

Fletcher was a young man in his early twenties, short blond hair, round-rimmed glasses on a small head, his features were untidy, like that of a student at University, his beige overcoat quite tatty and too large for his slender body. As for Shackleton, he was a tall, broad man, somewhat overweight by more than a few pounds, his cloths stretched over his frame tightly, making him look uncomfortable.

The snow continued to fall; and with the wind picking up along with the temperature dropping a few more degrees, the three men stood there in the doorway, the bitter cold biting at their faces, turning them blue with cold.

"Please come in and get warm by the fire," said Harold pointing to the welcoming warmth of the gas fire. The three men did just that, rushing over, hogging the heat from the fire, whiles Harold closed the door behind them.

Dad sat down in his usual fireside chair and mum brought out a tray of piping hot mugs of tea and a plate of Ringtones biscuits. DI Collins thanked her, while the three men tucked in.

I was sent to my room to play, so the adults could carry on their conversations, with me supposed to be out of earshot, but I could hear everything, especially mum crying.

The living room fell silent apart from the words of DI Collins. "Sorry to have to tell you this. We found the bodies of Mr. and Mrs. Parker by the peace park near the Wilsons arms; they were found laying on the road, their bodies were frozen solid, would seem they met a terrible end." His word lacking despondency but showed empathy. Everyone knew the Parkers were heavy drinkers and as popular as they were, the local residents knew poor Chris and Jenny were left with very little. "The report from the post-mortem at St James's hospital said that Mr. Parker had suffered a twisted ankle, but been as drunk as he was, would have felt nothing and passed out where he had fallen. As for Mrs. Parker, she stumbled over him, hitting her head on the pavement, causing her to be concussed, again it would appear they both died from hypothermia." Harold looked straight into the face of the DI, almost demanding, "How Long were they there?" the young DC Fletcher intervened, looking at the notes from his notebook, "It's believed the pub had a lock-in till 2 O'clock this morning, seven hours or so, not much longer than that! ...They were found by our local bobby on his beat around eight O'clock this morning. Poor beggars, how're the kids bearing?" He was genuinely upset, feeling the strain, his whole demeanour showed sorrow. "We were just about to call on the house to find the little ones when you called, but trying to contact social services proved futile" Dc Fletcher continued. Dad shook his head in disappointment, "What now for these kids?" he asked, "Don't Know Mr. Brown, need somewhere for these kids to stay until we can contact social services" came DI Collins answer.

It was as if the house had turned grey in colour; the mood was sullen; the Christmas cheer had faded to nothingness. A cloud of sadness had taken over.

It had been agreed that mum and dad would care for Chris and Jenny until the social welfare team were back at work on Tuesday 29th December or someone comes forward to claim them.

Joan had a sister, Jane, who lived in the Midlands, Coventry somewhere. However, she was hard to find, she travelled often, to some of the most exotic locations of the world. Her job being a model for a famous clothes designer, this would take her out of the country for most of the year. Never knowing when she would be back home.

Jane had never seen Chris or Jenny, not even during their births, never sent them a birthday card or anything come to think about it, Joan and her sister Jane were complete opposites. Jane wanted nothing more than her freedom and wealth, while Joan was in love with the idea of being married with children, and the notion of freedom, both Joan and Barry were stuck in the nineteen sixties and the flower power era.

With noting much more to say the policemen thanked mum and dad, closing the door behind them. No wishes of a merry Christmas, just a handshake followed by the closing of the door. The house left in a sombre mood, sadness where a joyous cheer should be had.

I lost track of the time, playing quietly in my room, my parents sat discussing the best way ahead and how to deal with the rest of the day.

"David why don't you go next door to see Elizabeth" mum said, wanting me out of the house so she could talk with dad. I didn't hesitate, I was around their house in record time, anything to take these horrid feelings away.

Elizabeth was my best friend; we had grown up as neighbours for nearly 3 years now; even back then I think I had fallen in love with her. She was going to be a beautiful woman in the years to come; this was evident in her looks now, her mum Janet was a beautiful woman too, Janet's life had turned for the better, she was seeing Mr. Green of late.

Mum and dad looked after Elizabeth on Friday nights, her sleeping in our spare bedroom, while her mum and Mr. Green did their courting. Mr. Green was sat on the worn-out ageing brown leather three-seater next to Janet; they were getting serious about their relationship. They met at the local workingmen's club. My parents had taken Janet out for a well-deserved break, a chance to meet others in a more social light rather than stuck at home, which was the norm for her. Janet had dressed up to please and was by far the most attractive women there, turning heads on every corner. Mr. Green's eye caught a glimpse of her, and the rest was history.

Janet is much more cheerful now, smiling more these days, Mr. Green the same, together they were the perfect family. Elizabeth had some new clothes bought for her this Christmas; this was something that had been very rare in her life. Things were changing for the better; the house was a much happier place to visit.

Janet no longer cried herself to sleep, nor did Mr. Green.

Earlier mum laid out the clean clothes at the foot of the bed, for children to change into. The two slept heavily as mum watched over them, all the troubles of the world disappearing, tears slowly fell from her eyes, lifting her arm and wiping her eyes on her sleeve, not wanting dad to know she had been crying again, with a deep sigh and a loud cough she cleared her throat, transferring her frown into a smile knowing the children were at least safe for now.

The woollen Christmas jumper with the snowman picture was one of my old ones that no longer fit, also the pair of jeans. Chris was smaller than me so these would fit perfectly, mum asked Janet if she could have some of Elizabeth's clothes that she had grown out of for Jenny. Janet and Mr. Green offered to help mum and dad in any way they could.

Mr. Green took this quite hard; he had been friends with Barry for many years, they had played on the same football team, until Barry gave it up a few years ago, due to his drinking.

The smell of the Christmas dinner had awoken Chris and Jenny from there slumber. Roasted turkey along with the roasted vegetables, the aromas wafting through the house.

Their appetite ready for a feast, the trials of the morning disappearing, this simple act of kindness transporting the children to new heights. Mum had decided that we were going to carry on with our Christmas no matter what happened.

With a mighty yawn, the two of them awoken, a little bit disorientated, finding themselves in a strange bed. Chris tapping his sisters shoulder, "I think these clothes are for us." On seeing the clothes, both excited and a little giddy, they hurriedly changed into them; we could hear them giggling and muttering to each other on how clean our house was and how they could almost taste the lavish feast. "Do you think they will let us have some dinner?" Jenny's little voice asked her brother, "I hope we can" came his reply, both desperately wishing this was to be. Apprehensively they slowly made their way to the dining room, fear etched inside them, frightful of rejection; their eyes opened wide, the sight of the two seats which had been prepared in readiness for them, the silver plate mats with a large plate, and silver cutlery, placed neatly by its side, with the wine glass filled with cream soda. I was sat at the table, my eyes wide open watching them. Nodding I acknowledge them to take their place at the table. Christopher climbs up effortlessly, while Jenny cumbersomely manages to get herself seated.

Unable to control their feelings, they burst into laughter, staring at the table. "Never had a Christmas dinner before, never had turkey or stuffing" whispered Chris across the table to me, "What does it taste like" Jenny joining in, almost bouncing on her chair. I was shocked, to say the least, who would have thought in this day and age they would be still kids who had never tasted a piece of turkey? Maybe this would always be, a world where the basic food types had not yet reached the many dinner tables across the globe, let alone on my street.

Mum set the serving plates in the empty aisle on the table, the steam rising from various dishes, the piping hot roast potatoes, the oven cooked winter vegetables and of course the turkey. Mum guided the two lost souls, reassuring them it was all Okay to be here and the meal was for everyone. Dad stood, carving knife and fork in hand, cutting through the turkey cleanly, slicing piece after piece.

The morning's events now placed in the past, it was as if they had never occurred, not one mention from Chris or Jenny about their parents, they just ploughed into their dinner. Dad could see this saddened mum a little. With a sorrowful tear, mum braved it through the meal, trying not to show her feelings.

It wasn't long before the festivities were in full swing, the party hats from the Christmas crackers, the weak jokes on the little slips, and the food piled high on our plates. Nothing to be heard but the munching from around the table, and the odd little snigger from our two little guests. Finally, mum relaxed and began to enjoy her Christmas. Our two little guest were a pleasure to watch as they tucked into their dinner, you could sense the happiness from them, they were truly comfortable and at ease in our home.

The meal was a success, leaving us all stuffed to the brim unable to move, watching the 36-inch black and white TV, Her Majesty the Queen giving her Nations Christmas speech. In an odd way, the day had been a success.

CHAPTER 9

UNWANTED

The days leading up to the 29th were quite eventful. The weather blowing a gale, the winds too harsh for playing out. Elizabeth joining us, playing with our two guests and me. The noise level reaching unbearable at times, without any intervention from mum or dad saying nothing, happy in the knowledge that we were having fun, yet no mention of Chris and Jenny's parents. The resilience of the two children upsetting mum. Never asking for their mum or dad, strange to think that they would never mention their names. Dad was a closed book never allowing his feelings to show.

The police had managed to contact Joan's sister Jane on the 27th. Jane arrived at our house to claim the children that afternoon.

She's a beautiful young woman, full long golden yellow flowing hair, clean fair-faced, no blemishes, full-lipped, sparkling bright blue eyes, and a figure most women would die for. You could see why this five -foot six woman was a model. The kind of girl who would snap her fingers and a handful of suiters would be at her beck and call.

She entered the room as if she was the Queen of Sheba, all heirs and graces, strutting around like a proud peacock. Even at seven, I could tell mum had taken an instant dislike to her. She gave dad that look she always gave when mum disapproved, but she would never say.

The young constable seemed intimidated by Janes' beauty, after all she looked like a goddess. The police man stood in his six feet and two inches tall slender frame, he could not have been more than twenty-three years old, his boyish looks displaying a shy inverted nature.

"Hello Mrs. Brown, may I introduce you to Miss Jane Turner, the children's aunty" Jane stepped forward holding out her hand, greeting mum with a handshake. It didn't take long for Jane to make up her mind, Jane took one look at the children, both looking up at her, projecting full smiley faces, full of hope, someone to take them away, someone to belong to, to be accepted by a family member, going to live with Aunty Jane was going to be great, or so they thought.

Janes face distorted at the sight of them, instantly we knew, Chris and Jenny were not going home with her, she wasn't the maternal kind. Dad was furious, how he managed to keep his feelings in, we will never know. You could sense him grinding on his teeth, let alone hear him. Jane knew he felt ill of her, she could see it in his eyes, the writing was shown all over dads' face, he didn't need to mention it.

Jane willingly smiled, no fear of despisement, she had no time for this, her world had no allowance for children, especially those that weren't hers by birth right, let alone those which could have been. Within ten minutes, she was leaving, she spoke to mum, brushing her yellow hair away from her eyes, shaking her head slowly. Her voice calm and soft "I can't take these two on" Why would she want two brats sticking around her hemline, holding her back from her jet-set life, her whole body repulsed at the thought. "Something must be done … maybe the social services can get them in an orphanage, or you keep them" she continued, dismissing them as being there, her nose up in the air as she waggled her finger at the two of them.

She may have been beautiful on the outside, but she was definitely ugly on the inside.

It was the last time we ever saw or heard from her; she didn't even leave a forwarding address in case of emergencies. Mum and dad were definitely not impressed. Mum was tempted to throw her out, but wouldn't lower herself, and for the sake of us kids, they had been traumatized too much already.

Without a goodbye or take your leave she was gone.

The police officer asked dad to keep a hold of Chris and Jenny until the social services contact us. Apologetic, the officer informed my parent they could had no power to force her take them and were happy to see the pair of them settled at our house. Jenny jumped up at mum. Her little face bright and cheery, "I love you Aunty Margaret" her tiny voice melting mum inside. Why would no one want these two adorable children, why should they suffer a life without a family, the love, compassion, or the caring nurturing a parent could give? After mum explained to Chris and Jenny, Chris turned at the door and said "Not to worry Mrs. Brown, we love you not her." Mum had to leave the room, too upset for words, she couldn't face the children.

The home of the Parkers was now boarded up and vacant, a small box of photos and personal possessions were sent over to us for safekeeping. Dad took it upon himself to burn Chris and Jenny's clothes, he knew they were just rags and hand me downs from the street, nothing they could hold dear to.

The twenty-ninth came, my parents apprehensive, walking on eggshells, waiting for the unbearable sound of the knock on the door. Nothing happened all morning, mum and dad not daring to move out of the house just in case.

The ringing of the telephone startling them both, leaping out from the comfort of their easy chairs and racing to the hallway where the phone hung, ring, ring it continued, suddenly a silence, the receiver in mums' hand. "Hello, Mrs. Brown how can I help you" answered mum, her voice shaking. "Hello Mrs. Brown, my name is Simon, calling from the social services about Christopher and Jenny Parker, how are they doing?" came the voice from the receiver. The conversation went on for some minutes. Mum replaced the receiver back onto the telephone. Dads eyes stared down at the children, "So what's happening with these two?" asked dad. "Come on, Chris and Jenny go play with David," mum said gently pushing them into the room. The front door opened, both mum and dad walked into the garden, shutting the door behind them.

"Ho Harold, he said they won't be here till after the New year, poor darlings" a slight quiver in her voice. Soon the tears were rolling down mums' face, her emotions taking over. Harold cradled Margret in his arms, standing in silence.

The second day of January and the big stores in town are beginning the winter sales. The best time of the year to bag a great bargain.

"Margaret get the kids ready, we're going clothes shopping" dad shouted from the foot of the stairs. He was beaming, tying his shoelaces, and eagerly throwing on his winter jacket. Mum was finishing with tidying the bedrooms; her heart skipped, she loved shopping, especially dressing up us kids. It took mum less than five minutes getting us into the car, and before you knew it, we were heading off up the road towards the Leeds city centre, ready for an exciting shopping extravaganza.

The city centre was bustling with shoppers pushing and shoving each other, chasing for the best bargains. Mum eyeing the window displays, lost in a shopper's paradise, Jenny breathless in wonder, clinging to her, pointing at the pretty clothes displayed.

Harold spent the day spending his hard-earned cash, buying us kids' new clothes. Dad really knew how to give a treat and spoil us. He never scrimped, he believed if anything was worth doing, then make sure you always give your best and he did. Jenny got three new outfits, was even allowed to pick her own dresses.

Poor Jenny had never picked her own clothes before, never had a new dress before, her stomach churning inside, all stressful, confusion raging through her like a tornado, unable to decide. Overwhelmed, finding this all too much, Jenny threw herself into mum's arms and wept despairingly, her poor little frame shaking. Lifting her up into her arms, mum cuddled her, her soothing voice attempting to calm her. "It's all ok Jenny, no need to cry, I will help you choose" Jenny held mum around her neck, squeezing tighter. "Ho Jenny, this is going to be all right, look I can help you," said mum placing Jenny down and leading her by the hand, soon they were both in giggle fits, trying one dress after another.

Chris was the opposite; he was in seventh heaven, getting quite hyperactive, racing around the store floor, flicking at the hung clothing swaying on the hangers, the attendants frowning upon it.

Dad didn't mind; he saw no reason to chase him. Seeing the joy on this boy's face was enough. Chris like Jenny had never had new clothes before, and as for me, it was just another day in the Brown household, I was spoilt, and I knew it, mum got me extra just so I wouldn't feel put out or despise my two friends.

I didn't need more outfits than them; this was mum's way of showing everyone I was her child.

I knew how much they needed there's, I was becoming more considerate, beginning to understand that some people didn't have the luxuries we have. I had also learnt how to share in the short time they had been with us. I loved having Chris and Jenny staying with us; I was growing very fond of them. I had decided they were my younger brother and sister and would always be.

Mum talked dad round, into taking us to the pub for lunch, wanting to treat the kids, again this was a new experience for Chris and Jenny, who unfortunately found it hard to handle. They weren't used to these acts of kindness. They struggled to choose from the menu, so mum decided what they were to have. Mum spoilt them with a knickerbocker glory for pudding, both mum and dad glowed as they watched us demolish every last spoonful. Closing our eyes, we savoured every mouthful, sent into a blissful paradise from the chocolate, strawberry and vanilla flavours dancing around inside our mouths.

The day had been a wonderful colourful day, Jenny and Chris went to bed joyful and in high spirits, calling my parents mum and dad as they said good night. We raced up the stairs to our rooms wanting the night to pass quickly so we could play again tomorrow. Sleep was going to be difficult, we were all hyperactive, in a buoyant mood, the day's events racing around our heads.

Margaret was very emotional; today had knocked her back a bit. Sobbing in dad's arms, she had never witnessed such sadness, where they should have been joy, overcome by the children's reactions. It was as if their parents had never existed. Mum wanted to talk with the children, but dad said a resounding no, and to allow them just to enjoy their time here with us. Mum seeing sense in this agreed to let it lie. Holding Harold's hand mum whispered, "This is why I love you, Harold, you are one of the most thoughtful people I know, and I thank you for that" her words sincere as she moves closer and kisses him lightly on the lips. Harold holds Margaret closer, they make love and gradually falling asleep, still cocooned in a blissful pose.

Over the next two days, we hardly saw my parents, we played for hours, Elizabeth, and Ryan joining in, they too had grown very fond of my Chris and Jenny. We were quite the little gang, always into something, going home dirty faced, cold, and hungry. We had become almost inseparable; mum was caught up in it too, this was going to break her heart, the day they have to leave.

The day of the Parkers funeral came and passed; it was a chilly day, an overcast sky hiding the afternoon sun. Everyone wrapped up on this grey freezing winter's day, the site deserted, hardly anyone attended, just us, the Backhouses, Janet, Mr. Green, and Elizabeth, also Mr. Graham Potts, the publican from the Wilsons Arms, he had a floral tribute from his locals, sending their condolences.

It was a dull day; the service was quick and dismal, no one spoke much at all. We left the cemetery grieved, feeling low. There were no tears spilt today not even their own children shed a tear. There were no more tears left to spill.

The journey home was serene; even the world outside had fallen into a lull. No birds singing in the trees or rooftops, no stray dogs to be seen, barking at whatever moved, the day was gloomy and grey, too upset to have a ray of sunshine shine down giving a warmth pleasing breeze to wipe away the chill and sadness.

Harold turned the key in the front door. I raced passed into the living room, switching on the gas fire to warm the room, at the same time deposing my hat and coat on the settee arm. Dad made his way to the kitchen to fill the kettle, and prepare the cups, ready for the hot drinks to warm us through. We no sooner shut the door, when the light knock-on-door sounded.

"Hello again." It was the familiar voice of Jenny's, the social worker, that came from behind the opened door. Mum to rush to the door, "Hello Jenny so good see you again" said mum excited. Jenny still had that teacher voice, "Good afternoon Mr. & Mrs. Brown," her face expressionless, she stood in-between two uniformed policemen. "I have come to collect Christopher and Jennifer; they have a place at the local orphanage." Everything just stopped dead. Dad moves mum to the side and allows the policemen to place the children into the police car.

Chris confused and not wanting to leave, yells out frantically "I don't want to go, mum, I want to stay with you" scratching the policeman and kicking the air from over his shoulder, his cry was an aching heart-wrenching cry, the policeman lifting him into the fireman's lift, then placing him into the vehicle. There was no feeling in his task, he came to collect two children and deliver them to the orphanage, and that was it, no personal feelings needed, after all, that wouldn't do, that would only get in the way of his job. This had mum in tears, not only were they being taken away, but he had accepted to calling her mum, Jenny was the same, kicking and screaming as she was led to the car, her screams could be heard across the street,

"Mummy, Mummy I don't want to go" the sound of her voice had mum helpless, breaking down to her knees, Mrs. Backhouse rushing to mum's aid, but no amount of comforting could console her. Dad asked them to get it over quickly, this was wrong, someone should have contacted us first. Elizabeth wrapped herself around me, tears streamed down our faces, but not a sound could be heard from anyone, she pulled me close, feeling my shaking body, she pulled me in tighter.

Jenny retrieved the children's possessions along with the newly bought clothes, placing them into the waiting vehicle, she wished mum and dad well and coldly thanked them for their time as she said goodbye. Dad, choked up, fighting back the tears, stood in the street watching the police car disappear. They drove away as swiftly as they came.

We didn't get the chance to say goodbye to the two of them; mum wanted to hug them, let them know they were always welcome, but not given that opportunity, it broke our hearts.

The funeral had no reflection on how we all were feeling now, the Backhouses and Janet just looked on in disbelief, not saying a word. Mr. Green placed his arms around the sobbing Janet and Elizabeth and took them home; everyone was too upset, unable to express their feelings, too gloomy to react.

Mr. Backhouse hugged mum then kissed her on her cheek; he shook dad's hand "Sorry Harold, I think we will go home" he said gathering his family, placing his arm around Joyce. Joyce wanted to stay with mum, but Mr. Backhouse said it would be best to let us find our own way. Ryan gave me a hug then left with his family. Leaving me standing in the middle of the room. Dad held out his hand for me, but this was too heartbreakingly, holding my hand wasn't going to help this time, I ran into my room and hid under the covers, tears rolling down my face, it hurt so much in my stomach, the pain almost making me vomit.

Mum sat on to her chair, not wanting to move. She was devastated, sobbing continuously. The feeling of hurt and loss, sweeping over her. Dad could not comfort mum, but he sat at her side and held her hand, he too was feeling empty, tears rolled down from his water clouded eyes, a massive void swooped inside us.

I had been in fights that hurt less, this was a feeling of utter bereavement, even though they weren't dead, our sense of loss and sadness, taken to new heights.

We never did see Chris or Jenny again. The local social worker sent mum a letter explaining that they had been deported to Australia with 600 other children in the care system, it read that they were to start a new life and opportunity in the building and growth of a new country. These were to be the last to be deported from the UK from within the British care system. It is said; most of these children never had much of a life, they ended up in institutions and workhouses, starved of affection and love, most of them turning to crime in later life.

Mum had tried to contact them through our local MP, but all was in vain as no news of them ever came our way. Some of these children suffered on route to their destinations with illness, some passing away before reaching their goal.

We never did find out, if they had reached their destination.

CHAPTER 10

A TIME OF CHANGE

With the dawn of the New Year came new prosperity to our streets, life-changing for the young and the old alike. A chance of a better life.

The Barnbow munitions factory in Cross Gates had been blessed with another MOD requisition of new armoured tanks and required some 700 additional employees. This was a massive boost to the local area; giving an employment surge to the male population in our area, most employed as semi-skilled operatives, working on lathes and CNC machinery. The knock-on effect giving the new wealth in the local economy, gave great strength in buying power. The high streets welcomed the extra sales, providing an increase in the employment of shop assistants. For the first time in many years, the pockets of the many on these streets were no longer empty.

Ryan, buoyantly came sprinting down the street, his blond mullet hair bouncing on his head, the excited look on his face.

Me and Elizabeth were playing football on the grassed area in front my house, the snow was disappearing leaving a boggy mess behind it. The sun shone out brightly, burning down on this glorious mid-January morning, which was unusual, to say the least.

The grassy field was a boggy wet mess, from the melted snow, leaving sporadic puddles. We joined in with Carl Fawcett and his mates who were playing football; they had placed their jumpers down as the goal post, avoiding the potholes filled with melted snow. Carl was nine-years-old, a small lad who stuttered when he spoke, but all that didn't matter when he played football. He was transported into another world, quick on his feet and very nimble, he could turn on a sixpence, his footwork was years ahead of his time. He could have been the next Georgie Best, so we all thought. Later in life, he played for Leeds United. His playing career was cut short, tragically killed in a car accident; returning to Leeds in the early hours of the morning, after celebrating at some birthday party in Chester in 1982, it was reported he had been driving while under the influence of alcohol. Footballers rubbing shoulders with the film and recording artist of their time, becoming household celebrities.

Carl had us on his team, Elizabeth could play too, she was quite good and very fast, made me look dire. My skills were non-existent when it came to football.

Ryan was always the one in goal; I don't know why, he was an excellent footballer, one of the fastest kids of his age. I was a defender, I wasn't the best player, in fact, I was terrible, and all I did was hack at the opposition, which worked. I was growing fast now, almost eight years old, I had started to fill out a bit, no longer that small thin coffee coloured skinned kid with the thick mop of hair stuck on his head, but a slender big shouldered lad, who was losing his infant school looks. Elizabeth had shown signs towards me that she cared more than just a friend. We both displayed affection towards each other. When we thought, we were alone we would often hold hands. Mum and Janet believed this was cute, a puppy love mum called it. We just thought it was normal.

The game was the usual sixteen aside, no subs just all us kids running, chasing the one with the ball.

To an outsider, this must have looked quite scary, thirty-two kids chasing a ball on a wet field. We had fun, no doubt about that, and we always finished the game with the next goal wins' scenario, no matter what the score was.

Ryan was excited by his news; his dad had finally got a job after four and a half years on the dole. Ryan was more than overjoyed, his parents could compete with others, now with a reasonable standard of living. "Hi, David" his usual greeting with the broad smile across his face. "Hello Ryan, what's up" I replied, there was never anything much up, we were just good mates and acted out in good mates' fashion. "Nothing, but dads' got a job," he said excited, laughing as he spoke. We already knew, news like this flew around the street, gossip was hype at the moment. Elizabeth cut in; a little frustrated just wanting to play, after all, we got all this from Clive last night when he told dad.

"Hello Ryan, now can you two shut up we all want to play the game," she said pointing at the football.

Six kids stood over the ball, all eager, and ready. Kick off, the first strike of the ball flew high and straight, hitting me; bouncing off my face towards the oppositions goal area. Mud covered my face, trailing streams of watery mud dripped out of my hair from the splatter of mud which flew my direction along with the ball. Elizabeth and Ryan stood there in fits of laughter along with twenty others', the sting from the impact causing a rush of blood, and a stream of tears, not that I was crying, it was the force and stinging of my face that caused it, but that never stopped the crowd of kids taking the piss out of me. Hurt, and upset, I made my way home to get cleaned up and too upset to return to the game. Elizabeth came running after me all apologetic, placing her arm around me, and making sure I was Ok. Mum was on hand, arresting the bleed from my nose, and wiping the mud from my face with the face cloth, Elizabeth watched mums tenderness, with my head now hung over the sink bowl, mum continued to wash the mud out of my hair. "Ah you're handsome again David" Elizabeth cried out, mum burst into laugher; watching my face burn with embarrassment.

Life was starting to change; financial gain in the area, new builds were being erected, old parts of the school refurbished, the colour schemes changing, vivid bright blues, yellows, greens, and reds replacing the dull, depressing battleship grey.

The old regime of seen and not heard replaced with a voice of free speech and attitudes, time for a new era, a new social revolution.

Colour TV became affordable to the masses. Unlike back in 1966, where only some two hundred and seventy-five thousand households could afford this luxury. Only the elite in this day's society, the rich and famous. We had to make do with the black and white for another four years.

The breakthrough of technology saw the 1970's leaping forward, invention after invention, the making of household devices, easing the labour on everyday task. Over the next two years, the colour Tv found it's self in over twelve million households across the UK, and our house was one of them.

Mum demanded we should have one, so before you could say Jack Flash, Dad was off to the radio rentals shop. I remember him sat there with mum, both as giddy as a kid in a sweet factory; I too was amazed at the sight of full colour transmitting through our television. Always amazed me how the pictures got there in the first place, dad did try to explain, but I lost it within seconds, with my concentration span, out of the door I ran, Dad's explanation going nowhere, all too technical for me.

Ryan's stood waiting with his football, another fifteen a side football game on the small grassed area outside our house. No doubt a fist fight over some insignificant quarrel will emerge, and our parents all ending up with an even bigger argument and a fight, which was pointless. We kids would just watch them after we made up within minutes of it starting, making us laugh and take bets on whose parents would be spending the night in jail, when the police turned up, and believe me they always did.

Our neighbours visited us, well the TV, to see how it looked. Standing room only, mum showing off her new colour Tv. She even got the biscuits out?

I had to go out, the constant barrage of questions, how much and where to get one, the noise level, ear-splitting, unbearable, all speaking over one another. Mum loved it, dad wasn't much better, both showing off. Bloody well surprised me, didn't know they had in them to. Me, I was told never to gloat, Really?

My parents should have asked for commission on the T.V sales; soon the whole street had one. The Radio Rentals shop at the Seacroft centre had never been so busy. Had some customers waiting up to four weeks, renting them out as quick as they came into the shop.

For the first few weeks, most of the parents had taken to drinking at home, leaving the pubs empty, with the landlords thinking of new ways to entice their regulars back. One idea was by placing a colour Tv into the lounge bar.

Our first day back at school. The Christmas holidays over. The reminder that Miss. Pointer had left.

We found this attractive, well-groomed athletic built man standing where our Miss Pointer uses to be. This clean-shaven chiselled chin face looking down at us. "Good morning class, happy to see you all after the holidays, may I remind you, my name is Mr. Preston, and I am your class tutor and PE teacher, so any of you who think a letter from mummy will get you out of PE, are very much mistaken" his voice confident but mellow in tone. He sat on his large wooden chair which he had placed at the side of his desk, his right leg crossed over his left, he reached for the class register and began to roll call out our names, one by one on our

97

reply. The whole of the class had turned up, apart from Chris Parker, who had not been removed from the register. "Anyone knows why young Parker isn't at school," he said gazing around the room. The room had suddenly turned black, a dark cloud hovering over me, all the kid's eyes turn to me to answer him. Nervously I stood up, my head hanging down, stumbling out my words "Sir! Chris has been taken away by the government." This sounding absurd, I began to cry all of a sudden, no warning just uncontrollable tears streaming down my face. The memories of the day they were taken, came flooding back, Jenny's screams ringing inside my head, Chris and his look of disappointment, the callous way in which they had to leave our house, the same day we buried their parents. The harrowing gut churning pain clawed up inside me, shivers running the length of my body. "They are in Australia sir" I stuttered … "his mum and dad died on Christmas day" the words spilled out from my mouth without any thought to what I was saying at the same time wiping my runny nose on my sleeve.

Overcome from memory, I sprinted for the exit, the door slamming shut behind me. My heart was racing; I had no clue where I was running to. I just knew I had to escape the class, that deep sinking sorrow etching at my very being, taking control. "Run David, just run" the words pounding inside my head.

I didn't get far before he caught up with me, I made it to the main doors, Mr. Preston gently placed his large hand on my left shoulder and accompanied me to the playground wall, I tried to run, but he held me tight to him with both hands, struggling was pointless.

Sitting there on the wall, I explained my story to him, he pulled me closer resting my head on his chest, "David, that's your name yes" he whispered smiling at me. "Yes," I replied looking up at him, tears still rolling down my face. "Well David I think it will be ok now and I believe we need to go back to the class and join your friends, they will be worried about you." his words were gentle, reassuring and caring, his sympathetic look sincere, giving me comfort in the knowledge he knew I was truthful and yet hurting inside.

He removed his handkerchief from his trouser pocket and wiped away my tears. We both stood up and walked back to join the others.

Entering the room, we were met with silence; the pupils sat, not saying a word, their heads facing down laid on their folded arms. A dark, gloomy sadness engulfed the room. Elizabeth's catches sight of me, jumping from her seat, and races forward, flinging her arms around me, tears streaming down her saddened face as she hugs me tight. Once again, I was feeling the strain, sobbing into her cardigan, my head resting on her shoulder.

Mr. Preston took one look at his pupils, and sensing how upset we were; he marched us to the playground.

In single file, with our heads bowed down we amble out into the playground yard. Standing there in the playground square we wait for his orders, like little soldiers, the sniffling turned into weeping, catapulting like a domino fall, me, Ryan, and Elizabeth, this followed like a sweeping epidemic around the class. "Right that's enough." His soft voice said, not truly understanding what had occurred during the Christmas break and having no idea who Chris was. "Stop your crying and go play, think of your favourite thing, your happy place, then return to class, in a happier mood" Mr. Preston continued, concern on his face, he didn't want to lose control on his first day. He knew if he could get us back from this dark melancholy state, he could win us over with pretty much anything. At first, we stood there in small groups, still sobbing, the bounce of the football on the concrete yard turning our heads, and soon we were chasing it, kicking, and shouting. The fact that it was cold and frosty had not entered our minds; we hadn't realised how cold it was.

It wasn't long before he had us all back seated on our chairs, Mr. Preston's grin stretched across his face, he stood there in the centre of the room contemplating over us, speaking to each of us, asking how Chris had affected our lives, and what we missed about him. The response was quick, finding ourselves interrupting each other's conversations, soon we were laughing and joking not realising we had stepped out that sorrowful dark shroud.

I realised then he was the right teacher to replace our Miss. Pointer; he was the one to step into her shoes. It was that moment that cemented what was to be a solid relationship between us. Him as my mentor and me the student for the next three years.

CHAPTER 11

THE WEDDING

Time passed quickly for our little gang; we were still getting into little scrapes. Like the one when the new boy joined our class. Gary Brotherton, a tall, scruffy, skinny kid, mousey lank hair reaching passed his shoulders, looked older than any eight-year-old I knew. His teeth were oversized for his mouth; they seemed to overfill it, his top lip protruding out from his face.

Ryan was the first to call him names, "Goofy Brotherton the rat boy" is what he called him, and like sheep, we all joined in. Needless to say, Mr. Preston would have none of it. This never stopped it from happening; the schoolyard was full of name calling and the odd fight.

Gary was the first fight I ever had. He picked on me because, I like him, stood out from the rest, he thought it would be easy to channel his frustration out on me, thought the other kids wouldn't be mind as much, after all, I wasn't white, I had dark skin. Surely this would single me out to be unworthy of any kind of support. He was so wrong; the fight got underway in the lower schoolyard, most of the class chanting my name, "hit him, David, don't let him hit you, you can beat him" then the usual chant "Fight, fight, fight". Luckily for us, none of the teachers had seen this. It only took about five exchanges of blows, and he had me down on my arse. He knew I had, had enough.

Neither of us cried, but he knew when to stop, the right-eyed shiner he gave me was enough, Goofy Brotherton held out his hand, his smile distorted across his face made me laugh, it never was a straight clean smile, his teeth made his jawline protrude out from his face, hence the rat boy name.

Reeling from the pain, I gladly took his hand. He assisted me back to my feet and brushed me down. "Sorry David, don't even know why I did It," he said unable to take his eyes off my purple-black shiner growing by the minute, almost closed, "No I'm sorry for calling you names," I said, my right eye now fully closed. With my only good eye, I notice Brotherton's lip was split, made me feel a little better knowing I had done some damage, at least I could hold my head up.

Ryan respected the fact that Goofy never went overkill on me when I was down, and that we had made up. He would have jumped in if Goofy Brotherton had continued to lay into me. Fortunately, this wasn't required. Ryan definitely could go over kill.

Out of this new respect for him, Ryan stopped calling Gary names, as did we all. Well for a day, because the silly thing was, after all that, he actually liked been named Goofy Brotherton the rat boy. Made him feel different, and the attention he received gave him a feeling of belonging, so the name stuck. As for my eye, it took a little longer to heal. Mum and Dad went crazy, wanted to complain to the school, but I managed to play it down and got them to reconsider.

This could have been embarrassing. Not only that, think of my credibility within my group of friends. Yes that would have gone down like the titanic.

Gary stayed at our school for seven weeks, turned out he was in the care system, and he move from one foster home to another, he had an attachment disorder, not that we knew what that was back then. This made it particularly hard for him to accept people, especially when things were good and showed promise. He was a misunderstood child, not able to gain or accept trust from adults, he was a vulnerable kid, but labelled as a disruptive, naughty, and challenging child by foster parents, doctors, and teachers alike.

Being let down by his own parents caused his loss of trust in adults, and this made his life difficult. Was a shame, he had become part of our little gang, he was a funny lad, always joking and prancing about like Ryan. He was a character, and we missed him at first, but with time, it cancels out friendships, people grow older, and new people and interest take over.

Months rolled past, gone were the days of the miners' strike, the blackouts and the state of emergency placed by the Prime minister Edward Heath, and gone was the three-day working week to save on electricity. It had been a hard January to early February for many industries, relying on the coal to keep the furnaces burning and electricity to keep the machines working, but all that's behind us now, was good to have them back on the five day a week, was hellish for us kids, the constant moaning on who was to blame.

The biggest story to hit the tabloids was the Nasa launch of the Pioneer 10 probe, sending it into space, reaching as far as Jupiter the following year, exploring the solar system as it travelled. Many star gazers believing and watching out for UFO's.

The seasons changed, gone were the cold snowy winter days transforming into bloom as March introduced the first days of spring, new life, and new hope.

During this period Mr. Green and Janet's relationship had blossomed too, they had gotten engaged. Mum was as giddy as a fruitcake, dad wasn't much better; it was the topic of conversation for weeks.

I benefited, got to play along with Elizabeth because she stayed more often at ours, giving me a companion, a friend to talk to, while her mum was to be courted, taken to lavish dinners and dances, Mr. Green had made an impact on her, she was quite smitten, even Elizabeth enjoyed having him around. Ryan began to sleep over too; mum enjoyed the challenge of keeping us kids amused. She would have us bake more often than not, rock cakes, chocolate cornflake buns and the like. The best part was eating the mixes out the bowls, using our fingers, well it was for Elizabeth and me. Our faces would be covered in chocolate. Mum joined in too. Ryan would just stand, not amused by our antics. It had to be some of the best times I had with mum, was made much better having my two best friends join in.

The year passed, and the new year followed on, promising to bring joy and happiness, and the offer of more than the previous year, and for some, it looked to be coming true.

It was Friday 12th March 1972 the day of the wedding.

I was stood outside the Leeds Registrar office all dress up in my new grey-blue suit, regular straight-legged trousers, new brogues, mum beside me, all dolled up looking every bit like a movie star, as were the rest of the wedding guest. Mr. Green had turned up with Clive (Mr. Backhouse), they had become good friends over the past 3 years playing football for the local working men's club. Dad found that amusing, with Mr. Greens build and strength, dad had him down as a rugby player or professional wrestler, often said the opposition defenders must have shite themselves seeing this hulk racing toward them. To be fair though, Mr. Green was very agile and nibble on his feet, and had one hell of a right foot, had scored forty-three goals last season and nineteen this season. He had tried for Leeds when he was in his late teens, but Don Revie the Leeds United manager thought the same as dad, well that was their loss. Mr. Green had a trophy cabinet any footballer would have been proud of and probably more silverware than United.

Mr. Green stood in anticipation with Clive waiting for Janet to arrive, both dressed in twin silver suits with golden ties. Both looking very dandy. Mr. Green was nervous for the first time in years; you could smell the fear. This muscular mountain of a man was not so cocksure of himself today, looking a bit peaky and nauseous. Clive who was some six years older stood there by his side, reassuring him, quietly so no one else could hear what was said. Whatever he said must have been funny, they both laughed. All that was missing now was the bride.

The sun reflecting off the white Rolls Royce as it pulls up outside the building, giving off a shimmering, ghostly appearance. Harold shuffles out, breaking the light rays, followed by Elizabeth.

The late winter weather, complimenting the occasion. Deep blue clear skies, with a bright yellow sun burning down, a light breeze blowing her long flowing dress. A beautiful white-pink silk dress, coloured with blue and pink flowers embroidered around the neckline, her shoes are pink with a 2-inch heel. Elizabeth unsure, wobbles a bit as she walks. Both Stood outside of the car, waiting for Janet to appear. Elizabeth gives out a mighty gasp, her eyes glistening behind the tears, "Mum you look so beautiful," Janet's ivory, satin bridal shoe rest on the pavement. Harold takes her hand as She stands there, radiant, glowing, absolute perfection, the look of a princess in her white wedding dress. Harold closed his eyes, the large intake of breath, followed by the loud exhale. His eyes now transfixed on this beautiful vision in front of him. "You look amazing, are you ready Janet?" he asked nervously, "Yes Harold, go on, make my day" replies Janet, with Elizabeth towing behind as they walk arm in arm towards the large open entrance.

The familiar tune of "here comes the bride" plays, dad arm in arm with Janet, and Elizabeth the bridesmaid following, holding the train. Slowly they walk down the aisle, step by step, passing her family and friends as they go, everybody smiling, women crying tears of happiness, the sound of chitter-chatter on how beautiful she looks reaches a high, almost drowning out the wedding march.

The music ceases to play, Mr. Green relieved sighs and nods at Clive in approval of his bride, Clive responses with a wink.

Groom and bride are now stood side by side, the room drops to a deathly silence, all looking on in awe.

"Welcome everyone I'm your registrar and by English law qualified to carry out marriage," came the voice of the large rounded man, dressed in his black suit, white shirt, and black tie. He looks warm, redden faced, but not nervous. Calmly spoken he gives the ceremonial speech, the bride and groom now settled, recite their vows.

With the ceremony well underway; we sit watching the registrar almost sings out his words. "Do you Harry Green take Janet May Stuart to be your lawful wedded wife" he continued singing out his words to what seemed like an eternity, then finally on the receiving of the rings, they kiss each other.

An explosion of noise fills the room, Mum and dad along with the wedding guest stood, cheering loudly congratulating the newlyweds. Illuminating flashes from the Polaroid cameras lighting up the room, every one of the guests wanting to snap this young couple on their wedding day. A reminder of this beautiful day.

Confetti spills out like snow, spiralling down over the newlyweds and the building entrance as they step out through the doorway. I'm running around like a madman hurling more confetti into the air, along with most of the guest, Ryan's running around out of control just like me.

Confetti spills into the street, the wind picking it up, propelling it around like butterflies fluttering in a cool breeze. Amid the chaos, the photographer is stamping around, frustration taking hold of him, cursing under his breath, struggling to get his pictures taken, not one person stood still for than one minute. He finally got his large group photo, after giving a bit of rant, protesting he was a professional and required order and sensibility. Everyone just looked at him, then erupted into hysterical laughter. Raising his arms, Mr. Green shouts "settle down and to allow him his time," we shuffled into place as the gaiety subsided.

The large square flash burst out like a million candles, the glow causing us to blink. Within minutes we were being loaded into the waiting vehicles, heading homeward for the wedding reception.

Christine, the head barmaid, opens the function room doors of the local workingmen's club.

Harry has spared no expense, this is his and Janet's day, the room is lavishly decorated, displaying highly decorative tables, immaculate white table cloths, each table seating eight. The ceiling a burst with colour, bright coloured streamers, silver, gold, reds, and blues. The table set up for the bride and groom, their best man and family stood out from the rest against the far wall.

We were on the main table too, dad was honoured to have given Janet away, Janet seeing my parents as her adopted parents.

Janet's' parents had passed away many years earlier before we had moved onto our street. Janet had grown very fond of mum and dad, relying on them in her time of need, just looking after Elizabeth or dad gifting her the odd five pounds to help her through the week.

I sat in between Ryan and Elizabeth, giggling most of the day away. Mum scolded us once or twice telling us to quieten down, Dad giving his look of discontentment our way, backing mum one hundred percent, "Be quiet you lot" scolded mum "The best man speech and all I can hear is you" her look says it all.

Meanwhile, Phil and Carl Backhouse are chatting up the barmaid, trying all they could to get served at the bar. Julie Fellows a twenty-two-year-old barmaid, just teased them, taking pleasure from flaunting her body, and fluttering her eyelids, knowing this was wrong, and getting them aroused, telling them that at seventeen they were too young. Out of sheer flirtatious mischief, she poured them both a pint of Guinness; their faces were a picture, their faces screwed up, disgust displayed with every gulp. Both boys swallowing the full glass, for bravado's sake, wanting to impress her. It wasn't long before they had to rush to the boy's room, re-emerging, looking a paler shade of white and a lot quieter, sitting next to their parents not daring to approach Julie, both flushed with embarrassment.

It would seem the whole street had been invited; Mr. and Mrs. Connor sat at the far table with their three boys, Darron, Cliff, Robert, and their daughter Lisa. The three lads were older than me, but Lisa was born a year later, her birthday 2 days after mine, she was quite a cute looking girl for an eight-year-old. Mum and dad had made up and became friends with the Connors again, dad wasn't one to hold a grudge, and Mrs. Connor had apologised for her outburst all those years ago. The Connor boys had taken a healthy interest in making sure no one picked on me, they like Ryan's brothers knew how to fight, in their earlier life when Grant wasn't wheelchair bound, he took it upon himself to teach his boys how to fight, and being an old Marine that was one thing he excelled in. Further down to the right was the notorious Mr. Flanagan and his family, now this family was known to be troublesome, always in and out of prison, makes you wonder why someone would mix with people like these. Their crimes usually involving physical attacks, I heard they were distant cousins of Janet. It was rumoured even the police gave them a wide berth, only arresting them in numbers. I couldn't see the whole gangster thing about them, yes, they dressed flash, fancy expensive dresses, and coats for Mrs. Flanagan and her two older teenaged daughters, and only a clean shirt and pinstripes for Mr. Flanagan. The three sons, all short and wiry, looked out of place, dressed in black slacks and white shirts with a pencil black tie. They didn't look like they could beat up anyone, well not looking at their physique, but apparently, they were a right mean bunch, and ugly with it. Saying all this, if you ever wanted anything, but couldn't afford it, they could always get you it at a knocked down price.

The celebrations were well underway. We were dancing and singing, the music echoing across the floor, mums, dads, and kids alike swaying and jumping, kicking, sliding. Me and Ryan sat watching the adults, they were getting drunker by the minute. Mischief was creeping in our heads.

Mr. Connor deciding to chase us kids in his wheelchair around the room, with uncontrollable laughter we dodged in and out of the tables. Eventually, we stopped rushing around the room, to our parent's joy and sat with him. Grant began his tale as he always did, telling us some of his war stories, about when he served in the Marines. One of his many exploits, racing against time to rescue someone or other or getting caught out in a Scandinavian snow blizzard miles from civilisation. With his drink in hand, he sipped until he fell into a drunken slumber. We all sat content, listening, imagining the adventures he must have had.

Slowly Grant dozed off, his glass rolling across the floor, something we all found hilarious, all apart from Mrs. Connor who disapprovingly dumped him in the corner of the room. Elizabeth picked up his blanket from the floor and covered him, her smile so sweet as she looked down at his old weathered face sleeping peacefully, her kindness shining through. Elizabeth was a very considerate girl, and at such a youthful age, Janet looked on, very proud of her.

By late evening Ryan and I had sneaked the odd half pints from the tables when we thought the adults weren't looking, thinking we were smart.

"You'll be sick later" commented Elizabeth, standing there, one hand on her hip the other pointing her finger at me, "What's it got to do with you" I questioned her, feeling a little tipsy, the odd wobble, using the table for balance. Elizabeth just shook her head and left Ryan and me to our first drinking session.

The night was going well until I began to feel dizzy. Consuming two or three more half pints of beer, and the room was spinning, unsure of this sensation and why I was feeling this way, had me disoriented, I fell to my knees, my head was beginning to thump, a heavy vibrating pulsing inside me, now unable to stand and very queasy. Ryan aided me to my seat, informing my mum. He always seemed to be there when I needed help; he was my guardian angel, my trusted friend, the one I could always rely on.

The next day I awoke in my bed, not remembering how I got there, my head was still thundering inside, and the room spinning as I sat up, that sickening sensation rushing over me. Without thinking I instinctively grabbed the bin by my bed, emptying the contents of my stomach, violently wrenching. Mum was stood at the foot of my bed laughing at me. "Serves you right young man ... maybe you won't drink alcohol in future." Her arms crossed, in one hand she held a glass of fizzy water. "Do you remember coming home?" she asked. I look at her, my eyes trying to focus, mum's blurred outline, not quite in view. Shaking my head in reply.

I drank the fizzy offerings out of the glass; it's got to have been the worst thing I had ever tasted, Andrews liver salts, how revolting was the taste, making my body shake as it passed through. Mum was now in stitches; I had never witnessed her laugh so much as she did that day, as for me I stayed in bed the whole of the day feeling really sorry for myself. Ryan had called for me, checking to see how I was, mum explained my predicament. I could hear them sniggering at the foot of the steps.

I closed my eyes and slept.

Six weeks had passed since the wedding day. Today Janet and Elizabeth were moving out from their home in our street and were joining Harry to live in his home. An empty feeling hung over my parents; they had grown very fond of Janet and Elizabeth over the years, Janet was like the daughter they had never had. Tears were aplenty. Janet accepted the bouquet of red and yellow roses from mum, it was a sorrowful day, hugs and kisses exchanged. Elizabeth gave me my first real kiss then entered Harry's car. It was a tender kiss, I smiled from the inside out, she was so sweet, I didn't want her to go, but I knew this was right for them. A fresh start. We waved them goodbye watching as Mr. Green drove out of our street, his car getting smaller and smaller as it disappeared out of view.

I wasn't overly upset, but still, I shed a tear, I knew Elizabeth had only moved to Cross Gates, in one of those big houses near the Manston Park, the kind of street dad wanted us to move to. Elizabeth would be still attending our school, and I could still see her, but I was already missing her. Janet said I was always welcome to stay the odd night, that was both Ryan and me. I knew we were going to miss her, we had become quite the trio, inseparable, until now.

Mum and dad treated Ryan and me to a visit to the Seacroft shopping centre for a wimpy dinner to cheer us up, burger, chips, and a large Pepsi, just the treat to make you feel better.

The years passed quickly, time seemed to fly by, growing up into our teenage years.

Four years had passed, life was rushing past us. Elizabeth not visiting as much as she used to, I missed her most evenings after school, not able to listen to music or play games with her. It was rumoured that Mr. Green was a disciplinarian and ran his home like a tight ship. When the opportunity did arise we took full advantage, with me walking her to the end of her street, it became apparent that Mr. Green did not want me in his house and barred both Ryan and me from sleepovers. I was starting to detest the man.

Ryan and me had grown to be the best of friends, we were like brothers, in each other's pockets, becoming familiar in each other's home.

We were changing, our likes and dislikes, our bodies maturing into manhood, we were growing stronger, as was our friendship, we had been friends from the first days of primary school. Ryan at thirteen years plus was a tall five feet eight, me and Elizabeth were the averages for our age.

It was a time of coming of age, Ryan and I were quite athletic in build; I was broader than him, my shoulders gave my frame a compelling look, made me look stronger than I was, even though Ryan towered my five feet five.

Elizabeth was transforming into the attractive young women I always knew she would, she was by far the best-looking girl in LEEDS, in my eyes. When she walked down any street, the boys would look, heads turned, made me proud, she only had eyes for me.

The streets were changing too, the passing away of the elder folk and the new families taking their place. The young couples with their kids moving in, some lacking pride in the appearance of themselves, their homes and surroundings, the street going to the dogs, the lack of respect from one neighbour to the next.

Clive and Joyce were mum and dad's best friends, often sharing the weekly gossip from the street. Who was who and what they did or not do? Crime had risen, the blame was on the solvent abuse and the creeping up of unemployment. We had been fortunate not to have been broken into; four houses had not been as lucky, the so-called well off had been targeted, the less fortunate taking a chance, stealing from their neighbours. Police sirens were now a commonplace on our streets, and at any hour of the day.

Dad was now the sorting office manager. Man, and boy he had served the mail, getting his reward. Now reaching the dizzy heights, placed in charge of the central sorting office in Leeds, responsible for the workforce. He enjoyed his job, he was very proud of his position and would always tell me he was the man who kept the mail running on time. I thought he was the king of the royal mail because everyone addressed him as Sir instead of Harold.

Dad took me on a visit of his work place; his office was on the third floor of the five-story building. At the desk outside his office sat a pretty young woman, about twenty-seven years old, this slender brunette with the perfect smile, and sparkling brown eyes with long lashes, her small nose, and thin red lips completed her good looks. "Good morning Miss Holloway, this is my son David, he has come to see how we get the post out on time," said dad greeting her, as he removed his hat and coat, placing them on the coat stand next to the wall. "Good morning Sir, your tea is made, also two rounds of toast set on your desk, would you like me to get David anything?" she replied, her wide smile and the wink of her eye directed at me. I began to blush; she was gorgeous and so graceful in her movements, her hands were well manicured, long smooth fingers with long white painted fingernails. Her finger touched lightly on her typewriter as she continued to complete her work, the ping of the page holder as it reached its end recoiling it back to its start. Dad chuckled as I hid my face, not allowing her to see my embarrassment.

Dad introduced me to his staff as he inspected the shop floor, I found everyone pleasant and kind, I had a blast of a day, vowed I would be sitting in dads' chair when I left school, this amused dad and his colleagues.

This had been the first time I had seen dad at work, and to be honest, it suited him.

Dad wanted to relocate, move out of the street to a much more respected suburb. A place which would have more standing with his position.

Harold could easily afford a new mortgage, his wage had doubled, cash to spare, but mum said no, and she meant it, no arguing.

Mum enjoyed our lives on these streets; she had grown to appreciate her friends. Mums' friends and my friends lived here.

Mum was held in high regard in our neighbourhood; she was the one they all asked to help them when they had trouble understanding how to fill in forms for their unemployment benefit or passports, the odd home delivery, where mum would assist the midwife, bringing a new life into this world. Mum had helped deliver more babies into this world than she ever did when she worked at the hospital. Mum loved this status and treasured the community spirit amongst us; Mum argued that we belonged in this neighbourhood. Dad wasn't in agreement but went with it for mums' sake. However, the community spirit was starting to decline with some of the new young tenants arriving. Many from outside the catchment area of Seacroft.

The biggest change was the friends we use to play with in the street. Time taking charge. The older kids now leaving school, no longer affording the childish behaviour, playing as they did only weeks before, but finding themselves transformed into adulthood, working in the factories or moving out of the area. Some joining the forces, while others taking a chance, with the search for a new life as they emigrate to the other side of the world, mainly to Canada or Australia, most of them never returning.

Time played its part on us too; our school days were almost at an end at Parklands. We had seen eight years there; the three of us excelling in our studies, working hard to achieve our goals, believing if we reach top marks we would have the world at our feet. Teachers came and went, but Mr. Preston had stayed the course, keeping an eye on me, making sure I got through school life with the minimum of distraction. We had formed a good relationship; he was very in touch with his pupils, always a good listener, rarely lost his temper with us. Mr. Preston was what made school worth going to. Ryan had become an active sportsman, he attended personal coaching lessons during the after-school activities with Mr. Preston. Our school had built a reputation for producing good sportsmen and women, laying the foundations to carry it on in higher education.

With the start of the long summer holidays, seven weeks of it, what would we do? We were lost. We had said our goodbyes to Parklands school, never to return. Some of the teachers were tearful, sad to see us depart, on to new ventures after so many years. It was a sad departure for most. They had nurtured us from infants, developing into young adults.

Without a second thought about the school we were leaving, we went Yelling and screaming out of the schoolyard, we raced through the gates for the last time.

We screamed immeasurably loud, you could almost hear us the other side of the world, ok slight exaggeration, to the bottom of our street. Hordes of young kids racing through the streets. Parents looking on in dismay unable to control us. These streets were ours for the next seven weeks. And we were gonna rule them.

Ryan and I would be going to Foxwood high school next term, a mixed gender school, for the last part of our education, before being pushed into the real world, working for a living. Elizabeth was going to be attending the all-girls school, Parklands high school for girls. This saddened us, thinking that this may break us up, the trio finally disbanded.

Advancing into our teens with the innocence of childhood lost. Now was the beginning of our lives in the adult world, along with the simple-mindedness that came with it.

With the influx of immigrants reaching our shores, racism was raising its ugly head. The race relations act was established in 1976 by the Parliament of the United Kingdom to prevent discrimination on the grounds of race. It included discrimination by race, colour, nationality, ethnic and national origin, covering the fields of employment, the provision of goods and services, education, and public functions.

As much as this was to help prevent the discrimination, it was rife throughout the whole of the United Kingdom, even spreading its ugly head on my street.

CHAPTER 12

REALITY CHECK

1976, found it to be the hottest summer in my years. The sun beating down well into the thirties, with no letting up. The green grass now tinged brown, the failed crops in the fields causing a twelve percent raise in the high-street prices, making it tough on the purse strings, what to do without was more the question, and with the drought had come so much devastation, not unlike the winter of my birth but the opposite. The deep cracks in the land stretched the length of the country, opening the doors of hell.

Construction placed on hold; transport lightened, railways closed, the infrastructure took it hard, short working weeks, and at the start of our summer holidays. We even had to collect water, yes water from the standpipes erected in our streets, not because we were a third world country, no, just because the drought had run us dry. This was a challenging time for most people and not just our street, but our nation.

The water supply was rationed, the government had finally stepped in, the reservoirs running low and now with a countrywide emergency set in place, you weren't allowed to use fresh water to hose your garden, heaven help those who did, and got caught. Mr. Connor had to use his triple used bath water for his garden; he was not going to allow his plants to be wilted away. He was proud of his garden, and with the weather forecast offering no encouragement, said it would be a few more weeks till we were to get any rain.

People were collapsing in the street, through sheer heat exhaustion, the emergency services now fully stretched, with the local police checking in on the elderly, for many this was a vulnerable time.

For us kids it was great, the daylight lasting well into the late evening, we terrorised the streets. We had gained a lot of control over those weeks, the heat keeping most of our parents and the local residential busy bodies inside.

Glen Stinton from number two, had lost some weight. He was the fattest kid in our class, he was picked on most days. Always scoffing a chocolate bar or some cake or other, always seemed to have something in his mouth, even he had lost his appetite in this heat, his constant gorging and this intense sun-drenched heat causing him to projectile vomit. This summer changed his life; he grew up to be a fitness guru for the famous. It was said he married some movie star in L.A.

It was dad's sixtieth birthday, July 22nd, Mum had booked a long weekend in Paris for the two of them, not that dad wanted to go to Paris, no this was an excuse for mum to visit the city of culture; I was to stay at the Backhouses for the duration. Four days of staying at Ryan's house, this was going to be a great weekend, with Phil and Carl at home on leave from the army, things were going to be a little wild.

Mum and Joyce had planned this months in advance, the fact that no-one cottoned on was amazing, this was to be mums best ever kept secret, mum was useless at keeping them, if anything she would pass it on, just so she didn't have to feel responsible for it. Mum hated secrets, always said nothing good ever came from them.

Dad got up, carried out his usual ritual, wash, shave, have breakfast, cup of tea, then brush his teeth. Ready to step out the door for work. Dad kissed mum as usual, then tried the door, to his shock it was still locked, this should have been opened an hour ago, the thought racing through his head. Mum closed in, placed her arms around him, kissing him tenderly. "Harold, there's no work for you today" whispered mum waving the flight tickets in her hand. Dads arms raised and with a confused look on his face and replies "What's this?"

"It's our flight tickets to Paris Harold, I got them for your birthday". It took a few more minutes for dad to register this. Mum's face just couldn't stop smiling as she explained how she and Joyce had it all arranged.

"Well Mrs. Brown, you devious little minx, you" he replied beaming.

My bag was packed, and I was out the door, walking up the road to number 16 Hawkshead Crescent. Joyce leant in the doorway, welcomed me with open arms, smothering me, my head almost stuck in her boobs, and kissing me on the head. She grinned at the sound of my groans as she teased me, "Get off me" I said wriggling out of her arms, the sweet scent of honeysuckles and magnolias, tormenting my nose. In truth, it was a pleasant smell, and as for her boobs, I must admit, I was more embarrassed, and I don't think I will tell Ryan what I was thinking. Two weeks earlier we had found some of Phil's adult mags under his mattresses; we spent hours looking at the naked women, laughing so loud we were fortunate his parents didn't investigate. After all, we were thirteen years old and who would be thinking we would be checking out a nudie book. To be honest, we thought they were just pretty face women and were shocked at the shape and sizes of some of the private parts.

Throwing my bag on the spare bed in Ryan's room, I stood there smug, he ran at me, a great big bear hug followed, "Gee up Ryan, you're killing me" I squealed out, almost unable to breathe. "Ok, David, just my way of saying great to have you here" he released his grip on me, taking a jump backwards, his giddy face all bright and smiley, me, well, I was doubled up, regaining my breath. Recovering my composure, I made my way to the gate, I kissed mum and hugged dad, then with teary eyes; they made their way to Dover for the channel ferry crossing to France. Mum promised me they would be safe and be back in four days. Sadness swept over me, I felt alone, tears formed and rolled down my face, it was the first time I had been left, parted from my parents. I stood there sobbing, Joyce placed her arms around my shoulders and pulled me in close, at the same time scolding Phil and Carl for teasing me, "Do you remember the train journey? When you went to Thirsk for the first time. You two cried and asked me if I would go with you?" her mocking tone drowning out their taunting, quietly they slid away, back into the haven of their living room. I could feel myself beginning to smile, her presence and cuddles were a comfort to me. Joyce was a lot like mum. I guess that's why they got on so well. Wasn't long before I was settled, Ryan saw to that, two chip butties, loaded with salt and vinegar. Phil and Carl already sinking their teeth into theirs.

It was that time for Joyce to set off to the Leeds city market for their meat run, this was repeated every Saturday, just like Clive and his ritual visit to the bookies, he loved a flutter on the horses. He wasn't bad at it either, winning more often than he lost.

As for me, I went to visit Elizabeth's in Cross Gates, leaving the boys to play fight in the backyard.

She was sat watching the television; the afternoon matinee was showing, I didn't mind, it's was John Wayne, in the Sons of Katie Elder, I had seen it twice over the years, westerns are my favourite kind of movie.

I slid next to her on the sofa, she snuggled up all cosy like, and kissed me, this made me smile inside, the softness of her lips touching mine, within minutes we were cuddling. We were happy together; it felt right. We weren't sexual with each other, just stealing kisses now and then. Janet was pleased we got on as we did. Always commenting on how handsome I was, she always joked with my mum that we would be giving them grandchildren in the near future. Elizabeth, like me, knew that we would always be in love with each other, forever. We would be that perfect couple. It was to be our destiny. We were well tuned into one another, we cared for each other, never wanting harm or hurting to ever get in the way of our relationship. This was love, problem was we were young, and didn't know this yet.

Having a beautiful girl on my arm like Elizabeth wasn't always pleasant, it wasn't always easy on us, some kids in her street would be cruel and call her names, but she didn't care, "Paki-lover" they would shout in the street as we walked arm in arm towards the Arndale shopping centre. This just encouraged her more. She was pretty much her own person, not easily swayed.

I left Elizabeth just after two thirty, making my way back to Ryan's house. An uneasy feeling creeping over me, The sound of two hidden voices chanting "Paki bastard". I wasn't taking any chances, I legged it out of there in record time, exhausted by the time I reached the Backhouse house. I didn't say anything to the others, not wanting any trouble. If I had, I knew they would go over looking for them, and that wouldn't do. Someone would have been badly hurt. Definitely hospitalized.

Staying at Ryan's was great, his mum Joyce would often put out finger food, real meals were rare in their house, Joyce was a terrible cook, Clive joked with mum and dad about it, on many of their visits to our home. Joyce had become immune to his taunts over the years.

Fish finger butties, chips, pork pie slices and an abundance of cakes. Life in the Backhouse household was easy going, Clive and Joyce would be drinking their real ale, pint glass after pint glass, watching the T.V until captured by sleep, slumped in their chairs. Usually were asleep by ten or half past, Ryan would sneak extra crisp or a few slices of beef dripping on bread with onion, the stupidest thing was Joyce always knew, after all his breath stunk of it the morning after. She never said anything, just smirked to herself.

Joyce was still in town shopping. She always went late in the afternoon, because she got the best deal from the meat market traders. Wanting to clear their counters. Poor Joyce was always fully laden on her return, but she didn't mind.

I got back from Elizabeth's a few minutes before the wrestling ended. Phil already had me in a headlock, sat there on the settee, he tugged hard, straining my neck, I couldn't cry, needed to be the big boy, but the pain was immense, his woollen bobbled sleeve rubbing under my chin. "Phil go easy with him, he's not one of your barmy army mates" Clive shouted as he entered the room, returning from the bookies, and sixty-four pounds better off. Phil instantly released me. I replied with the stare of death, Phil just laughed at me, brushing me aside.

Within minutes the boys and I were wrestling in the living room. Pushing the settee to the far wall, creating our make-believe wrestling ring.

We were imitating the great Mick McManus, Jackie Pallo and Shirley Crabtree aka big daddy and the likes, doing flying head kicks and dropkicks on each other.

It all started with the standing dropkick from Phil on Carl. Carl was flung to the other side of the room, crashing hard to the floor. Phil raced and threw himself onto Carl, punching him in the eye as he landed, Carl gave out a loud yelp, kicking himself free, stretching out his arm to Ryan, their hands slapped as he tagged him.

Phil was almost stood up now, his balance a bit weary, rising back to his feet. Ryan took his chance, driving his forearm across Phil's chest, the sound was almost felt by the rest of us, he staggered back, almost losing his footing when Ryan connected with the reverse kung-Fu style kick, his foot landing square to Phil's chest.

The gilded glass bar cabinet rocked and shattered as Phil's body drove through it, falling to the carpeted floor, the cabinet following, breaking into several pieces, sending slivers across the room. Clive stood there flabbergast, not wanting to believe what he had just observed, you could feel the rage building up inside him. All of us stood there not daring to move or speak, our heads lowered, fear crawling over our bodies like malignant cancer.

The longest silent minute ever, then he exploded, like a whirlwind, scolding the boys, he had his belt to them, yelling at the top of his voice. Phil and Carl were in their late teens, but they were still wary of their dad. He had a right temper, however, calmly, he turned to me and just told me not to get involved in the future, I was shitting it, thinking he was going to scold me too, but when he spoke, I gave out the biggest sigh of relief, Ryan told his dad, that would not happen, it was the best! Me living with just mum and dad meant I wouldn't get the chance to do this much. This met with a clout around the head, "Shut up you idiot" Clive retorted to Ryan, who now stood in silence, not daring to speak. With a few deep breaths, Clive settled down, and knowing this had been an accident, told us "Look boys don't break anything else … Your mum's already gonna kill you when she gets back from shopping, best get this cleaned up". He was smiling as he spoke, the knowledge of knowing the boys had another crack coming pleased him. He told me to keep scarce.

Sure enough, when Joyce got home and found her glass display cabinet in the bin, she lost her blob big style, upset just didn't cut it, no she was boiling mad, the boys didn't hesitate, they just ran out of the house avoiding her, hoping she would calm down. "What the fucking hell have you done" you could hear her screams across the street. I still had a key to mine, Ryan followed me, we sprinted out of the door as if our lives depended on it. Joyce wasn't one for swearing, but when needed she could swear like a trooper, and this occasion had cause.

Clive stood there taking the brunt of Joyce's anger. Repeatedly she slapped him across the face, his face now swollen and bruised. The pain gave way to Clive's love for Joyce; he could see she was hurt, Clive grabbed her arms unable to take any more punishment, "Ok Joyce, need to stop now" his voice loud, tapering off softly as he cradled her tightly, kissing her forehead. Joyce wept nonstop, "Ok darling we will sort it out later" he whispered. The two of them stood in the middle of the room, silent, not a sound, not even a whisper.

It was late in the day when the boys returned home. Clive collected Ryan and me from my home, said it was safe to return, just not to say anything about this.

Joyce had calmed down somewhat; she had a restless night, too annoyed to sleep. Both Phil and Carl had agreed to pay for the display cabinet now they were in the army and earning their own money.

To Joyce this gesture made no difference, she didn't want to speak to her boys. That night I wished I was back home with mum and dad. This house had a terrible atmosphere, a sickening feeling. I think it took us all a while to fall into slumber.

The new day approached, the atmosphere was still edgy in the Backhouse home, Joyce looked ok and calm. However, the slamming of the cereal bowls gave a different impression.

Not a word was shared at the table.

Ryan and I went to see Elizabeth; Clive said it was probably for the best. Phil and Carl left for camp two days early; they knew there was no getting through to Joyce. Clive promised to call them and get their mum on the phone. Carl was upset, unlike Phil who just let things blow over, Carl fretted pretty much about everything, but most of all about upsetting his mum.

I rapped on the door, three times as I always did, my signature knock for Elizabeth. Janet answered the door; she stood there crying, she had bruises on her face as if she had been fighting. "Are you ok?" I asked, perplexed and concerned. She looked frightened, afraid to speak to us, as if she was hiding a secret. Trembling Janet just nodded her head and asked us to leave and to come back another day. "Please David just go, I promise all is ok." She left us stood there, as she shut the door; I could hear her walking back into the lounge. The shouting started between Harry and her; we couldn't work out what they were saying. I thought I could hear Elizabeth crying too.

Ryan's gaze was as mystified as mine; shaking our heads, we turned and headed back towards our street.

Just like the most of this summer, it was another blazing sweltering day, dressed in our Levi's and sleeveless round neck t-shirts, the sweat was dripping from us, the temperature had risen dramatically from a hot twenty-two to a blazing thirty-three in the last hour. We continued to walk down the Avenue where she lived, even the shade from the huge sycamore and beech trees couldn't offer refuge from the heat.

"Hey Paki," the harsh words projected from the garden we had just passed, Ryan looked at me "Keep walking Dave ... Let's get outta here" his face showing dread; this was not like Ryan, I knew he could fight, to my knowledge he had never lost a fight, for some reason this spooked him.

Every step was as painful as the next one; we could hear at least four sets of footsteps behind us. The anxiety was overtaking our very being; we wanted to run but couldn't, my bladder was aching as if I needed a wee, Ryan was like me that day, so scared, that we dare not turn around. We were out of our comfort zone, out of our street. I was shaking inside, my body reeling, the swarming of fear rising through me.

The next I knew, the sting from the curled-up fist hitting me hard behind my right ear, I fell hard to the ground almost bouncing off the tarmac, "Kill the fucking Paki bastard ... shouldn't be touching our fucking white girls anyway" the shrill from the same voice as before. I could feel the burning sensation uniting through my body with every blow.

Ryan was on the ground, curled up protecting his head, as was I. The baseball booted feet striking us both repeatedly. The groans loud, deafening, echoing inside my head. Each blow penetrated hard, sending the blood rushing to the surface of our skin, causing the bruising. With the harrowing pain injected kicks to the body increasing, the group of thugs continued, laughing and joking aloud. "As for you Blondie, what are you fucking doing hanging around with a dirty Paki? not enough good white kids for you, just like that slag at number six, you fucker" his menacing words spat out, another boot to the stomach strikes Ryan, he's stopped moving now, laying there barely conscious. "Get the fuck out of our country you black twat" came another voice, full of malice and hatred, followed by another torturous volley of kicks to my body. Unable to feel any more pain, we stopped moving, almost unconscious. Our four assailants dispersed on hearing the tell-tale sound of the police sirens screeching in the distance, their footsteps fading out of earshot. Abandoned, both quivering and shaking, lost in sorrowful grim darkness, our badly bruised bodies lying, bleeding on the tarmac road.

We don't know how long we had been lying there, but when I came around, I found myself in a Seacroft hospital bed. To an outsider looking in, I must have looked like the invisible man, my body covered in white bandages, against a white-sheeted background. I must have been in quite a bad shape, being propped up with four pillows. The pain was gone, this helped by the pain-relieving drugs drip fed into me.

Mum opened her eyes, she heard me stirring, gave a massive yawn, arms stretching as far as they could. The relief on her face, seeing me awake for the first time since they arrived back from their holiday.

Dad and Mum had slept there all night, wanting to keep a vigilance. It was Tuesday 27th July; I had been unconscious for nearly three days. The duty ward doctor swiftly appeared by my bedside and carried out a quick check over me. His large hands gliding up and down my body, checking my eyes, and limbs making sure I was not blind, nor any more of my bones broken, they had checked my lungs as I had four cracked ribs. I was bounded in bandages around my chest and stomach. Restricted tightly bound, causing little movement, I found it hard to breathe at first. I was disorientated, unsure as to where I was, confused, finding it hard to remember why I was there. Mum filled in the gaps on what had happened, tears rolling down her face, both mum and dad taking the blame, guilt-ridden for not been there. I was going to be all right, and chances are this would have happened anyway. The sad reality, this was inevitable, just a matter of time for the hardship of adult life to catch up with me. The burden I carried, just for looking different.

Don't get me wrong; it's not just skin colour that gets you into this situation, no, you could be white with ginger coloured hair, wear spectacles too, have a lisp or just look odd, or may be from a poor family and wear unfitting hand me downs. People can be very cruel, trouble is no one ever looks at themselves and their own down falls and sad to say it's usually the kid who's beaten at home or having some other infliction, being the one that ends up being the bullies.

With my parents making a fuss over me, overcompensating for my well-being, I felt safe; I didn't need the extravagant gifts, all I wanted, was to know how Ryan was. Where was Ryan? I couldn't see him anywhere; I started to panic thinking the worse may have happened, obsessed by these thoughts, my eyes welled up, it took nearly an hour to calm me down, reassuring me that Ryan was okay. "He's in the next ward to you, but he needs to rest for now" came mum's voice, soft with her caring reassuring smile, the one I've seen so many times before. It reminded me of my first day of school, me panicking, all the time worrying over nothing. Mum told me I could see him in the morning. I was to rest for now.

It was late in the afternoon when my parents left, telling me they would not be back at evening visitors time, they had been so consumed with worry about me, they had not had a chance to unpack from the France trip or even think about the time they had over there. Their concerns were about me. I could see they were exhausted and needed to rest. Mum kissed me, leaving with dad who may I add was still blaming himself for leaving the country.

My first glimpse of Ryan, was him laid there in his bed, wrapped up in bandages, pretty much a replica of myself. I knew he was in pain, the beating, almost to his last breath, and why? Just for being my best friend.

A burst of relief hit me the minute he sat up. "Hiya David, how are you, I feel rough, god they did a job on us didn't they?" the jubilation in his voice surprising me. Seeing me for the first time since the incident. Apologetic I sat on the edge of his bed. "Sorry Ryan, they only did this to you because of me" I chirped, a really sorry looking face, not that you could see with all the bandages. "Not your fault David, you didn't hit and kick me, and I would never, never leave you to face it on your own, you're my best mate, and best mates stick together" he was a genuine friend, a best friend anyone would be proud of, a true comrade.

I couldn't help it, but I welled up, tears raced down my face, he sat there all pleased to see me and all I could do was feel sorry for the both of us. "Hey, come on David, it's all over now and look, we got a thumping, but where still here mate," Ryan declared shuffling over to me, laying his head on my shoulder.

Over the next few days, Ryan and I were causing chaos, back and forth to each other's ward; it was awesome fun having the nurses chasing us. We were getting quite a lot of attention, and we loved it.

Shame we were just kids, we had these beautiful nurses eating out of our hand.

Our time on the wards was ending; the doctor was happy to inform me I would be going home in the next few days. In truth, I was missing home. Missing mum and dad, and ultimately missing Elizabeth.

Then came my favourite day, Elizabeth came to visit. The bandages removed from our faces, revealing a

135

swollen lip and two back eyes. She kissed me as she always did, shame we couldn't hold each other, the pain was still immense, the slightest touch sent currents of pain firing through my aching body.

Her smell was sweet; a vanilla scent enticed my senses, she looked as good as the sweet aroma. Seeing her lifted my day. A true vision of beauty.

Perched on the edge of my bed. Elizabeth's story unfolded. Relaxed and glad to see us both sitting up, she told her tale. Mr. Alfred Toomey, an eighty-two-year-old frail old man, from number eleven across the road from her, had helped us. He had called the ambulance and police. Seeing it all on his way home, returning from his afternoon drinking session at the Crossgates working men's club, he had given the police the names of our assailants, without question, a selfless act without fear of retribution to himself, and not many people would do this, for fear of retribution. Alfred explained to Elizabeth, that at his age, he had nothing to fear, and was waiting for God, after all his wife has passed away over twelve years previous.

The thugs who had attacked us had been arrested and in custody. Our assailants were a lot older than us, apparently, in their early twenties, and all in college. Two had admitted the offence, giving all the names concerned. Without any reason other than the colour of my skin, gave them cause to attack us. On this occasion, the police had got a result. The courts had found them guilty, and the penalty for their crime was a three-year jail sentence. Four lives spoilt by the simple minded act of violence.

136

The nursing staff waved us goodbye; it was good to be leaving, going home, the comfort of my own bed and mums' delicious dinners.

Dad and Clive helped us both into the car, still bandaged up, I got the odd twinge of pain as I scuffled across the rear seat allowing Ryan to clamber in behind me. It wasn't long before dad was driving along the road home.

Mum was there, waiting at the front door, her arms welcomed me in, "My poor little boy... come here" she said smothering me, her face next to mine. I could feel her tears rolling down my left cheek, pulling my head back I look into her eyes, they weren't those sparkly eyes, but gloomy water glazed. "Mum I'm Ok you know ...I'm glad to be back," I said reaffirming this with a strong hug, squeezing her small frame into mine. Her hand reached out and brushed across my hair, we turned and entered the house, dad closing the door behind us.

Over the next few weeks mum never let me out of her sight, or let me off the street, we were healing well, but still had a few bruises and the odd niggle of pain, but all this was subsiding day by day. Joyce was just as bad with Ryan; we were transferred from one house to the other. Not even allowed to play the street football games.

School had restarted, the summer holidays now ended. The streets had silenced, no more yelling and screaming from the kids in the street from sun up till sun down, a new-found freedom for our parents, who now felt safe to walk the streets, the elevated temperatures had subsided into lower calm, breezy days, and the estate had found its normality once again.

I settled into our new school well, with Ryan already placing his mark on the student fraternity, he had two fights in our first week, which if I can add he won. These were not fights he had started; it was just because he was tall and athletically built and looked quite intimidating, the bully boys in our year wanted to stamp their territory. Would seem they were a new cock in town and he just so happened to be my best friend.

The school was good for most part. I found class work easy for the year we were in. The days flew by, all rolled into one; time went by very quickly, Ryan was growing fast. He towered most of the teachers, he had a strong athletic frame and was becoming a handsome young man, his blonde mullet hanging down to his shoulders, with his steely blue eyes and wide-mouthed smile, showing off his perfect set of teeth. He had the girls eating out of his hands.

I was five feet six now, the right size for a thirteen-year-old, was well respected by my tutors. I was doing well academically, and Ryan being the all-around sportsman, got away with the odd altercation.

Ryan had been given the captain's armband on the school football team. His parents were so proud, Clive very rarely missed a game; it was only when he was working night shifts did he miss them. Ryan was the talk of our year, the local star everyone wanted to be friends with. Ryan enjoyed the status but kept his friends to a minimum, mainly just me and him along with his footballing buddies.

The rest of the year passed quite uneventful. Ryan was fast becoming a leader and no longer a follower, he had his own fan club. A queue of girls wanted to go out with him. The lads were envious, I wasn't, but then I had my Elizabeth.

I rarely visited Elizabeth's now; she always made her way to ours. This was a mix of her mum and Harry having their troubles and me not wanting to go; there was still a part of me that feared the walk into her street.

She often stayed on Fridays; this was the working man's club night for our parents. Harry would be extremely drunk and Janet not too far behind, mum always a little tipsy, while dad always staggered home, he enjoyed his Friday night drink. His night to lose his inhibitions.

It was mum who offered Elizabeth to stay, said she would be good company for me. Janet agreed, Harry on the other hand argued, it wasn't healthy for two young adults to spend so much time on their own, both mum and Janet would laugh it off saying he looked too deep into it, just looking for something that isn't there.

All way through the winter nothing changed, apart from Elizabeth, who was not the same, she was full of life and giddy when she came to visit, but always seemed to be upset and drawn when she left. It had to be more than just leaving me; I knew something wasn't right, just couldn't put my finger on it. I told mum how

I felt; she asked me to stop worrying, saying, "Elizabeth was starting to reach female maturity, and her body inside was changing," mum gave her usual reassuring smile, saying "you will see, all will be fine." She knew best.

My fourteenth birthday came and went, as did Easter. Time flew by.

Dad took up baking as a hobby. He was the worse baker ever. His staff at work would encourage him, feeding the ducks at lunchtime by the canal, then telling him how delicious they were. It took mum three months to talk him out of it, and hundreds of foul tasting cakes I had to endure.

CHAPTER 13

TEARS FOR A FALLEN STAR

It was a warm Saturday summer morning, the last day of July 1977, the school had broken up for the summer break the week before. Donna Summer was No.1 in the UK charts (I feel love), the song playing out of the radio. The smell of mum's full breakfast wafting through from the kitchen.

Ryan had stayed overnight. Mum seemed quite sprightly to say she had not gotten in till after twelve last night, Clive and Joyce had joined my parents at the workingman's club. I realised the landlord had a few of his regulars stay behind for a lock-in, our parents joining them. It was about half past one in the morning when they decided to return home, dad worse for wear. I listened to him clamber up the stairs, one step forward two steps back; I couldn't hold it in, erupting into a burst of laughter, waking Ryan in the process. He just mumbled and fell back into slumber. Mum was howling too, trying to help dad into their room. The house fell silent about two O'clock, all apart from the snoring.

"Be quiet you two, dads asleep in bed" mum yelled at us from the kitchen, her yell was much louder than our singing. We were singing along with the radio, the Sex Pistols "God Save the Queen." Replacing the Donna Summer hit.

Ryan and I were jumping, crashing together, bouncing off each other as we met, falling over the furniture. Many parents were trying to ban this kind of music, saying it was offensive and gave out the wrong signal, sending a petition to Downing Street. As I recall from my history lessons, my mum and dad went through such a change in their youth with Elvis, Cliff Ricard, the Beatles, and the likes of. Lucky for me, my parents believed in a natural progression.

We did as mum said, the enticing smell of breakfast was fast taking over our senses, the hunger pangs aching inside, it wasn't long before mum had it dished up, and we were sat filling our faces, mopping up the last of the egg yolk with the last slither of bread. Mum loved seeing us empty our plates; she was unquestionably a feeder.

This was a time of anarchy, a time of change, punk music played just a small part, gone had the old do as your told ways of public life, in came the right of speech and movement. Immigrants were flooding in, filling the jobs nobody else would do. It was an uneasy time for the far-right political parties.

Lewisham in London was one such place, trouble and chaos arose, the clashes of the National front with its five-hundred members marching in the streets voicing their beliefs, meeting an angry four thousand crowd of demonstrators protesting the march. The streets were bloodied, and many were arrested, with many more hospitalised, this again proving nothing positive comes from violence. The country was divided, a fear of change was gripping the nation.

The voice of the young being heard, and noticed, no longer afraid, standing in the shadows unable to speak. For most this proved to be a good change, for the minority it prove to be a trying time. For our street not much changed.

The week was the usual boredom, nothing to do, Dad at work and mum doing some volunteering work at the local youth club. This leaving me to fend for myself, more often than not finding myself in Ryan's house watching TV with him, and being fed fish finger sandwiches for lunch, slurped down with a large glass of dandelion and burdock. Joyce's food choices had grown on me.

Elizabeth was staying the weekend at our house; I couldn't wait to see her. This weekend was going to be fun and a chance to get Elizabeth smiling. After all, everyone knew there was trouble at home.

Her parents, Janet and Harry, had gone to Spain. Harry said they needed to get out of Leeds, needed a small holiday. Needed time to themselves, to rekindle the romance in their relationship.

Her presence just picked me up as soon as I saw her. Ryan arms flung around my shoulders, "Look at you going all soft" he said shaking me, his smile was more a smirk as he took the piss out of me. "Shut up Ryan, you know I like her a lot" I replied, I couldn't hide the smile, it was beaming all over my face like a Cheshire cat. "I'm gonna leave you two to kiss then shall I," Ryan said childlike, laughing. He began to walk up the street to his house still mocking me, "See you later David," he said waving, "see you" I shouted back, not taking the time to look at him, my eyes transfixed, mesmerised on her beauty.

She carried herself stunningly as she walked up the street. The sun giving her hair aglow, her face fresh and perfect. Her beauty was second to none, she was blossoming, developing into womanhood nicely, her long legs defined in her tight jeans, her swaying hips giving that extra swagger, tossing her head side to side allowing her hair to flame out like tendrils in the wind. I never once took my gaze away from her.

Swinging on the gate, I let her through, watching her wiggle her arse from behind. Jumping off I followed her through the door. We stood face to face in the middle of the hallway; I couldn't stop smiling. "What you so happy for," she said pushing me lightly. "Just you, you make me happy" I replied, the grin on my face wider. Without any warning, she plunged herself forward, kissing me. Wow, my head was all over, wow she really likes me, I couldn't believe my luck, Elizabeth was stunning. Her smell was divine, a floral mix with a hint of vanilla, you could taste it. My senses were going bonkers, I was in love, but didn't know it.

We sat there sipping from mugs of tea and munching on chocolate biscuits, watching Abbott and Costello, the old reruns flickering on the T.V screen, our stomachs aching from the laughter.

Mum and dad had gone to town for a shopping day, wouldn't be home till late they said. I was to peel the potatoes and cut them into chips ready for when mum got home; she was doing rump steak and chips as a special dinner for Elizabeth.

The room was in semi-darkness, just the flickering from the T.V illuminating the room, we were on our own, daringly we snuggle up together, kissing every now and then, comfortable in the knowledge we wouldn't be disturbed.

Our snuggling soon heightened into a passionate embrace; we found ourselves lost in time, exploring each other. The sound of the television fading into the background, before we knew what we were doing, we found ourselves naked, lying next to each other in my bed, two nervous adolescent kids making love for the first time.

Her kiss on my shoulder as we spooned together was tender; the touch of her fingers ruffled affectionately through my dark curly hair sending shivers down my spine, we were relaxed, at ease, fulfilled and complete, silently we fell asleep.

Just after five that evening, mum and dad arrived home laden with shopping. Mum was concerned, the house was in darkness, empty, and silent, not a sound could be heard. By instinct, I had locked the doors and turned off the lights before we venture to my room. Mum wondered where we were, nor had I cut the potatoes ready for our steak and chips supper. Dad told mum not to fret, said he would check upstairs.

He made his way up the stairs, trying not to make a sound, popping his head around my bedroom door. His face said it all; it was there he found us both naked under the covers, snuggled up together sleeping. At first, anger engulfed him, but just like dad, he took a minutes thought; he knew a scene wouldn't help anyone. Shaking his head, he quietly retreated down the stairs, placing his arms around mum, he said convincingly, "No one home dear, they probably went for a walk, you know what it's like been kids at their age, and in love." Mum nodded, "Let's go out for a drink Maggie," not letting on where we were, or what he had seen. This wasn't for my sake; he knew mum would take it badly. He never did tell mum.

My parents returned from the Wilsons arms at ten that evening; mum was a little drunk, unsteady on her feet; dad was much the same, holding the wrapped-up supper in the local newspaper, the smell of fish and chips enticed our senses, you could almost taste them.

Freshly cooked fish and chips smothered in salt and vinegar.

Me and Elizabeth were fully dressed, sat on the sofa listening to mum's records playing on the stereogram player. "So you win again" by hot chocolate, echoing around the room while mum plated up the supper, dad gave me a cheeky grin and a wink, it was then I knew, he knew. I turned sharply towards Elizabeth, who began to blush and lowered her head, she never uttered a word.

"So where were you two when we got home from shopping?" mum asked, handing over the fish supper, giggling at me. The smell from her breath almost overpowering the supper. "We went for a walk mum … just forgot the time," I said, my face reddening by the minute "Sorry about the spuds," mum just smiled. She ruffled my hair in reassurance all was Ok, then kissed me lightly on my forehead. Mum sat next to dad and joined in with the supper. "Just think if you two marry each other, how lovely our grandchildren would be?" Dad started laughing, just never said why Elizabeth began choking on her supper. "You Ok love" mum said bending over to look at her face, "Yes Mrs. Brown, just a chip going down the wrong hole" she replied, the look of mortification covered her face. As for me, I didn't know where to look.

Sunday was met with a loud knock on the door. I ran down as a matter of urgency, after all, it was only twenty past eight in the morning, and most folk would still be sleeping. I didn't want mum and dad disturbed.

Dressed in only my blue pyjama pants, tied at the waist with the threaded white cord, I unlocked the door and opened it. Guess who stood there? Ryan, all giddy jumping about like a primary school kid "You coming out Dave … Gotta few quid off my brothers Phil and Carl, both home on leave from the army for the next week.

Phil and Carl now twenty-two, had been in the army some four years now, both attained the rank of corporal in the Yorkshire mechanised infantry regiment based in Germany. Phil had married a local girl from Celle; they had a two-year-old daughter called Petra. Joyce and Clive had never met them but was planning a visit in August after the boys returned. Ryan was to stay with us that week.

Elizabeth followed me down, fully clothed and washed, she leant on me from behind, her arms around my shoulders, "Hi Ryan how are you" she said winking at him, his face instantly flushed red, Elizabeth had that effect on boys. "Hi, Lizzy (that's how she liked to be known) you Ok … why you here" his face now smiling back at her, "Mum and Harry have gone to Spain for the weekend, should be back Monday night!" came her reply.

The three of us sat there on the sofa, "It's not even nine O'clock, most people are still sleeping, it's Sunday, and we all sleep in on Sundays" I said getting up and walking towards the kitchen to make the three cups of tea. Ryan just shrugged his shoulder, sniggering with Lizzy.

We were happily sat there drinking from the steaming mugs, when mum bumbled down the stairs, feeling worse for wear after her night at the pub, the stale smell of our fish and chip supper lingering from the wrappers sitting on the formica worktops in the kitchen, making mum gip.

"Morning kids you all Ok? Want any food, anyone?" she said scratching her head.

Ryan was straight in. His voice boomed across the room "Please, what you got on offer my darling?" a big cheesy grin displayed on his face. Mum looked over in our direction, "Oh hello Ryan didn't see you there you cheeky young git, some cheese on toast if you like" mum always liked Ryan; she sometimes teased him saying how dashing he looked. He'd always blush, nothing changed there, something I found quite unusual, mainly with the way the girls chased after him.

Within twenty minutes we were all sat there chomping into the toast. Mum took a tray up to her bedroom for her and dad.

We left my parents at ten, relaxing in the room, watching the midmorning telly, saying our goodbye as we headed off to Roundhay Park for the day.

The mighty trio back again, all arms linked, singing, and prancing as we went. Dad treated Lizzy and me to one pound and fifty pence each. More than enough to spend and have a great day out. Nineteen sixty's pop music filled the air; the local fairground was vibrant, hordes of fun active teenagers were filling up on candy, chips and drinking fizzy pop. Screaming and shouts erupting from every ride.

By the end of the day, we trekked home, all feeling queasy and a little dizzy. Too many swings and waltzer rides. The walk home taking longer than usual.

Ryan said his goodbyes as we entered our street. Racing up to his house, his mum stood there at the gate, welcomed him into her arms, Joyce looked upset, her the boys were returning to Germany in two days, she wished they could stay longer. It had been good to see them at home, after two and a half years, that was the last time they had visited their parents. The day they left after the breaking of her glass bar. Clive and Joyce missed their boys; the house was calm, but empty without them. Joyce missed the mayhem and the untidiness they use to cause. She had more than forgave them for the accident all those years back, she just missed them so much.

Elizabeth and me were canoodling by the gate, Dad's imitation cough disturbed us, both responding rather sheepish. Dad had been to the off license to buy a bottle of sparkling wine, tapping me on my shoulder as he passed me, "See you two in there, mum got dinner ready, mum thought we should have a glass of wine as a special treat for Elizabeth, so don't be too long" his face showing urgency. We followed dad to find mum had laid the table all fancy, had even got the silverware out. The Coq au vin dinner was a smash; mum had every reason to pleased. The weekend passed, and the daunting feeling of Monday evening finally catching up.

Lizzy had to return home. She changed from the energetic fun loving girl into a quiet, withdrawn person. I assumed it was because she was leaving us, going back home, but it was more, something I had seen in her before, I would even say she looked frightened, not wanting to return. She held me tighter than she had ever done before, pressing into me. "I love you, David, please don't come over for a while ... mum and Harry are having a tough time at the moment" she whispered, kissing me one last time before she disappeared down the road. It was obvious to me Elizabeth wasn't happy at home, bemused I turned to mum who shrugged her shoulders, "I'm sure it's all Ok David, come on let's get some dinner." We returned to the kitchen and set about making our meal, nothing more was said on the matter.

Over the next few weeks, Lizzy and I had some great days together, Ryan tagging on behind. Lizzy always met me as I was still not allowed to visit hers. There was something not right going on in Lizzie's home, Elizabeth would never tell me what it was, she just said her mum and Harry were having troubles. We would often sneak into my room when mum went shopping and dad was at work. Each time being more daring staying there longer than we should.

16th August 1977, it had been a scorcher of a day, I came home late in the evening, after hanging out all day with Lizzy and Ryan at the cinema, Roger Moore playing James Bond in the spy who loved me. Ryan going on about how dashing Bond was and how he would love to be a secret agent. Lizzy teased him, "Oh James, James please help me escape the clutches of my lover" she would play the part of the damsel in distress, I followed on in my villainous prowess, "You will never succeed Bond, the girl is mine" followed by an evil laugh. Ryan, who was now embarrassed joined in," Mr. Brown remove your hands from this fair lady" in his most upper-class Bond voice, high spirited, we fell about laughing all the way home.

Harry was waiting in his car outside our house; his face was moody, sullen. "Jump in Lizzy, your mums waiting," he opened the passenger door, Lizzy gave me a peck on the cheek, and with her head down she sat in the car, Harry put his foot down hard, driving off at speed. Ryan shook his head in disapproval as did I, no words were spoken. I bid Ryan a good night.

With the memory of the look on Elizabeth's face, I entered my house still shaking my head.

I entered the living room hoping to tell mum how I was feeling, and how confused was I, how I couldn't understand Lizzy's mood changes, she's my girl and I should be able to help her.

To my surprise, the room was deserted, mum would usually be watching the TV, she wasn't there. The T.V in the kitchen was sounding, I took the few steps to the doorway. Mum was sat on a chair at the kitchen table, sobbing, distraught, her pleasant, cheery glow had gone, she looked so small, shivering, crumpled tightly, rocking back and forth.

The news on the portable television was blurting out something or other, I never notice, wasn't that bothered, that's when I saw mum was crying. Approaching her, I asked what was wrong, mum never answered, she just continued to sob.

Her head hung, her hands covering her face. I tried my best to comfort mum, with my arms placed around her slender frame hugging her tight.

"You alright mum," I said feeling a little distressed myself. Mum was shaking, she felt so tiny in my arms, childlike. I knelt in front of her, placed her hands in mine, her face was the saddest face I had ever encountered, all life had disappeared. Images of Chris and Jenny at our door, Christmas 1970 flashed in my head, the two of them stood there lost, this is how mum looked now. I could feel myself crying, tears trickling down my face. No reason just feeling sorry for mum.

Had she received sad news about a relative? "Mum," I repeated "You Ok."

She looked directly at me from behind her tear-glazed eyes, saying, "He died today," confused I replied a bewildering "Who?" lacking any feeling in my words. Truthfully, I just wanted some food; I was starving.

"Elvis ... David, Elvis has died today" shaking, even more, pointing to the news on the TV. I could see the gates of Graceland in the background and some reporter blabbing on relentless.

I knew mum was a fan and loved his movies and records, but I never realised she had felt so strong for a man she had never met. Wiping away my tears, now feeling quite foolish. I hugged her anyway, after all, mum had always been there for me.

Fortunately for me, dad walked in from the late shift to find me comforting mum and sparing me the chance of embarrassment, saying something I shouldn't. Dad placing his arms around mum's shoulders and kissing her softly on her cheek. "It will be okay love, I am here for you," he said, whispering in her ear. Dad looked at me, his look, sympathetic and thoughtful "Go out lad, Go get yourself some chips, I'll look after mum" followed by a wink of his right eye.

I stood up and cuddled dad who placed a pound note in my hand, "See if you can stay with Joyce and Clive for tonight." I knew then dad had a tough time on his hands because mum idolised Elvis Presley. Mum must have owned most of his albums in her record collection, and we knew it, by the number of times she played them. Crying in the Chapple was her favourite song. Ironically the tune was now playing in the background, following the report on T.V, which made mum cry even more.

I walked out of the room looking back, dad knelt beside mum, his arms around her whispering softly, mum just sat there continuously sobbing.

The news of Elvis's death had sent shock waves around the world. He was only forty-two, found dead in his bathroom. The world was in a sombre mood, the sun no longer shining for many this day.

The world was in bereavement for the loss of an entertainer.

Clive and Joyce welcome me in with open arms, I told them about mum, Clive and Joyce said they too felt the loss, saying the world will be a little sadder now the King has passed away. At first, I didn't get it, probably never would, Ryan stood there laughing at me for not understanding it, (not that he did.) but he was, however, chuffed to have me staying over; this meant he could stay up a little later than normal.

Thanks to Clive paying for fish and chips, I became one-pound richer.

CHAPTER 14

ACCEPTANCE

Friday 19th August 1977, the deep orange sun burns down on the Seacroft estate, high in the blue but hazy sky, 06:20 am in morning, the street is silent apart from the engine from the taxi idling, picking up Clive and Joyce, excited about setting off for Germany, to visit the boys, their first time abroad.

Clive looks straight into Ryan's eyes, "Now you, just make sure you don't give Harold and Maggie any trouble while we're away" his face stern and solemn. Ryan's arms reach out, he hugs his dad, kissing him on his right cheek, "Don't worry dad, I will be on my best behaviour, promise." Ryan smiling, still half asleep. Joyce throws out her arms and grabs her son in a tight embrace, tears racing down from her eyes. Guilt beating her up, this being the first time she has left him, alone. "It'll be all right mum, David's mum and dad will keep an eye on me, mum I'm fourteen" Ryan's cheeky face exclaimed. Joyce kisses him on his forehead, "I know, look at you all grown up now, my little boys gone" followed by another kiss.

Now alone he watches the taxi disappear out of sight, before swaggering the few doors down to our house. Mum is stood waiting at the gate. She waves at Joyce as the taxi pulls away, heading out of the street.

Ryan feeling pleased with himself, chuffed to be trusted and treated as an adult, his face expressing his self-pride, heading towards our gate.

Full of excitement, he throws his Adidas holdall onto the bed, "Should be a fun week Dave, got £6.00 off mum and dad for the week" (today's equivalent would be £38.00). Was a lot of money for a kid when you take into consideration the average wage was £62.00 a week, but, this was his holiday money.

We squeezed each other tight, then throwing a high five (couldn't tell you what we called it back then), laughing we fell onto our beds. We were looking forward to tomorrow, going to the beach for a week's holiday, I had never been to the seaside before, neither had Ryan, sleep didn't come easy, we sat up in bed imagining what we would do when we got there, sounding like two toddlers waiting for Christmas day. Sleep did win through; the house was silent once again.

Dad was on annual leave; the car was packed to the brim. Listening to Elvis on the radio cassette player as we set off on our journey. This was for mum, she said she missed Elvis so much, I never could understand how you could miss someone you had never met, but who knows maybe I would learn that in time.

It was a clear blue sky Saturday morning with very little wind; the temperature was starting to rise, as we hit the summer highs. We sang along to the Elvis tape, travelling along the motorway towards Scarborough.

Dad's new Ford Granada. It was brown in colour with leather seats and wooden trim. Compared to the old Morris Traveller we were travelling in style. Dads foster grants protecting his eyes from the glare. The dry asphalt road shimmering in the heat wave.

We were going to be staying in a two-bedroomed chalet for the week at the Butlins camp in Filey. Ryan and I had never seen the sea before, apart from on television. I don't think we knew one kid in our street who had. I couldn't wait.

The anticipation was so overwhelming that I had car sickness, luckily for me, we had time to pull over to the side of the road before I had the chance of emptying my stomach contents over the car seat, and as usual, mum was on hand to clean me up. "No more food for you David till after we land there!" mum pointing at the goody wrappers on the car seat, and looking rather disappointed at me, as she spoke; I had eaten more than I should have. Left me feeling like a toddler rather than a fourteen-year-old teenager. Ryan was leaning out of the window laughing and ridiculing me as mum scorned at me, Mum swung around, her face fiercely staring at Ryan "Don't you laugh at my boy, could be you down there, now sit down!", Ryan just smiled back at dad, who in turn returned the smile, this just annoyed mum more, and with Ryan having his condition, it was never going to happen, he never ate sugary foodstuffs like sweets and cakes. He had however managed to scoff eight bags of crisp.

Butlins was buzzing; the noise could be heard a good 300 meters before entering the camp. Temperatures were soaring as the sun blazed down on the resort, cloudless skies with hardly any breeze, elevating the temperature to a sweltering heat.

We watched the colourful holiday reps huffing and puffing, red-faced as they rushed excitedly, herding the holidaymakers around like cattle, Ryan and me were in fits of laughter, wasn't long before mum and dad joined in. How comical it all looked, we were in for a fun week.

Dad parked up, bringing the car to a halt outside the reception block, he entered the low flat-roofed building to collect our keys. We sat in the car glaring out of the windows watching the holidaymakers racing around struggling with their over-packed suitcases, cursing as they dragged them to their holiday homes.

A family with three teenage girls about our age passed by; one of them turned, winked and blew a kiss our way. Mum was giggling at us; she watched as we fought for ownership of the blown kiss.

"What a pair of fools you two are," she said mocking us. Embarrassed we smiled back at her, feeling our faces warming as we blushed. Dad saved us from more of mum's ridicule, returning to the car, and driving us to our new home for the week.

Mum opened the door to an interesting sight; we all just stood there taking in the décor, it was dad who first set us off in fits of laughter, the room was bright yellow with a brown and blue checked sofa with a white background. The wooden framed four-legged television set stood in the corner, the windows gleaming in their white wooden frame, pink lace curtains draping from the curtain wire. Looked more like a dolls house than some where to stay. The bedrooms were spacious, mum and dads had a large double bed, and ours had two single beds. I took the one on the right leaving Ryan to toss his bag on the left one. "David ...Ryan come on, helps us get the rest of the stuff in here" dads voice demanded, huffing, and puffing, removing the cases and the box of toiletries out of the car. It didn't take long to complete our task; mum had three ice-cold lemonades set up, ready to quench our thirst, they were the most welcome drinks ever, with the sweat dripping off us. Dad was getting old now and was finding it harder to do the minimal of task. He was going to see the doctor when we got home as his breathing was difficult at times and mum worried. Dad just said it was his age. Mum didn't argue, but knew better.

Once we were settled in, Ryan and I did our tour of the camp. Excited and in buoyant spirits, we were making a nuisance of ourselves, running in and around of the other holidaymakers, annoying some, but being fourteen-year-olds and boisterous, we didn't care much, or consider others feelings the way we should have.

Ryan clumsily bumped into the girl who blew the kiss, almost knocking her to the ground. Just as she was about to hit the pavement, Ryan had her scooped up in his arms. His face flushed red with embarrassment; his voice stuttered out "Sorry are you Ok ... didn't mean to knock you down" the girl now stood unaided but irritated replied "You gormless oaf ... you could have killed me" brushing her long mousey brown hair from her face with her right hand. She then did the head tilt,

159

swaying her hair back and forth as it found its natural lay. "My names Kathy what's yours" her smile broad on her beautiful freckled face, standing there in her printed god save the queen, sex pistols t-shirt and jeans. "Ryan ...Ryan is what they call me" sounding like some half-wit, he blurted out, "So your Ryan Ryan then," she said teasing him. "No just Ryan that's all ... Ryan Backhouse at your service" he said as he bowed in front of her.

She giggled and pulled him back upright, offering her hand. For a split-second Ryan seemed unfocused, shocked, then he realised she actually liked him, finally, he placed his hand in hers. He looked across at me, I gave him the thumbs up and walked in the opposite direction, leaving Ryan to get to know his new friend better. It was some four hours later before I saw Ryan again. He had a smile so broad he could have had a flip back head. "David she's great ... I really like her, and she's funny, and she loves punk rock" he cried out eagerly. I nodded back at him putting my arms around him, "glad for you buddy ... Where's she from?" I replied. "She's called Kathy, and she's from Wakefield," he continued to say as he flopped onto his bed. "I'm meeting her tonight at the concert room, there triplets you know" again smiling, he sat up "There are Kathy, Joanne and Mary, and there fourteen like us." He lay back down, hands behind his head, closed his eyes and fell asleep. It wasn't that long before I followed into slumber too.

Five O'clock, we made our way to the canteen for tea; it was awful, following a long queue of people, standing in a line, it was like being at school dinners.

It was a large room full of square tables with four or six chairs around them. The place was packed out; we were lucky to find the four-seater table. The food was terrible, fish fingers, chips, and peas. Not much of a choice, the decor was the same as the chalets, bright and bold. Mum decided there, and then, we would be eating out from now on. She hated what she called plastic food. A good hearty meal was what mum was about.

We made our way back to the chalet to get spruced up ready for an evening of onsite entertainment. Mum was excited, looking forward to a dance with dad.

Eight O'clock in the evening and the resort was full of sounds and flashing lights, the adult holidaymakers rushing over to the concert rooms, all dressed in high collars and beige trousers, shiny shoes, and the women in floral patterned dresses. The holiday reps were busy shepherding the holidaymakers into their holiday village clubs. The celebrity host speaking loud, alluring his audience, the crowds pulled in by his wit and charm. Mum and dad had befriended a couple about their age; they sat at a round table, a checked tablecloth draped over it, with a token vase with a solitary red rose. They sat in light conversation, drinking their alcoholic beverages, entertained by an artist of yesteryear, tonight it was Gerry and the Pacemakers, they were a massive hit back in the sixties, spinning out many popular tunes.

Meanwhile in the room next door, a huge spacious hall with a square dance floor in the centre, with rows of tables with the plastic chairs surrounding them. Teenagers filled the room drinking from cardboard cups full of Pepsi, cream soda, or lemonade. Apart from the sound of the music playing not much was said, the teenagers too shy to integrate.

Ryan entered, arms linked with Kathy, and me trailing behind. We found an empty table, the four blue plastic chairs vacant, the DJ was playing David Soul's "going in with my eyes open." With only a few couples dancing on the dance floor, the two young reps were pulling at the boys and girls lining the walls onto the dance floor, trying to inspire them to join in.

The voice of the DJ boomed, "Baccara with yes sir I can boogie, for all you disco dancers out there," as it travelled through the speakers; the dance floor was filling fast. Ryan and Kathy were there too, strutting their moves, swaying their bodies in time with the music, leaving me sat on my own, David no mates. Out of all the people in the room not a single hello came my way.

"So, your David" came the voice from the mirror imaged Kathy. It was obvious this was one of her sisters, "Hi, yes, I'm David" I Replied looking up at her, not looking too bothered, "Do you mind if I join you?" she asked pulling up a chair. She sat opposite me sipping on her cardboard cup of Pepsi, we sat there in silence, just staring at each other, our mouths breaking into a smile, within minutes we burst into laughter, "So what do you want to do" I asked, my arms outstretched as if offering a gift. "My name is Mary if you're interested," she said, slightly embarrassed "Sorry," I answered, not very convincing. "Hello Mary, my name is David how do you do" as I tried again, introducing myself, she reached for my hands, her touch was light and soft, "I'm fine" her face beaming as she replied.

The track changed to Elvis's Suspicion, I instantly thought of mum.

Mary stood up and offered her hand. "you fancy a slow dance." Her body was typical of a girl her age, long legs, firm tummy, firm small breast leading up to a slender neck which housed a cute, attractive face, full-lipped, high cheek boned and wide eyes exaggerated with black eyeliner. I stood and accepted her hand, thinking hey why not? Nothing to lose. We walked over to the dance floor and began to dance, swaying close together, in time with the beat. I could see she liked me and I knew I like the look of her. Over her shoulder I noticed Ryan and Kathy heading for the door, leaving the room, into the warm evening sun, they walked; teasing each other as they ran and climbed on the junior playground frames, not saying a "see you later David" which would have been nice.

It was getting hard to dance; almost unable to move, the floor was now packed with young couples swaying closely together. Without thinking, we were kissing, full on the lips, holding each other close, lost in each other, moving to the sound of the music, as if we were the only two there.

As the music began to fade out, we found ourselves surrounded by a group of older boys, all wearing the uniform of skinheads, the closely shaven head, Dr. Marten boots, and baggy jeans with large turn-ups. They were all a slighter build than me and not one of them could have probably held up on their own, but collectively they were quite intimidating. The twelve of them poking at me, Mary whimpered, taking a step or two back from me scared. I could feel the room getting smaller, shrinking slowly, closing in. The crowd behind the gang of boys had grown by some fifty or so out of the eighty or ninety teenagers in the room.

Peter Fletcher, a short lad for his age of seventeen, was the leader of the gang. Peter had travelled up with a group of families from the Coventry area, mums, and dads with their hoard of siblings.

Peter takes two steps forward from the rest. "Here what are you doing snogging and dancing with one of our girls?" He hissed through his teeth. I didn't answer, just stood there, I could feel their eyes penetrating me, I knew what he meant, (a white girl). Fear rocketed through my body. This familiar feeling taking over. The strain in the lower part of my stomach churned inside. I knew this wasn't going to end well.

Mary trembling, terrified pushed further back squeezing through the crowd, crying as she went, her eyeliner combining with her tears as they rolled down her frightened sobbing face, she was forcing her way out, now heading for the door.

"What we gonna do with the little Paki boy Fletch" came a cry from one of the boys behind me. I didn't respond. Peter raised his cup in silence and spat into his drink, hurling it towards my face, the drink explodes on my chest as it shortfalls its destination. He then starts to chant "Nigger nigger pull a trigger bang bang bang" within seconds a chorus of the words filled the room, the crowd began to chant too, missiles of cardboard cups full of drink, targeted at me like missiles on an enemy target, exploding the contents as they find there target. Soon the floor was coated in a sticky liquid mess. All the while I stood there head down silent.

The pain as the solid mass hit my head and body was distressingly painful, blood began to flow from my nose as a cup hits it square on. Unbelievably I still gave no reaction. I was hurting, shivering, cold and wet, cocooned in a room full of hate. The room disappeared into darkness, an empty void, closing in on me. The noise in the room catapulting into a volcanic eruption of chants. Their vile words echoing inside my head.

The two reps made their way to Peter. I saw a glimpse of salvation, but none came, Instead of breaking up the chaos, the young girl just looks me up and down. Her face, a twisted evil look "You should be with the bloody blacks and Pakis on Caribbean street, where they play your coconut music," she said laughing, the others followed, "Yeah monkey boy get your arse out of the white man's room" came Peter's remark. This followed with another volley of some thirty drink missiles. I couldn't cry, I just stood feeling small in the middle of this human ring dripping from head to foot in sticky fizzy liquid. I could feel myself wanting to run away, but my feet couldn't move. Tears finally began to fall, some of the kids felt sorry and sickened, and slowly left the room, not daring to look back.

Gerry and the pacemakers were well into their routine, the audience singing along, and the odd couple dancing in the aisles.

Suddenly the concert door swung open, a young teenage girl stood there, crying hysterically, forcing her way up to my mother's table, exhausted through her tears, confused and fearful from the bullying towards me, the words would not release from her mouth. The music ceased as Gerry stopped singing; the chants from the room next door enveloped the complex, vibrating from all sides, getting louder and louder. Mum knew instantly I was in some kind of danger and was already heading towards the door. Mary stood there as mum passed her; she had not had a chance to tell mum, she just stood there quivering and sobbing, her mum was soon comforting her, getting the full story, poor Mary fell to her knees, shaking, crying, and shivering in her mother's arms.

The heavy door of the dance hall flung open, mum just stood there, the noise of the chanting faded as the teenagers looked on, like a domino effect the chanting stopped, silence, not even the wind dare blow. The room reeked of fear, but not from me this time; you could cut through it, something bad had happened, and was just about to get worse.

The teenagers divided like the parting of the sea, revealing an aisle, there at the end stood a solitary figure dripping wet, head lowered, shoulders stooped. Without hesitation, mum made her way towards me.

Most of the parents had emerged, snatching at their children; the wailing started, their parents being quite aggressive after seeing me stood there, the cracks around the teenaged heads echoed throughout the room. The words that followed were unrepeatable. Ashamed of them, they dragged them out. The room emptied in seconds.

Mum walked past Peter not acknowledging his existence, she placed her arms around me, helping me escape the ordeal, dad joined us taking my left arm to assist mum.

Peter stood in the middle of the empty room, silence fell all around, his face twisted as he shouted out, echoing around the deserted room, "I don't get it ...He's just a Paki". His voice filling the room.

Frank Fletcher entered the hall, a young twenty-two-year-old man; he was on holiday with Peter and his parents during his leave from Scotland. He was serving with the Royal Navy Commandos.

As cool as you like, he stood upright, face to face with his brother. "You are an embarrassment," he said calmly, tugging at Peter's shirt, "Just get lost, he asked for it Ok" replied the vile little man. Peter found himself doubled up on the floor; Frank swiftly punched him hard in his stomach; Frank looked down and sneered at him "Get to the chalet now," retreating, leaving Peter curled up in the river of fizzy liquid on the dance room floor.

How ironic the very person who had caused the mess. Now lay in it.

Dad opened the door to our chalet; I headed for the shower, stripping off and allowing the hot water to rain down, washing the nights' torment away. Dad was consoling mum. "First thing and we are out of here" mum cried as tears fell. Dad looked on holding mum in his arms, "Let's see what tomorrow brings Maggie" he whispered to her.

The rain of hot water couldn't wash away the pain; I found myself scratching at my flesh, screaming "Get it off" repeatedly I screamed, Mum came racing in followed by dad.

Witnessing the distress, I was in, had mum break down, falling to her knees, tears streamed down her face, "Bastards …Why can't they leave him alone" screeched mum pulling at dads' shirt, dad aided mum back to the sofa, sitting her gently down, just as Ryan came through the door, "Look after Margaret for me Ryan … I'll be back in a minute" dad said, heading for the shower room once more. Ryan looked lost, not knowing what had happened, he just sat and talked with mum.

Dad kneels next to me in the shower, his arms cradle around me, pulling me in. "You're a beautiful young man son, you have nothing to be ashamed of," his words heartfelt, his head resting on mine, "Why won't it come off Dad," I asked still trying to scrape it off, blood starting to seep out from my scratch wounds. "What are you trying to do son?" said dad holding me tighter. "This black skin dad! It won't come off, why don't they think I'm a white man, dad? I'm English, aren't I?" the tears spilling down my face like a waterfall, unable to stop myself from sobbing.

"Yes, you are son" tears developing, start to roll down dads' face as he places his head on my shoulder, rocking me for comfort.

Dad turns off the shower and dries me off with the beach towel. Gently picking me up in his arms, without any thought of if he could manage or not, unstable on his feet, he manages to place me on my bed. Within ten minutes, I am fast asleep in my bed, whimpering in my sleep, exhausted from my ordeal.

My parents and Ryan cuddled up together, sat on the settee in conversation, discussing the night's events over a hot mug of Ovaltine. No one slept well that night, as for me I had reoccurring nightmares, crying in my sleep. Ryan sat for the first hour on the edge of my bed; he held my hand as he watched over me, stroking my head, as I whimpered in my sleep. Tiredness gained the better of him, he reluctantly went to his bed and slept into the daylight hours.

The following morning dad had taken mum into Scarborough, while Ryan met up with Kathy.

I was still sleeping. It was ten O'clock Sunday morning; the day was bright, but breezy, the temperatures a mild 17 degrees. Mum had wanted to stay and fuss over me, but dad said no and that I would come around on my own and I had to now accept who I was. Dad said I was to take on board all the changes adult life brought, both the good and the bad. Mum was reluctant towards dad's words but knew he was right.

The mirror reflected my image, a five-foot-six well-proportioned young teenager, all I saw, was a sadly downtrodden child staring back, pick yourself up David you're better than this, repeated the voices in my head. It took nearly an hour for me to finally decide to get dressed.

I made my way to the settee and sat in silence. I could hear the gaiety from the outside. Holidaymakers doing what holidaymakers do, the sound of laughter and the screams of joy as the children ran about in droves, the constant yelling of parents trying to control the kids, unsuccessfully. I wanted to hide, couldn't even bring myself to get a drink of water, just sat there staring out into nothingness.

Hours passed into the mid-afternoon; I was sat watching the television when mum came through the door, paper bags full of rock candy in her hands. Mum placed them on the wooden sideboard against the far wall, and then swiftly made her way to me. Dad followed, carrying a couple of pizza boxes. Ryan, Kathy, and Mary followed, must have been the smell of the pizza. Mum had her arms around me, holding me close; my head leant on her shoulders as we watched the Sunday afternoon movie.

Ryan looked over to me chomping down on his slice of Margarita. "You Ok David ...I should have been there!" he said scooping the melted cheese in swirls around the edge of his slice. "I will be from now on" he continued.

"There was nothing you could have done ...And anyway I don't want you getting hurt again because of me" I replied as I tackled the hot Italian spiced meat slice. The first bite, reminding my stomach I hadn't eaten anything all day. I was feeling a little better now, especially having the people I most care about around me.

"I didn't get hurt because of you pal it was because they were knobs," Ryan said defensively, I gave him thumbs up. Mary tried to apologise to me but was cut short as they were nothing to apologise for, she raised from her chair and approached me, giving me a kiss on my right cheek, then returned to continue the feast of pizza and a glass of dandelion and burdock. The evening was pleasant, just watching TV and eating our pizza. Mum was happy to have me next to her. You could see the sadness in her eyes as she gazed at my arms, long scabby scars from my attempt to rid myself of my skin colour.

As the week went by Ryan and Kathy had become very close, spending as much time as they could with each other, with me not too far away in the background. Ryan had taken it upon himself, that if anyone tried to hurt me again, they would have to deal with him first. I had no more trouble. We never saw Peter or his family in the camp after that night. The two holiday reps had also left.

The week turned out to be the holiday mum and dad had planned. The site manager took time out to visit us. He couldn't apologise enough; mum reminded him he was not to blame and thanked him for his concern. We got a weeks' worth of vouchers to use, saving us money, and free transport to the beach.

As for Mary and me, we both told the truth about the special person in our lives, for me it was Elizabeth, and for Mary, it was someone called John. We still had the odd snog which was fantastic, I think, had we not got that special person in our lives, our relationship could have blossomed, we really fancied the pants off each other. To be honest to myself, Mary made my week; she made me believe in me again, she was a beautiful girl who wanted to be with me no matter what colour skin, I wasn't that much different after all.

The weather continued to be fantastic for the rest of the week. The bright blue, sunny skies, low breeze, and warm sea air, the tantalising brush of the surf flowing over your feet, entering the sea for the first time, surprisingly cold to the touch. Ryan and I stood for ages up to our knees in the surf, amazed at the sight, the horizon and beyond, nothing but water, the endless blue. "It's amazing David" the words from Ryan's mouth, falling out like a child, I was the same, "Wow Ryan, how far it spans" we must have sounded stupid to an outsider, but we were truly taken aback. Our first experience of the sea, the unstable feeling of walking, the sinking into the bed, soft silt covering our feet, finding every nook and cranny, losing our balance the further we edged in, the force of the waves rising over our heads, mesmerized us, we took it all in. Kathy and Mary joined us, the four of us splashing around. Mum complained most of the time, she had gotten sunburnt and was always uncomfortable, while dad went a golden tanned. He was sometimes mistaken for a Spaniard, which was hilarious when the Spanish waiters served him, always adding extra on his plate. I think Dad put on an extra stone in weight this week. He had never had a beer belly till now, and he looked hilarious, he wasn't too pleased about it, he had to buy some new shirts because his shirts wouldn't button up over his stomach. Mum teased so much; he almost lost his temper, this didn't help, just set mum off into a giddy fit.

In truth, we were quite sad to leave the chalet. The week had been good, even hard some days, but overall, very good, Butlins had been fun.

Leaving Butlins was a harsh time for Ryan; he silently cried, tears trickled down his face, he had left his first love behind, someone he had bonded to, someone he had dared to care for more than he would have liked. He was hurting all the way home. We left him alone, leaving him with his own thoughts and his coming to terms with his feelings, in truth, none of us wanted to talk, the week had exhausted us. Mum was just thankful we were allowed to continue the holiday as we first intended, free from hurt, just enjoying the time, the sun, and the sea. The last week had tested us on our frailty as individuals and our resolve as a family. We came out quite well, showing each other what a great strong family unit we were.

As for Ryan, he never saw or heard from Kathy again.

CHAPTER 15

DAYS INTO WEEKS

Waiting for her best friends to return home, Elizabeth patiently stood by the gate, emotionally charged on a high, a chance to escape her dull life with Harry and her mum and their constant squabbles.

Dad slowly brings the car to a halt as he parks up outside our house, the engine silenced as he removes the key from the ignition; exhausted dad gives out a big sigh, and slumps back in his seat. "So good to be back home, a nice cup of Yorkshire tea," Mum agrees, smiling back at him, pleased to be home again.

Ryan's parents had returned home, after their visit to Phil and Carl's in Germany. Both stood by their gate, waving to mum, mum replied by waving back and shouting "Hello Joyce, hope you had a lovely time with the boys?" handing Ryan a brown paper bag full of sticks of candy rock, Joyce not hearing her just nods in approval. Ryan says his goodbyes to mum and dad, then briskly walks up to Lizzy and kissing her on her left cheek. Lizzy hugs him close, "Look after him, Lizzy, He's in love with you, you know," he says looking straight at me smiling, at the same time giving me the thumbs up, making his way off up the street, and back into the arms of his parents.

Elizabeth wraps her arms around my neck and kisses me hard on the lips, releasing with a loud smacking sound, she breaks into an even louder laugh. "It's great to have back home ...I have missed you so like total crazy" her head swaying back and forth, her hair flowing like dancing flames. To her it was as if we were the only people on this planet, her inhibitions' all disappeared, her eyes only seeing me. "Ryan's right, I do love you, Lizzy ...I really do" the words departing from my mouth before I had really thought about what I was saying. She just kissed me again. I honestly do love her.

Through our two lives from being primary school kids till now, she had taken the most special place in my heart and would stay there, always.

Mum smiled at us as she watched, signalling dad with a nod of her head. Dad snatched at mums hand, squeezing it a little tight, mum turn to face him, thinking she had done wrong, but not the case, he kissed her tenderly on her lips. "Let's give them a minute love," he said, his nose wrinkled up. Mum blushed not expecting his tenderness. They enter the house hand in hand closing the door behind them.

We stood face to face, tears in her eyes, "David I have missed you so much, I don't like it when I can't see you, I love you, David, please believe me when I say this," her words were genuine and true. I knew this, and I also knew I felt the same, I held her closer, kissing her face and rubbing noses. Elizabeth wept as she hugged me tightly, "I don't want to go home anymore David, I want to stay with you. It's not good at home; we're having a terrible time, so much anger, I don't want to go home." We must have stood there for twenty minutes before Elizabeth calmed down, and we entered the house to join mum and dad.

We had a beautiful afternoon, mum talking the most, not giving anyone else a chance to speak. The sandwiches and cake for tea finished off the day.

This was spoilt by Harry, turning up and demanding Elizbeth return home with him to help Janet with some chore or something? Mum asked him to calm down and not to intrude in that manner, he apologised quickly but reaffirmed he had to be going. Elizabeth got into his car, her face was strained and saddened, she asked mum to allow her to stay and phone her mum, but Harry was persistent she was needed at home, mum saddened by this said a sorrowful no. I felt a little empty and useless, so went to my room, mum was doing her best, but to me, it was as if she didn't try this time. There was something not right at Elizabeth's, but what it was I didn't have a clue, and this was tormenting away at me, not knowing, not able to help her. I felt totally useless.

The days flashed by, turning into weeks and the weeks into months. Before we knew it, the year was nearly over.

During this time, the three of us stuck together like glue, helping each other with homework, making sure we all hit the grade at school, Elizabeth was by far the smartest out of the three of us, not just a beautiful lass, but brains and common sense with it. Her escapism was me.

We took it on ourselves to find Ryan a girlfriend; this was to no avail, we hung around the shopping centre on the weekends, along with the kids our age.

The teenaged girls pushing towards Ryan, trying to sneak a kiss here and there. Ryan seemed indifferent to them, had no interest in them and would always politely ask them to leave him alone. He was quite a mope sometimes, probably yearning for Kathy. Wasn't like he couldn't get a girl, they were throwing themselves at him.

Going to the cinema to watch some movie or other was one of our favourite pastimes, we loved watching the iconic stars on the big screen, John Travolta was making his mark in the Hollywood circles, and becoming a household name, even mum thought he was dishy looking, telling dad he had competition.

Lisa Connor had started hanging around with Lizzy. She had befriended Elizabeth, both going to the same girl's school. Lisa was a year below Lizzy, but they both hung about together in their break times, they had become best friends. Lisa was well ahead of her peers in her age group and sat with Lizzy in English and math's in the year above hers. She excelled in both subjects. They swapped boy stories. I just hope Lizzy was kind.

Even though Lisa was only thirteen, she looked older and was sassier than Lizzy, but not as beautiful as my Lizzy. Lisa could still turn heads in a crowd, being a natural beauty. Looking at her mum you wondered where she got her looks, not saying Mrs. Connor's unattractive, but her constant scowl took it away, She had the makings of a beautiful woman, just needed to take a little more pride with her self-grooming.

Mrs. Connor wasn't too please Lisa hung with us, but she never interfered or said anything. Mrs. Connor took comfort from Grant; he was the sensible one, she knew she had to allow her little girl to grow.

With her boys all grown and flown the nest, all her attention was given to Lisa and Grant, and with Lisa becoming more self-reliant, she felt quite redundant, just like mum and Joyce.

Dad was feeling the strain a little more these days, he had four more years before retiring, which I knew he was dreading, but dad always tried to hide it, mum knew he was starting to feel less desired. At work, he was given less to do and only had to do four days a week now, and it was going to get less as the years passed. He was guaranteed a great pension, had even been asked if he wanted an early retirement. That apparently offended him; this was never an option. Harold was at a loss every Friday. He was up no later than usual, but sat in his chair looking out of the window, watching the world go about its regular business. Dad was saddened to think he was now at the twilight of his working years, he knew he had to find something to fill his time, but for now he just sat there.

Mum was also finding it a little harder to rule the roost; the world was changing in our house, our opinions, and beliefs, also we'd aged a bit more. For me, it was understanding the much wider world. The world was beginning to shrink, the media was now the new face of the world, taking away the adventure and yearning for unchartered knowledge, television had crossed over the seas into foreign lands, the new satellite links from space, communications speeding through, easier and now less expensive to make a phone call, rather than write a letter, a skill decaying and outdated.

It was official now, me and Lizzy were boyfriend and girlfriend, and everybody knew, Ryan had said it was about time we admitted it. Mum and Janet celebrated over a can of larger; however, Harry didn't look too pleased, in fact, the opposite, dad told him. "It's been on the cards since they were four" offering him a can of Worthington ale, mum and Janet agreed, Harry gave a pretentious smile' accepting the can, but there was no fooling me, I knew he didn't approve, but, Elizabeth and me, well we didn't care what Harry thought.

The most significant thing to change our lives in 1977 was the December premiere of Star Wars the movie; every cinema countrywide was showing this, it had to be the biggest and the best movie we three had ever seen. Ryan was running around with his invisible light sabre, fighting anyone who would join in, coming out of the cinema he had his pick of fellow Jedi. Lizzy, lisa and I were left in fits of laughter watching him play. Whizz, whoosh, swish were the sounds coming from the playful Jedi, jumping around the cinema forecourt, everyone from twelve to sixty were joining in, this was one hell of a sight to see, there must have been about one hundred people running around acting like children, emulating the scenes from the movie. The local Bobby's stood applauding the exhibition. Not one person caused any trouble; it was a night of peaceful, light-hearted fun, enjoyed by all.

School had a topic day on the subject, mainly about the possibility of Star Wars ever being possible. Could a man indeed possess the ability to mind control? For us pupils, the answer was a simple yes, we had to do as we were told, so therefore if the teacher or an adult said jump, then this is what we did. The world had gone Star Wars mania crazy. The biggest selling toys on the Christmas shelves.

Once again, the school gates closed for the December break, leaving us kids with too much time on our hands.

Mum was finding it tiring having me home twenty-four-seven; she would invent jobs around the house for me to do, like sort out old clothes to be taken to the rag and bone man or clear the leaves from the garden to stop us slipping on them. I would do my chores without question; I knew I was getting under her feet, mum even asked if I was going out or to see Lizzy, anything to get me out for a few hours. Mum had gotten used to and loved her afternoons alone during the week; she could sit down, listen to her favourite music, and read her Mills and Boon. Now, all my school holidays did, was to interfere with her regular routine, after all, what did she need to do for me? I was fourteen years old and had grown out of the motherly pampering. Mum like many mums had kind of grown out of their nurturing days. Mum was happy to have dad home on Fridays, and dad had become a custom to being home now; they enjoyed an afternoon tea in the local market and a brisk walk in the local parks.

As for me I just spent my days with Ryan and Lizzy, we didn't do much, spent most of the time in Ryan's room listening to music, Lisa would join us on the odd occasion. This year's Christmas holiday was uneventful, I had grown out of the father Christmas beliefs and wasn't as giddy or enthusiastic about the morning. No longer playing with toys, I think as teenagers we lost the innocents and joy of all the build-up and anticipation of the day. Wanting to grow up too quick, denying ourselves of the true joy we craved. Playing with our old toys, transporting ourselves into our fantasy worlds.

Christmas day arrived. A warm Christmas day, no snow today, the sun spilled out its warm rays, brightening up the street. The previous day's snow lay compacted on the ground, the steam rising upwards towards the skies giving off a hazy rainbow spanning the street.

The knock on the door got mum a bit panicky, mainly because the roast potatoes weren't quite fully cooked, and she was running behind with her Christmas dinner. Dad answered the door to see the Greens all stood there in their Sunday best, Janet looked radiant, she was pregnant with Harry's child. They were both over the moon, Lizzy was pleased for her mum, however, over the last year she had withdrawn from Harry, but never said why.

Dad welcomed Harry with a large tumbler of whisky. Both men trying to prove who's the alpha male, necking them straight down; it was comical to observe, with both men coughing violently and spluttering, Janet just looked on shaking her head at the bravado; the two men drank the next glass slower than the first, both speaking as if they were experts on the subject of whisky making. The sitcom, Are you being served was on the BBC, Dad loved this program, said he could never understand how the BBC got away with the sexual content in this program. Dad and Harry continued to drink, laughing at the slightest innuendo. "Mrs. Slocomb, I bloody wish" yelled dad, not realising he had blurted it out. "Mind your manners Harold" shouted mum from the kitchen. Dad sunk in his chair, Harry burst into laughter, ridiculing dad, who now sat quietly. I guess Harry was the alpha male.

Janet made her way to the kitchen; mum was busy, still preparing dinner, "Hello Margaret could you do with some help" Janet said smiling at mum, leaning on the door frame; mum turned, her eyes met Janet's, looking all aglow with her bump showing underneath her smock. Joyously she replied "Hello, Janet …I don't mind if you, and your little bump do" pointing at the serving pots ready to be placed on the table. Janet joined in, the two of them busy, both in and out of the kitchen, arms full, while dad and Harry sat there in front of the T.V.

Lizzy made her way to my room, finding me laid on my bed with my headphones plugged in, listening to the latest top of the pops LP, Ain't gonna bump no more (with no big fat woman) was playing as she walked in. I laid there; eyes closed lost in my own world trying to mimic the words and doing a hand jive. Unknowing to me Lizzy stood there grinning at me, while I made a fool of myself. Opening my eyes, and seeing Lizzy, I quickly removed the headphones, almost throwing them to the floor, embarrassed, sitting up within a millisecond. My face was as red as a beetroot; she just stood there laughing, the moment soon passed. "Hello David, happy Christmas" she looked stunning in her thigh length mini skirt and black stockings covering her beautiful long legs, and the loosely fitting Star Wars woolly jumper draping over her torso. "Happy Christmas Elizabeth, you look great" came my reply, I grabbed her onto the bed. Our lips met, we kissed, smiling at each other, shuffling over, we sat up on the edge of the bed, cuddling each other, swaying to the music. We were all loved up; we could have stayed in that time forever.

Christmas dinner was, like all those before, a remarkable success, we had the usual full plates of turkey roast and winter veg, followed by the hot Christmas pudding complimented with the brandy sauce.

Slumped back on the settee, with our swollen aching stomachs. Most of the conversation was about the expectant child and when he or she was due.

As usual, we all sat there stuffed to the brim watching the Queen's speech. Dad would have it no other way.

"The Queen's speech is addressed to all in her kingdom, so all should listen" dad would say pointing his finger at the T.V, I found it annoying, but sat there all the same.

CHAPTER 16

EMOTIONALLY SCARRED

January 14th, 1978, my fifteenth birthday.

Met with a big kiss from mum, her sparkly eyes meeting mine. "Happy birthday son, look at you all grown up" mum said softly, her hands on my shoulders, mum beamed the biggest smile, I could see how proud she was, mum's arms slid around my shoulders, and mine around her waist, we cuddled up close, I could feel her warmth. Mum kissed me again on the cheek, then let me go. Dad flung out his right arm, thrusting a Wilkinson swords razor in my hand, like handing me the coming of age prize. "Time you learned how to shave properly my boy," he said in his commanding daddy voice. Bursting his bubble, I replied "Dad I started shaving last year ...Mum got me my first blade then" looking at him blankly. Shrunken and a little-disheartened dad scorned. "No one tells me bloody anything in this house" shaking his head in dismay. Mum had told him, it was just dad had more to think about this past year than me shaving.

Dad wanted to treat me, wanted to make me proud of him, I was already proud of dad, after all, I had the best dad in the world, and I loved him dearly, he wasn't just my dad, he was my friend. Over the years he had shown me so much, been there when I needed him, and cried with me in time of sorrow and lifted me out in times of sadness, he was a hero to me, and let no one say otherwise.

My parents had arranged to take me in to town for lunch today, they said I could take Ryan, Lizzy, and Lisa.

I raced around the street to give out my invitations. Within minutes they were all at my door, Harry dropping Elizabeth off, his normal frown displayed on his face. "Happy Birthday David" he smirked, forcing out a smile. "Thanks, Harry, say hello to Janet," I said waving back at him, as he drove off at speed. Elizabeth smelt great, and tasted just as nice. Her lips met mine, Ryan shook his head, "Is that all you two do?" Releasing me Elizabeth replied "Yes it is, and we like it," her stance annoyed at him. Ryan backed off, passing me my cards from his parents, "Happy birthday David", I took them, ripping open the envelopes. I have received seven cards in all from my parents and friends.

Dad, all excited, drove into town. We parked in one of the multi-car parks in the town centre. The chill of the wind gripped you, penetrating your inner being, it was one of those cold frosty days, where the wind blew a crisp chill in the air, frosting up most of what it touched. Our footings were dainty, one steady foot at a time, the odd wobble and scream, no one excused as we chuckled as we watched each other's mishaps.

Looking through the large Window of the restaurant, we all stood there mouths wide open. The interior of the building, it looked expensive, too much for dad's wallet?, the large oval tables, surrounded by eight tall, elegant wooden chairs, crystal chandeliers illuminated the room.

We entered some Italian restaurant on Mill Hill street, escaping the cold of the outside world. The heat from the reception area gave you a welcoming warmth. The tall well-groomed man in his black tuxedo greeted us, taking our coats and having the young girl behind the small lobby counter take them for hanging. We followed this well-presented male to a large oval table covered in a white linen tablecloth. He seated us all individually, then bid us a "bon appetite." The food was to die for, each morsel as tasty as the last, this was food heaven. They made us feel like royalty; the service was second to none. Dad even had a second main dish of creamy salmon pasta with fennel and herbs, he said he had never tasted anything like it. The room was glitzy, polished glass and chrome fittings, very reminiscent of the old Chicago movie mob style restaurants you see in the movies, even went as far as having a Nat King Cole tribute act on the stage. Mum was in heaven, the air filled with the velvety voice of the singer. "Thank you, Harold, this has been wonderful," she said leaning over and pecking his cheek. I think dad actually blushed with embarrassment, Lisa and Lizzy thanked dad too kissing him also, causing him to blush further, oblivious, Ryan and I just continued to eat.

It had to be the best birthday meal day out ever.

Dad bought me a few bottles of beer to share with my friends that evening; we were elated, full of joy and a little drunk. Leaving us in our house, our parents went to the local pub.

Lisa and Ryan found it a little uncomfortable when me and Lizzy began to kiss. Lisa causing a distraction, the rustle from the crisp packets, distracting our snog. Lisa raided the crisp box, Bovril flavour, washed down with a bottle of Indian pale ale. We were in our element, sat there watching the Saturday night entertainment on T.V. Starskey and Hutch, our favourite detective program, then match of the day, Leeds United had won the day before 3 - 2 away to Birmingham city, Arthur Graham scoring a hat-trick.

Ryan slept at ours, due to it getting late, the time now half past midnight, and the fact that he was already sleeping in the spare bed in my room.

By the time our parents had gotten home, they all looked worse for wear, staggering, and slurring their speech. "Ello Kidz how's yer doing" followed by a hiccup came mums greeting as she walked through the doorway. The two girls and I were still on the settee discussing what was in the music charts and who we fancied in that world, regular chit chat for kids our age.

With the jingle of the whiskey tumblers, mum handed out a nightcap for the adults before they left for the night. Lisa took one look at her parents, "Goodness sake look at you two?" her face askew, her mum slumped on dad's chair and Grant swaying in his wheelchair, almost ready to fall out. "Best get you two home," she continued, helping her dad back home. Mrs. Connor kissed dad and mum and waved as she followed, staggering the few yards down the street.

Lizzy kissed me goodnight and followed her mum in the taxi; Harry gave me the dirtiest look as the taxi set off, it was evident he absolutely did not approve of Lizzy and me. Dad waved at the taxi as it drove out of the street oblivious to anything around him.

Standing at the door watching our guest disappear behind closed doors, you could feel the dampness of the night creeping in, the temperature dropping quickly, sending a chill throughout the house. "Come on son, let's get in and get warm," dad said, his arm around my shoulders, ushering me in. It must have taken all of five minutes for the house to be silent and fall into a slumbering darkness.

The days that followed were pretty much the same as usual, school, hanging about on the street, watching rubbish TV, you know the kind of thing, same old, same old. With being in our last year of school not helping much too, all we did was prepare for our final exams, so nothing eventful there.

Saturday 28th January. My day started like most others, the smell of bacon from the kitchen wafting through the house; it was the best wake-up call ever. I was up and in the living room within minutes, planting my backside firmly on the sofa, Dad sat on his old carver chair reading the morning paper. Mum served dad his cup of tea and placed it on the side table next to his chair. "Thank you love" he'd say from behind the paper. Always said thank you to mum no matter what she did for him, mum looked at him, the smile said it all, you could tell she adored dad, he was pretty much her world, and she was his. Mum almost skipped back into the kitchen to fetch the bacon sandwiches.

Noel Edmonds swap shop was on the TV, the swap shop gang up to their usual antics. Mum and I loved the show; we sat there eating our bacon sandwiches while watching the TV show, almost choking as we laughed. Dad was still hiding behind his newspaper taking no notice of us. The room was cosy, the heat flowing through the room from the gas fire.

The ringing of the phone interrupted our viewing, making us sit upright, gave us a little fright if the truth to be known.

The phone hung on the passage wall to the right of the front door; I raced to get it, Lizzy was on the other end, "Hi Lizzy you Ok" I shouted, just so mum and dad knew who was on the other end. "Not bad … Just wondered if you fancy coming over this afternoon, (came her voice down the crackly line), Mum and Harry are going out to town, Harry sold his shop, so he's taking mum out for a slap-up meal in celebration," "Sure thing what time?" I replied, "About two-ish," she said. We continued our conversation over the next thirty minutes just talking about each other, getting lost in our little world.

Time flew by, before I knew it, I was in our street shutting the front door behind me. The snow had almost vanished, leaving a slushy mess, and boggy fields, the sun was out, but cowering behind the clouds. Feeling the cold, with a nip in the air, I wrapped myself up in my green parker, fastening the stud on the hood, so my face was protected from the gust.

Ryan came sprinting down the road, "What you up to Dave" almost out of breath as he reached me, his breath vaporising in the cold. He too was all wrapped up in his heavy parker, zipped up and studded closed, his face peering out of the fur trim. "Going over to Lizzie's, her mum and Harry are going out this afternoon," I chortled, the widest smile I had ever given, beaming across my face. Ryan fell into a fit of giggles, almost shouting "No need to ask what you two have planned" placing his hands on my shoulders, "Hey quiet... mum's home, don't want her knowing", my right index finger in front of my mouth, trying to shush him up. Ambling down the street, we chatted more.

Ryan turned off towards the Melbourne pub to the right to meet up with his parents; knowing they would be a little tipsy after their liquid lunch. As for me, I turned left to follow the road to Lizzie's.

I was feeling the chill, couldn't wait till I reached her house, and get warm, cuddling up next to my Lizzy. I still dreaded the walk up to her street, the memory of the day I was attacked still haunted me.

I leap over their gate as usual, and oddly found the front door was ajar; I could hear the TV blaring out some rubbish.

It was strange to find the door left open, Elizabeth would never leave it open, always said there were too many break-ins on these streets, too many rich pickings to be had. I stepped through the doorway trying hard to listen for voices, but could hear no one; it was as if the place was deserted, the house had an unusual eerie feeling to it, it didn't add up, something was unusual about the house today. I Walked further into the passageway, popped my head around the living room door, hoping to see Lizzy sat there waiting, only to find it empty. I walked back to the front door and closed it. "Lizzy, Lizzy I'm here, you ok, where are you" I shouted. Apart from the TV blaring out, the house was silent. Still, no reply, was she playing a game with me, could be hide and seek? And the prize would be mine. Switching the TV off didn't help, the house now in deathly silence, not even a pin drop could be heard, well only my now heavy breathing, this was startling me now, as I explored the downstairs.

I searched the kitchen and dining room again, only to draw a blank.

Step by painful step, I slowly made my way to the landing. Something didn't add up; this was defiantly not normal. Fear gripped my insides, knotting me up, I knew something was not right, but what?

At the top of the landing, the four doors were wide open, the three bedrooms and the bathroom. I shouted out her name "Lizzy are you there," still no reply, only silence, anxiousness gripping me, my heart rate racing, I shuddered as a shiver ran down my back, I felt uneasy, the palms of my hands clammy. I could sense something evil; unpleasant was lurking behind one of these doors, the silence was killing me. I took another step towards her bedroom door.

My stomach tensed, knotted up, my bladder welling up, the feeling of sickness filling my body as my knees gave way, almost falling.

What I saw in the room, the image that I took in. This sight would be engraved in my mind forever.

The sight of the white bed linen sheets, soaked in a dark crimson red, a young woman's body laid there. The butcher's cleaver deep-rooted in her back. Her dead body, naked faced down, blood stains engrained from the several wounds on her back and legs.

My Elizabeth's face was unidentifiable from the beating she must have taken, her eyes so engorged they were closed, her delicate chin broken. The large bruises on her arms where she must have been forced down, the blood stain in-between her parted legs, evidence he must have raped her. I tried to walk towards her but couldn't. I knew she was dead, her body laid there, all life beaten out of her. Vomit spilled out as my stomach churned. The sound from my body was unhuman like, I dropped to my knees, tearing at my hair, tears flooding like a torrent river down my face, now crumpled over rocking back and forth, I needed to call my mum, I tried to shout for her, no words formed only a terrified scream.

The front door shot open, rebounding off the hallway wall. Lizzie's neighbours came rushing in, a little terrified from my wailing. Taking two steps at a time, striding up the stairs towards the unbearable noise delivered from Elizabeth's room.

Mrs. Ryder doubled up at first sight, churning out the contents of her last meal, followed by a scream, filling the landing, I was still rocking back and forth, deaf, and blind to the outside world. Mr. Ryder took one look then raced down the stairs and dialled the police. On

193

hanging up the phone, he raced back up the stairs, two steps at a time.

"Tom, please get up here" screamed Mrs. Ryder, a small petite woman in her early thirties, her face as white as a sheet, she stood at the bedroom doorway of Janet's room, sending an urgency in Toms climb to the landing. Janet was sat in the far corner, her arms folded around her stomach. Colour drains from her face: Janet's sat, pain etched deep inside her, her body, torn, battered and bruised. The sight of the decorative brass open fire poker protruding from her pregnant stomach sending shivers down his spine. Blood glistens, gliding down the sides, leaving a puddle of a thick red stickiness as it hits the wooden floor. Janet is still breathing, just, her face, not unlike Lizzie's, savagely beaten unrecognisable, numerous cuts running across her face, along with her nose broken and her lip split, and swollen. Mrs. Ryder stands there shaking, sobbing, her word stuttered out "PPP...please, Tom, help her, oh my god why? And that poor boy" turning around facing Elizabeth's door, seeing me rocking back and forth on my knees. For the first time since taking in the scene did Mrs. Ryder compose herself, her protective mothering nurture taking hold of her, she helps Tom to support and remove me from Lizzie's room, staying by my side, taking care, and comforting me until the medics arrived.

Tom redialled the police explaining what they had found, then returned to the bedroom; Tom raced to help Janet with her wounds, all the while staying focused, not allowing the strain to seep through.

Where was Harry? He was nowhere to be seen, why was he not here? Everyone knew he had sold the business and said he was going to be a man of leisure, taking care of his wife and family, there was even talk of moving south, and setting up a home in Kent or those surrounding areas.

Within minutes an outbreak of activity occupied the street, sirens ringing out, three ambulances and four police cars took over the road space, the medics had already got Janet down, and was already on their way to St James's Hospital. The cry of the sirens sounding out the urgency.

John finally broke, his stomach churned, and tears fell from his eyes, he had never witnessed such a horrific scene. His thoughts went out to Janet and Lizzy "Poor Janet, why? Who would do such a thing" he whispered to himself. It seemed like an eternity, but only minutes had passed. Mrs. Ryder joined him, both tearful, unable to accept the bloodshed. Not something that happens in this part of town. "

Hello Son my name is Duncan, and I'm going to help you," the medic said as he knelt next to me. Wearing his rubber gloves he started to wipe my face with a large damp cotton cloth, removing the blood and sweat from my face, I had cuts on my head from the frustration, pulling at my hair, removing clumps revealing a few bald patches. I couldn't see him, only guided by his calm voice, the trauma causing temporary hysterical blindness. I sat there motionless in a daze; in total darkness. Tears continued to flow, Elizabeth's image tortured me, I had died inside today, empty of feelings, no life existed.

Duncan placed his arm around my shoulders, and slowly guided me to the ambulance, one step at a time, no more fear fusing my being, just oblivious to my surroundings, not really knowing who or where and what was happening. Reality of the outside world had diminished from my thoughts.

Mrs. Ryder stayed with me at the hospital until Mum arrived. Mum was shaken to learn the horrors from Mrs. Ryder's story, the terror she had witnessed.

Both women wept, unable to take comfort from each other. Mum almost collapsed the instant she laid her eyes on me, she had seen me in a bad state before, but never witnessed anything like this. I laid on my bed trembling and cursing, tears still falling from my eyes.

Back at the Greens home, the forensic team had completed collating their data from Lizzie's room, allowing the medics to take her body to the mortuary. The street was full of onlookers, all trying to get a glimpse of the crime scene, finally dispersing as the last of the police cars left the scene.

It had taken three days for my sight to fully recover, images slowly appeared over time, causing many tears of frustration, losing my vision was only part of it, paralysis had taken my right side, denied the comfort of movement. I was spoon fed for the first two days, then as time passed by, I regained the use my right hand, slowly the feeling of pins and needles tingled down my right side, causing me the shakes and an unstable footing.

My state of mind was fragile, confused at what had been real and what had been a dream, haunted by the trauma of Elizabeth's image of death. How was I to carry on from this?

The nightmares, tormenting me, awakening the other patients on the ward, my screams of terror erupting across the ward, like a volcanic eruption, my body temperature excelled, sweat soaking me and the bed linen through. Sedated, I calmed down, my temperature subsiding to normal, and then the decision to move me into a single room, monitored regularly by the duty nurse, to feed my dehydration.

Six days later I returned home, my eye sight had returned, a solid 20 / 20 vision, but I was still rocky on my feet, falling over on the odd occasion. Ryan was always on hand to help mum; there was nothing he wouldn't do for her. His primary task was to help me find a way to get past this bereavement I was suffering, mum knew this was going to take some time to heal, but who better to help me with this process than Ryan. Mum gained comfort from this; she believed he was the best remedy I could have.

Dad was besieged with torment; he blamed himself for agreeing to walk her down the aisle to marry this monster, this was the darkest moment in his life, he struggled to speak to mum let alone anyone else, he cocooned himself in his room, rarely willing to venture out. Clive was struggling with his own demons, sickened for having Harry as a friend, Joyce told him, it wasn't something he should blame himself for, everyone who knew Harry thought he was a gentleman. Clive's trust in people lessened.

Over the next few weeks, the manhunt for Harry had heightened, it was believed he had travelled to Guernsey. Harry was born there; the family home still stood on the island, his childhood home. A place he thought he would be safe.

The newspapers reported that Elizabeth had kept a diary, inside she had written about our relationship and how often we would secretly meet to make love and spend time close to each other. This was a shock for mum, not believing her boy was sexually active.

The darker side was also written. A girl of thirteen forced to have sex with her stepdad, continuing for sixteen months to the day, and how he would send Janet out to the market or wait until the twilight hours while Janet slept, creeping into her bed, he would rape Lizzy. Elizabeth's ordeals were graphically described, leaving nothing to chance. The news reporter herself was weeping, getting her story to the press; this was without going into detail. Many readers across the country were sickened by reading this; the country was wanting swift action from the police, this monster needed to be found and removed from the public.

Elizabeth had grown up faster than she should have, especially when it came to sex. Knowing what she did to me, repulse me at the thought he must have forced her to do that to him. The diary stated he touched her at least once every fortnight. I never knew, she would never tell me. I went to my room I couldn't read anymore. Feeling lost, like someone was ripping me apart from the inside out, Mum wanted to make it all go away, she knew that wasn't possible, she didn't know how to console me; mum knew a part of me had died; consumed by my hatred of Harry, I just couldn't face the world. All our worlds were ripped apart, normality no longer existed.

Depression hit me hard, the lack of sleep, the moody silence, the outside world had become a sinister place, a place I didn't want to be part of. Secluding myself from the outside, not even allowing my best friend Ryan the chance of helping me, shutting the door to all.

My body was weak, I ate very little, rejecting whatever was placed in front of me, losing my appetite, I was losing weight rapidly, too sick to attend school.

Dad wasn't well, he too became ill, unable to get motivated, not wanting to get out of bed. He loved Janet as his own daughter; he couldn't accept Elizabeth, the beautiful blossoming young woman was gone, taken away from our lives, dad like me suffered, the depression consuming our bodies, taking control. Leaving us nothing more than a shell. Mum was the one who handled the lot, face on. With the help from Joyce and Clive, she was able to manage our home.

Ryan continued to try and gain away into my world. He too was hurting, she had been one of his closest friends too, after all, we had stuck together, the three of us for over the last ten years. Ryan did his crying for both me and Elizabeth. He was losing two best friends and felt helpless.

During this time of sadness came a glimmer decency, a change in perspectives.

Mrs. Connor had become our guiding angel, her kindness, and empathy shining through, the bitterness of past years had weakened towards me. Mrs. Connor felt for us as she did for Janet.

Mrs. Connor knew she was helpless to support Janet, so gave her support to mum, helping with the arrangements for Elizabeth's funeral. She arrange to stay in our house tending to Dad and me when mum couldn't handle it and needed to escape. This was when mum would do her own crying, Joyce would always take mum in and settle her down, mum would always be back home within an hour, thanking Mrs. Connor for her time. Mrs. Connor would brush it off, "Maggie no matter what has gone before us, I really do care for you and your family, and even though I was cruel to you, Harold and David all those years ago, you and Harold still helped me and Grant when times were hard." Both women embraced each other, "You have done more for me these last few weeks than I could have asked anyone, and if anyone owes, it's me" replied mum.

Most of the residents in our street visited, leaving flowers and kind thoughts for our loss. Most of the kids my age, moped about, the street had a deep sinking feeling, it was like a fog leaching over, sapping out all the goodness from life.

The days past and time was a healing hand, Mum was gaining a new confidence, able to do her daily chores with minimal help. For mum, the world was restoring to normality.

Mum and Lisa set off to visit Janet in the hospital; Mrs. Connor offering to stay behind and care for dad and me, giving mum free time to do what she needed to do.

At the hospital for mental health, Janet was recovering gradually; her body was healing up fine, but her mental state had regressed, caused by the loss of her unborn child and the death of her daughter Elizabeth.

Miraculously Janet had managed to inform the police of her horrors over the past eighteen months. Harry had decided he didn't want a child from her, recalling her nightmares. Harry, in a mad bout of anger, had to threaten her with her life, controlling her with fear. Harry had told her, he married her because he loved Lizzy, and this was a way to get to her, a young virgin, so he thought until he found and read her diary.

In total disgust, he wanted to punish her.

Janet believed he killed Elizabeth, because to him she was no longer pure.

He turned on Janet when she had tried to protect her daughter, and threatened him, she had enough and was calling the police. This was before his evil attack had taken place, just moments before raping Elizabeth that day. Janet recalled the pleasure Harry took from punching and kicking her across their bedroom, and as she fell, swearing vile and disgusting words at her, then grabbing the brass poker and driving it into her stomach, leaving her for dead, before he set about her daughter Elizabeth.

Elizabeth didn't stand a chance, his giant fist plunged into her face, with her kicking, and screaming, he dragged her about like a rag doll, forcing himself upon her, tearing off her clothes.

Her screams were too late and unheard to anyone who could have helped. Janet tormented by each plea, as Elizabeth cried out for him to stop. It went silent as he finished. Elizabeth lay there sobbing, then the sobbing ceased.

Harry stood over her, looking down at this naked harmless little girl. The bloodstained meat cleaver sunk deep into her back, he began to shake uncontrollable, his stomach knotted up with agonising pain, his head held in his red-stained hands, he broke down with the realisation, his eyes glazed over as the tears streamed down his face. In the other room, Janet slumped against the wall, dying from her wounds, sobbed inwardly, unable, and too afraid to make a sound. The memory too painful, Janet blocked it out, along with her adult life, regressing back to a child.

Janet sat on the edge of her bed, mum spoke softly, of pleasant things, the niceties of our early life, reminiscing of when they first met. It made little difference, Janet had regressed too far.

It was the day of Elizabeth's funeral, we were all dressed up in our Sunday best, Dad was looking frail, not the man I knew, he had aged a good ten years, unable to walk for prolonged periods, he had deteriorated over the last few weeks, depression absorbing the life from him. Clive pushed the wheelchair with mum by his side. I walked with Ryan, one frail small step at a time, the memory haunting me inside. Joyce held my hand, giving a side glance to mum, reassuring her all was well.

The horse-drawn carriage led up the street to the local church, we followed behind, it seemed as if the whole estate had turned out, lining the way, street by street, a mixed community, whites and blacks stood together heads bowed in respect, as the horse-drawn carriage passed, displaying the coffin.

Janet wasn't there, her mental state had deteriorated so much, she could not recognise who was who, nor did she know who she was, her state of mind had regressed back to her childhood days, she played out the actions of a small child. Janet was always accompanied by her favourite doll. Janet was sectioned under the mental health act, and never again saw life outside the hospital walls.

Every seat in the church was taken up; the walls were lined with her school friends, teachers, the investigating police officers and many of the estate residents. Countless tears fell as the vicar played his part well, versing the eulogy, he touched the hearts of many this day.

The route to the cemetery was long and tiresome; the trail of mourners stretched over a mile. Many residents paid their respects outside the cemetery gates as Elizabeth's handful of close friends laid her to rest. The day was still, and sombre, not a breeze, no birds in the trees, no barking stray dogs, the only sound was from the tears that fell.

I soon found myself alone, mum kissed me, told me she would return if I weren't home within the hour.

Sobbing I gazed down, looking at her coffin, placing a single rose on her grave. My heart heavy, isolated in a wilderness of sorrow, crying like a small child reaching out for his mother's aid, but no one came. All alone looking down at her. Her image danced in front of me; it could have been her, but possibly my mind playing tricks on me. I will miss her so much, never knowing if I dare to love again, emotionally scarred.

The horrific news surrounding her death shocked the nation. News spread fast, the police had finally caught up and arrested Harry in Guernsey and were deporting him back to Leeds to stand trial.

CHAPTER 17

NO REMORSE

I slowly walked down the corridor to my classroom, each step echoing, telling the students I had arrived. Conversations halted midsentence, and silence took over; all eyes trained on me. I could hear my own heart beating, like a hammer bashing against my chest, a rush of dread suffocated me, I wanted to go back home. Was I ready for school life? My body said yes, my head said no.

The hallway was lined with pupils from all years, heads lowered paying their respect for my loss. Ryan stood at the door. I could hear the world outside, the unnatural silence penetrating deep inside my head, the creek of the door opening as I stepped into the room, a sound I had never heard before, usual noise levels prohibiting the sound.

Mr. Clemence greeting us with a smile, a large round overweight six-foot-tall man, bald headed, wore round rimmed glasses. He may have looked odd, but he was a great teacher, always available for his pupils. He would make up stories, working out riddles and just using general chit chat was the way he got his message across. He was a very likable and a very smart teacher.

As we all sat, he stood proudly at the front of the room. His presence felt as he bellowed "Good morning class", then lowering his voice, a gentler, soothing mellow tone "Let's take a minute to pay our respects to a young lady who lost her life in such a horrid manner" his head bowed, the class followed his lead. After a minute, they were all talking amongst themselves apart from me who sat in silence. After registration, the class dispersed to their lessons, Mr. Clemence held me back, "David can I speak with you" his voice was tender, not the standard harsh spoken voice we were used to. "Yes sir," I said. He sat me back down and began to ask how I was coping, and if I felt as if I should be back. I was pleased with his concern for me and told him I was getting better every day.

He began to recollect about his time when his wife passed away and how he became more encouraged to help others and put all his efforts into education. I took his words literally and studied hard to ensure I made the grade.

Ryan was overjoyed to have his best friend back, as was I.

Harry found prison life easy, with his physique he was quite intimidating to most of the prisoners and the prison officers alike, he was smarmy and rude, pushing all the time, getting his own way, showing he was not to be messed with.

Isolated, sitting in his cell, his back against the wall, taking large gulps of his hot tea from the pint-sized tin mug, burning the back of his throat, his bravado all gone, no one to impress, no one to see him feeling small, and all alone. The moon sends out a ray of light through the tiny barred window, he lays down on his metal sprung bed, the smile on his face gone.

He still sleeps peacefully, no dreams or nightmares hounding him, terrorizing his sleep, not like me, I still cry at night. I miss her so much, my Elizabeth, never again having the pleasure of her face looking into mine, never again will I taste her sweetness, the softness of her lips. Never again will I hear her voice.

My Elizabeth was gone forever. I so want him to die, die a painful, horrific death, the same he gave to her. I bet he wasn't reeling in pain most nights, not able to sleep, seeing the repeated images of Elizabeth, that keep rolling around in my head.

Harry's trial date of April 10th came sooner than we expected. The tabloids and television covered the broadcasting of the case; this was one of the most disturbing cases to hit the UK in years.

Inside the court, the judge, his honourable Mr. Harrison Fielding's takes his place. At sixty-four, he has sat on this court for over two decades and had never come across such a gross malevolent evil case. A case that would etch into the very heart of him a case he would rather not have.

The jury was distraught by Harry's acts of evil; Harry's defence solicitor was struggling to convince any of them, that Harry was innocent. The hype of the case had been sensationalised, to the point of an outcry for the death penalty to be served.

The court was silent, only the voice of the prosecuting solicitor called out to be heard. He described, how Harry, had over a period of sixteen months, put Elizabeth and Janet through their ordeal. The rapes, the beatings, and then ending with the murder of Elizabeth and the attempted murder of Janet (who in reality was as good as dead). No one spoke, coughed, or dare breathes while the statement was given out. With the visual aids put on show, for all the jury to see, the pictures of Elizabeth's broken, beaten body laid face down dead. This elevated the tragic horror, and the madness of the ordeal. The sound of sobbing could be heard from the gallery as the prosecuting solicitor closed his opening statement.

Harry just stood there, smirking at the jury, as if he was untouchable, his eyes, penetrating through them, you could feel the hate seeping out of him, he loathed them all.

Mum and Joyce attended the hearings, wanting to know the outcome. Mum sat there; this was personal, the detestation welling up inside her, her eyes resting on one person and never letting up, he glanced back once or twice, sniggering, leering back at her, his own repugnance seeping out.

The pair watched in horror as the forensics describe the unjustified torture Elizabeth had endured and how she had gained her injuries, many of the Jurors found this distressing and disturbing. A request to leave the courtroom to recompose themselves was granted. The case adjourned for two hours until they had resettled. Judge Fielding was very sympathetic towards the jury, this case being very sensitive and the eyes of the world watching down on them.

Dads illness had him bedridden again; nothing we did seemed to help, it was as if he had given up on life, the doctor said he was making himself ill, he had no other reason, dad looked frail, mum and I found this heart-wrenching. Watching someone deteriorate before your very eyes, someone you love, and not been able to help. The feeling of usefulness non-existent, however, Mrs. Connor was there, solid as a rock, she made him eat and drink, she pushed him. "Not losing anyone else this year" she would say to my mum. To mum, Mrs. Connor had become her saving grace.

It all was dredged up; every detail of the harrowing crime was in every national paper and on TV.

I cared for dad when I got home from school, Mrs. Connor was always on hand as I got in. "He's taking this very hard David … You need to make sure he takes his fluids" she said, her hand on my shoulder, "His last cuppa was at two-thirty, so he'll be due another soon" she continued, now hugging me. She kissed me lightly on my forehead and left through the front door. Her positive attitude helped me, who would have thought, I would be rubbing shoulders with this woman and liking her, really liking her, as a friend, I didn't.

Ryan just walks into our house now; he would knock once then make his way to the kitchen, usually grabbing a piece of pie or quiche that mum would have made the day before. Mum didn't mind; in fact, she thought it was great, said it was like having two boys instead of one, in fact, she would always question me why I felt the need to ask? I would always ask because I was just polite that way. Dad sometimes got frustrated with this, he, like me always believed you should ask out of courtesy. Ryan would say "It's all right dad, mum said I can get it if I'm hungry, didn't you mum" which I could tell would make dad's blood boil, trouble was mum would just smile back at Ryan, saying "Yeah, he's ma little boy."

Ryan made three brews; the tea was piping hot, Dad's two sugars as always, the odd few tea leaves floating on top. Ryan filled the tray with assorted biscuits and the three mugs; he made his way to dad's room at the top left of the stairs, he found me reading the report from the daily newspaper, on today's findings. Ryan never understood why he would want this if it made him so ill, Dad had to know; maybe once justice is served, he might start to recover.

Ryan had noticed a change in me after the funeral, I had become more impersonal to the world around me and lost my spark in life, he understood I had gone through the most traumatic time I may ever go through, bar the passing away of my parents in the future.

He saw before him a young man, who was no longer going to allow himself to be hurt again. People would say I had become stronger, more resistant to the harshness to what the world threw at you, but sadly in reality, I had just become an introvert, not wanting to speak or join in any of the street games we use to play.

Mum arrived home sometime after six, she looked drained, Ryan was in the kitchen brewing up again, but this time four mugs of tea. Mum went upstairs to see dad, to tell him her news of the day and hug him, let him know he was loved and needed.

She felt she was losing the man she loved, her Harrold, her best friend; mum wasn't going to give him up though, she forced him to eat some cereal, admittedly only a few spoons full, but it was a start.

The trail dragged out over ten harrowing days.

Wednesday 19th April was the final day of the trial, the streets surrounding the courthouse were packed with onlookers, an excuse for the coffee vendors and hamburger vans to ply their trade. Traffic had come to a standstill. The crowd anxious, awaiting the verdict. A large police presence was needed and deployed, borrowing the neighbouring town's police force.

The courtroom was packed out, not a vacant seat could be seen; the gallery was bursting at the seams.

Judge Harrison Fielding entered the room, not a sound was heard as he seated. He sat upright looking down on the accused, his eyes meeting Harry's stare, he had made his mind up, but in the end, it was up to the jury. What they decide is final.

Harry stood there in the dock; he looked smug, and pleased with himself as the prosecution interrogated him, they would be no doubt about the outcome now as he flaunted his answers to the room. He couldn't care less what they thought; he had ridden the world of a dirty little slag of a whore, in his eyes she was better off dead than screwing around with some darkie, as he put it. Judge Harrison Fielding's had to stop Harry's foul mouth from speaking anymore and closed the prosecution saying he had listened to enough; he took time out for the jury to decide the fate of this horrid evil wicked man.

It was forty minutes before the courtroom reassumed, and the Judge requested the verdict. The gallery was silent as if it was holding its breath in anticipation.

Harry stood there, bold as brass not flinching nor feeling any kind of sorrow for his actions, in fact, he was the opposite, just standing sneering at the judge.

Mr. Gary Plintoff stood up, the appointed head of the jury. When asked if the plea of guilty or not guilty was requested, he showed no hesitation in giving the guilty verdict.

Judge Harrison Fielding gave his summary "Ladies and gentlemen and members of the jury I must conclude that the evidence presented before us is without any doubt one of the most horrific, I, in my twenty-four years as a judge has ever come across.

Mr. Harry Green in my mind is a foul, disgusting man, who without any remorse has taken the life of a young girl, who in her mid-teens with her whole life before her was stuck down, after the cruellest torture of over a sixteen months' period. This man is in no doubt an evil, dangerous person, and who has no law-abiding given right to be a part of our society." His eyes watering under the strain. "I now must pass sentence… Mr. Harry Green, do you have anything to say before I pass sentence". Harry stood looking square on at the judge, he lifted his arm and displayed two fingers.

Judge Fielding never faltered, he calmly looked over his courtroom. "Mr. Harry Green the city of LEEDS has found you guilty of murder ...You shall serve a sentence of thirty years, and no less than twenty-two years of incarceration in her majesty's prison, a sentence for the killing and torture of Miss Elizabeth Stuart, for the torture of Mrs. Janet Green, and the murder of her unborn child, you will serve a sentence of seventeen years, totalling your sentence to forty seven years. How do you plead?" he pronounced knowing justice had been served.

Harry gave the two-fingered gesture again yelling out across the gallery "Fuck you all."

"Take him away," the judge said, gavel hitting its block. He had seen enough of this man over the past ten days and was glad to be rid of him. The two bailiffs led Harry away, down to the cells.

Outside the news spread fast, the cheers catapulting throughout the streets of every city, town and village. Justice had been served.

CHAPTER 18

PENNY ON YOUR THOUGHTS

Dad was slowly recovering four weeks on after the trial. He was managing to get out of bed and spend time with us, watching the television for a few hours a day. Mum was smiling more now the worst was over, and dad had found his appetite again, his weight was resembling that of his former self. The trial had taken so much out of him; we thought we could have lost him.

As for me, I was getting back to my old self, hanging around with Ryan and Lisa, it wasn't the same, Elizabeth wasn't there and that sometimes made things difficult for me. Ryan and Lisa were starting to form a relationship, you could tell by the way they looked and toyed around, as usual, they couldn't see it. Friends are what we are, they would say, I could see them blossoming into an adorable couple. They were well suited.

School time again, another day in the prefabricated buildings, moving from one class to another like herded sheep. "Walk don't run" the words would echo along the corridors from various teachers, as the pupils rushed in all directions getting to their lessons. I studied hard, excelling in most subjects, now in my last year of regular schooling and starting our mock exams ready for the real thing next summer.

I made my way to the maths class, were the usual geeks would be seated. I was doing well in school, and this was one such subject, the problem was I was too advanced for the normal maths class, so they moved me up one stage. I seemed to suffer a bit in this one, the scientific maths class, and enough to spoil my final exam results.

Mrs. Cunningham stood by the blackboard chalking away symbols and figures, all of which seemed gobbledygook to me, for the first time in any class, I had to admit, this was too advanced for me. These were scientist in the making. Mrs. Cunningham made her to me, traversing in between the desk, "David I think you could be right … But you were finding the other class relatively too easy? So we had to challenge you, You do understand that don't you" she said nodding at the same time. Her face was kind and not sarcastic, she seemed genuine when speaking to me. "You can stay and try in this class or return to your old one, I don't think moving back will help you or stimulate you" she continued, I look back at her "If I stay what exam would I be taking? ...Chances are I would fail the one for this class" I said looking unsure of myself. "You will enter the standard school exam on which, I will bet you will excel and get a straight A, as we would expect of you," she said answering my question. I nodded and sat up on my chair. Mrs. Cunningham leant forward on my desk, looking me in the eye, exposing her cleavage, and a nice cleavage it was. She was a mature woman in her thirties, she was slender in stature, but very curvy where it counted, her shoulder length brown hair surrounded a small round face, was quite heavy on the makeup too, but probably didn't need to as she was an attractive woman. Her big brown eyes hiding behind large rimmed glasses, if anything they made her look seductive, especially when she pouted her full red lips. We often saw the male teachers falling over themselves trying to help her.

She had said something to me, but I didn't hear her, my mind was thinking impure thoughts at the sight of her cleavage and the hypnotic smell of her perfume, encapsulating me to places I shouldn't even be. "Sorry, Mrs. Cunningham I missed that," I said feeling embarrassed, my face flushed, reddening, she knew but didn't say anything, just smiled that dirty slutty smile, she placed her hand on my shoulder, beckoning me towards another set of tables. "This is Tracy Clarke ...She's a first-class pupil and very knowledgeable on this subject, and I think if you two work together, you will learn a lot from her David" she said introducing us both to each other. Tracy was a plain looking girl, she resembled a boy more than a girl, her clothes heavy and dark draped over her body hiding any trace of her feminine features she may possess.

Her hair a mousy brown, short wedge cut and a boyish face, she housed a little stub of a nose which made her look quite cute along with her freckles.

Tracy's attitude was sharp; she hated the fact she was mentoring me. She was good at it, even though she didn't realise this; her future profession could easily be in a teaching capacity.

The days were long and drawn out. I found myself walking alone at break times; no one really wanted to approach me, too afraid they may say something wrong.

Ryan was too busy being the most popular kid in school, he was the school football captain and had most of the girls chasing him. He never went out with any thought, said they didn't interest him.

Out on the playing fields, time for our afternoon sports lessons. The school was gearing up for the annual sports day. Mr. Bracey our PE teacher was stood in his red and black tracksuit, yelling out his orders "Come on lads gets your backs into it, this is the one hundred meters' sprint. First, five will represent the school in June, so please let's just get into it". There were seven pupils in a group, and nine groups. I was in the last group; Ryan was the same group too. The races got underway, Mr. Bracey stood there stopwatch in hand, nodding, smiling, also shaking his head in disappointment. They had been some excellent times; the pace was fast; other schools would have to have a champion runner on their side to beat us this year.

It was our turn to run, the gun sounded and off they sprinted, me, I just walked down the track, I just never saw the reasoning in sprinting, unless been chased.

Speaking about been chased. Mr. Bracey was on my tail screaming countless obscenities at me. "Brown who the fuck do you think you are, you are nothing more than a horrible stinking spoilt brat" his breathing erratic as he chased me around the football pitch. I would, in fact, say, had he been timing me, I would have had the fastest time out of everyone.

The class stood there on the touchline, watching in amazement, howling at the sight of us. I sprinted passed the class closely followed by Mr. Bracey who stopped running, halting in front of the class, his faced flushed with anger. "Get to the fucking showers you lot... as for you Brown", he bellowed "You're in detention you twat" his eyes almost popping out of his head along with the vein crossing his temple. I smiled replying "Ok sir, see you there" acting rather cocky. It was then Mr. Bracey burst into laughter, as he now saw the stupidity of chasing me around the football pitch. He apologises to the class for his language as he entered the changing room. However Ryan was to join me on detention, being caught imitating Mr. Bracey in the changing room, just as he entered, he stood a little while watching Ryan's rendition of him chasing me and blurting out words in his almost perfect Mr. Bracey voice. The class found this hilarious, Ryan's face change from the sarcastic to the horrified. This put a grin on Bracey's face.

It was the end of the last lesson, and the bell rang out for the end of the day, the doors opened simultaneously along the long corridors. Pupils hoarded out, screaming into the schoolyard and out of the main gate homebound. Not for me and Ryan, our invite to detention, class seven C on the second floor was calling. We made our way, along the empty, quiet corridors, moping miserable towards the class.

The room was full, the bully boys and girls as usual, but to my surprise, there in the far corner sat Tracy, my mentor. I briskly made my way up to say hello, "Hi Tracy ...Why you here?" I asked looking down at her as she sat on her plastic chair. Raising her head she said "I punched Gregg for trying to touch my tits in class" grinning, almost breaking into laughter. Gregg was a skinny kid, but tall, he looked weird, his spotty acne face and ginger mullet, along with his bizarre dress sense, black loafers on his feet with checked Rupert bear type pants and green polo neck jumper. There he was, sat at the middle table, sporting a great shiner on the left of his face. "Wow you really got him ...so why is he here?" the question seeming obvious, "For touching my tits! You arse" came Tracy's reply, both me and Ryan burst into fits of laughter.

"Backhouse, Brown! Sit down and shut up" the words from Mr. Graham bounced around the room, the deputy head teacher strutted in like he was the Lord Almighty himself. He positioned himself at the front of the class. Scanning the room with his beady eyes, his rotten stained teeth showing as he snarled at us, he didn't want to be here anymore than we did , but he was, and we knew it. He was probably the worse teacher I had ever had the displeasure of knowing, he had no tact or teaching ability that I could see. He was as much a bully as the boys doing detention.

"So, what do I have the pleasure of today," he asked, his arms folded, "let's start with the girl at the back" pointing at Tracy. Tracy stood up and introduced herself "Hi my name is Tracy Clarke, and I'm here today cos I punched Gregg for touching my tits in class," she said, her head dropped to one side as she slumped against the wall.

"Ha, you don't have any tits, you flat-chested git. Anyhow, we all call you Tracy no tits" yelled the giant monstrous overweight kid. His face a constant purple, "Shut up and sit down Frank Shackleton, by the way why are you here again" said Mr. Graham, frowning, Frank looked foolish and bowed his head, "I got caught smoking again in the toilets sir" he said in a low voice. "Is that all Shackleton" yelled Grahams; "No sir I was picking on some of the younger kids, making them gives me stuff" he replied, again his head bowed in shame. Mr. Graham launched the board rubber at him, floating through the air like a dart, hitting him square on the forehead, leaving a chalk mark to show the world he hit his target. Shackleton stumbling, almost falling flat on his butt. The room fell to a deathly quiet, none of us dared to move. Mr. Graham walked around the desk to where Gregg sat, "As for you, you little pervert, if you don't keep your hands to yourself you may find yourself locked up in later life" he said prodding Gregg. "Tracy get out of my class, you don't belong here with these reprobates" he continued breaking into a smile as he addressed her. Tracy left instantly, making her way to the door. "See you tomorrow David," she said raising her hand, giving me a wave, I returned the wave but remained silent.

"Brown what to do with you and your bloody shadow Backhouse," he said smirking at the thought of Mr. Bracey chasing me around the football pitch "As you all know I don't see eye to eye with Bracey, so Brown take your shadow with you … Go now before I change my mind."

"Can I go too" the voice, smooth and mellow, almost sang out across the room. She stood there, Miss Penny Ambrose Walters, an utterly stunning fifteen-year-old. A vision from heaven. Her long shapely legs with womanly hips and a slender waist, her blouse undone enough to expose the shape of her firm round breast following a slender neck with the most beautiful head of blonde, red hair cascading over her shoulders, her face was that of a goddess (maybe Venus herself). She had the wow factor; I just couldn't take my eyes away from her. Mr. Graham's voice broke my thoughts.

"Why should I let you go," Said Mr. Graham looking unsure at her. "Because Mr. Bracey sent me, and you don't like him" she replied flashing her eyes lids at him.

"Really! Miss Walters? So, you think I should just let you go?" he said raising his arms, hands outstretched, "Please," she said batting her lids again. I was still stood there watching the two of them in debate, mainly taken in by this incredible sight in front of my eyes called Penny.

"Why are you here?" he said with a great big sigh, "Because I didn't turn up for PE today sir" she replied.

Mr. Graham looked at his watch then looked back at her "Get out Walters, I can't be arsed to deal with the likes of you."

Now there were three of us descending the stairs towards the main door, Ryan first, me behind then Penny following. "Wait up guys," she said almost stumbling down the last three steps. I caught hold of her and helped her steadily back to her feet.

"Why thank you, young sir," she said flashing her big green eyes as she took a curtsy. Ryan smiled hitting me on the arm sharply, (which hurt a bit). "I'm going David ...see you later, going to see Lisa Ok?" he said halfway through the door then disappearing out of the school grounds.

I was left, stood there with probably the best-looking girl for miles, definitely the most beautiful girl in school. Awkwardly, I just smiled at her; my face was going red, I could feel myself getting warmer. Penny linked arms with me, leading me through the doorway into the school grounds; we stopped and turn to face each other, without warning she hurled herself at me and kissed me hard on the mouth. What a kiss, took me by surprise, soft cherry tasting lips. "Wow what that's for?" I asked, a grin as wide as you could ever imagine stretched across my face. "Just wanted to, I've always fancied you ever since you joined here," she said, her head lowered as if ashamed of what she had done.

I grab her arms and pulled her into me, then embraced into a lingering kiss. Lost in our embrace, we didn't noticed the rest of the detainees had emerged from the classroom and started to make their way home.

Colin Parker stood there, disgusted at the sight of us kissing "Why kiss a black twat like him when she could have me" he moaned at Shackleton. For all Shackleton was, he didn't care for that kind of talk. Not impressed he thumped him in the eye "Shut up knob head it's a boy and a girl kissing not black and white making grey." He punched him again, just because he could. Colin was almost crying from the pain inflicted punches.

Frank was some seven inches taller than Colin and massively heavier, Colin was a skinny kid who uses his wit to get him through school, he was known as the class clown, not a bright lad, but one who would always just make the grade. "Leave me alone will you, sorry didn't mean anything by it, Just he seems to have all the girls after him" Colin said, the green-eyed monster of envy creeping in. With that, Colin sprinted out of the schoolyard, leaving Frank on his own.

Penny held my hands, looking right into my deep brown eyes, she cooed, almost a whisper "Will you talk to me tomorrow or just ignore me?" I looked puzzled by her remark "Why would I ignore you?" I replied. She looked at me square on, "You could have any girl in this school, so why settle for one" she said doubt showing on her face. "You're kidding me aren't you," I said, "You're like sex on legs, and I think I'm the one who should worry about who talks to who." My eyes wide, and my mouth dropped open. Wow this girl thinks she should be worried about me straying? Not a chance, if you ever got a girl like this interested in you, take it from me, you don't cheat.

Our hands gripped tighter; I kissed her again, the taste of her sending my senses wild, the light touch of her lips touching mine had me in heaven, a place I thought I would never visit again.

We parted saying goodbye to each other; she travelled the opposite direction from me. I stood watching as she disappeared into the maze of brick buildings.

I turned and headed towards the school gate; I was light on my feet, a little light-headed and giddy. Wow what just happened, the thoughts running around my head. Frank met up with me as I passed the gate and started down the dirt track, this made over a period of years of cutting over the field towards our estate. "You lucky bastard Brownie, what have you got the rest of us don't? And that Ryan, What is it with you two" He said stuffing soft sweets in his mouth. "Don't know what you're on about Frank?" I said looking up at him; he was a giant of a kid, must have been the tallest kid in school and with only one teacher taller, he was intimidating to look at. "Well you two get all the girls, are good at sport, and have good results in all the test we do, you know what! You kind of make me sick" his tone had turned aggressive, "Hey slow down big fellow, maybe if you stopped stuffing that shit in your mouth, and you could be a decent looking guy too" I said, waiting for him to knock me out in reply. He didn't; in fact, we got on well, we walked through the streets, talking as we headed for home. It was as if we were the best of friends, talking candidly to each other.

"Do you think Tracy has any tits?" Frank said unexpectedly, which caught me by surprise as I almost choked on laughter. "Yes of course she has, it's the shabby clothes she wears that hide her," I said. Frank looked down at me, he looked sad, frowning saying: "Do you think she could fancy me then."

"Why cos she has tits? What you bloody talking about, Frank? You like Tracy?" I questioned.

"Yes, I like her" he bellowed, pushing me away, then grabbing me back by his side. "Even if she doesn't have big tits" Frank now looking unsure, and a little hurt. I was in fits of laughter; Luckily for me, Frank realise how daft he sounded, and saw the funny side, and began to laugh too. We laughed all the way to his house.

Today was a good day; I had made two new friends.

Frank waved me goodbye, as he made his way through his front door.

I continued up the street, three hundred meters further up Hawkshead Crescent to my house on the corner of Alstone Lane.

That night I couldn't get Penny's face out of my thoughts.

I just couldn't wait for school tomorrow.

CHAPTER 19

RELATIONSHIPS

I awoke feeling aroused, the thought of Penny kissing me today gave me a tingling feeling down below, reaching down, and adjusting myself inside my pants, getting out of bed, feeling awkward as I got dressed, not wanting to be on show at the breakfast table, how embarrassing that would be. Last thing I need is my mum wondering why my pants are pointing at her.
 Lucky for me the feeling passed as I strolled down the stairs, and the thought of my parents looking at my crotch.

I entered the kitchen as I did most days, carrying out the school day morning ritual, to my surprise, there was dad, for the first time since the trial, sat there sipping on his morning cuppa, paper in hand and fully dressed for work. Mum saw me, just as I was about to say something, she shook her head, instructing me to say nothing. Her face was aglow. You could see how delighted she was, her bright eyes shining. She danced over to dad, gliding across the floor with his full English plated up. She places the plate in front of him, followed by a kiss on his left cheek. Dad emerged from behind the paper and begins to tuck into his breakfast, knife, and folk working there magic, mouthful after mouthful; he never said a word, just smiled at mum. I ate my toast, happily in knowledge dad was back on his feet and looking well.

After my morning wash and the brushing of my teeth, I left for school. Mum did the ritual kiss on my forehead, "Have a good day love; things are going to be good, Dads back" she said, with a chuckle in her voice. I wiped the tears from her eyes, "Your right mum, I think it will" I replied, kissing her on the cheek.

Ryan, as usual, met me at my gate, I told him the good news about dad and about Shackleton, and that I was going to call for him, and if he wanted to join me, just to come. Ryan agreed, but then he was always going to because he was my best buddy in the entire world. He was my oldest friend, and I cherished this. Ryan was one of the most important people in my life, alongside my parents. No one could replace Ryan; he was my rock, my saving grace, he was the one who always brought me back from the dark place, the unhappy sad place. I owed Him.

The skies were darker than usual for this time of day, possibly a storm today. We ran down the road towards Franks. When we reached the Shackleton's home, we were greeted by an enormous roar; their front door was wide open. The voices from inside were booming, but not frightening, quite the opposite. Somebody was playfully roaring like a wild bear.
Out ran a little toddler, must have been about three years old, he was giggling hysterically, almost falling over the concrete doorstep as he leapt off it, heading down the path towards the gate. The bear growls and heavy footsteps grew louder as the bear got closer to the door. Out jumped Mr. Shackleton now in a pose ready to pounce on the poor little lad, with one enormous

growl he scooped up the boy in his arms and began to gnaw on his tummy making the little boy giggle more.

"Hello Detective-sergeant," I said, surprised to see him. I was shocked to see the detective sergeant there, I remembered him from that Christmas back in 1970, when the Parkers had tragically died, and Chris and Jenny had stayed with us. Frank had never let on his dad was a policeman, let alone a detective. He stood looking down at me as he placed the little boy back on his feet. "Go on Michael run to your mummy," said Shackleton pushing Michael gently towards the door. "So, what can I do for you two?" he said looking at us suspiciously as if we had committed a crime.

"Come to call for Frank, see if he's walking to school yet," I said nervously. The weather must have been as nervous as me. The clouds were changing and moving swiftly, in the now dark grey sky. Droplets of rain started to fall hinting this was going to get worse, the wind had picked up too. "Best come on in lads, looks like it's ready to pour down, anyhow, lazy bugger isn't out of bed yet," said Shackleton inviting us through the doorway.

Frank's mum got the teacups out and poured us a brew from the green teapot sitting in the centre of the table. His mum was a tall round woman who hadn't lost her womanly features, after giving birth to her three children over the last twenty-one years. You could tell she must have been an attractive young lady in her day. She still had long slender legs and a girlish face, full of freckles, her eyes were a pale blue, but bright, and she smiled a lot too.

She made her way out of the living room and headed for the stairway. "Frank, your friends, have come to call for you, so move your bloody arse" she yelled from the bottom step.

Frank was down in a flash, bouncing down the stairs, "Hiya guys … you calling for me" he said stupidly. "Of course, they are you nutter, who else goes to your school?" his mum chirped in clipping him around the head swiftly. We all just laughed, mocking him, shaking our heads.

Michael watched us intensely, sitting on his mother's knee. Wow, the shock when I saw his sister, Marie, a twenty-one-year-old, very attractive drop-dead gorgeous lass. Who would have thought he could have a sister looking that good, she was in her nightdress, and it didn't take much of the imagination to see she was a well-proportioned girl with all the right curves. It must have been that time in my life when urges just happened; lucky for me Ryan almost blocked me out, not so lucky for Ryan as he was on full display. And his mouth was touching the floor in a manner of speaking. Mrs. Shackleton placed the palm of her hand below Ryan's jaw and eased it up gently until it closed.

"Need to control yourself, young man," she said softly, looking down at his zipped area, Ryan made the quickest exit ever, his face flushed red like never seen before, thought his head would explode.

I walked out behind him smiling back at the female duo, who were now in fits of laughter at poor Ryan's expense.

Frank finally emerged, a large toasted sandwich devoured in seconds as we passed his gate.

The weather had changed for the worse; it was pouring it down, even the odd flash of lightning seen on the horizon. We ran the full mile or so to school.

Totally soaked, we entered the school building, drying ourselves off the best we could with the paper towels in the boy's toilet room, before separating for our lessons.

It was dinner time before I saw Penny, she looked up from her seat and waved, the girls sat with her broke into a giggling fit. I waved back as I stood in the dinner queue, awaiting my turn to pick the bland cooked food on offer, meat pie, mash, and peas, it looked disgusting, the crust was overcooked the meat tough, and the mash was gloopy, the peas were even shrivelled and dried up.

I sat at the table opposite hers, gazing at her momentarily, Ryan sniggering to himself, poking fun at me. "Shut up Ryan; you're making me look like a twat." "Never mind Dave, you are a twat" came his reply, still sniggering.

Finally, it was in the school grounds, that I got the chance to see her, I instantly took her in my arms and kissed her, a crowd of girls started taunting Penny.

"Why do you want to kiss him" voiced the leader of the group, "He's gonna give you little black kids if you marry him" came her malicious words. Penny was calm, and she never let go of me, her arms reached around my neck as she pulled me closer, her kiss was more intense, as we snogged hard displaying ourselves for all to see, no shame to be had.

The group turned, started to walk away when the leader spoke, her demeanour was that of hate "You're just a slag Penny Ambrose Walters ...You are". Frank caught the last part of the hateful words and promptly stood up to her, interrupting her mid-sentence. "Watch your mouth, Claire Curtis," he said grabbing her blouse collar, she was almost on her tiptoes. Colour drained from her face as Frank looked into her watery eyes, the tears starting to flow. Frank whispered, in a surprising calm voice "Look, Clair, she likes him and so do I, he's a good kid." He paused to take in a gulp of air, "Ok, maybe if you were nicer, you too could end up with a good-looking man yourself?" he slowly let her down, realizing he was hurting her. Claire's colour draining from her face as she almost choked, allowing her to run away, crying, but chuntering all the same.

Penny gave Frank a peck on his cheek and thanked him. Frank blushed red instantly, turning away all coy. Must admit this was amusing, who would ever have believed the great hard bastard Frank Shackleton would have turned all coy over a kiss?

The main door opened, and the duty dinner teacher blew his whistle, indicating the break had finished, The rush began to get indoors and back to lessons.

Sat behind my desk I watched Mrs. Cunningham traverse in between the desk, stopping now and then to answer questions from her pupils.

Me and Tracy were engrossed in some math's equation; I must admit I was still finding this hard to get my head around. It was time to hold up the white flag and surrender and say I didn't get it; Tracy, on the other hand, was racing away, scribbles here and there, trying to explain the relativity of the equation, against the formula for the derivative. She may as well have been talking a foreign language. Mrs. Cunningham also admitted the fact that this was not going to work; I could not understand the terminology let alone the math. She said she was sorry to see me go and this was a waste of a good brain, never the less I still found myself back in Mr. Graham's class.

"Welcome back Mr. Brown ...Not as smart as you think you are?" he stated, his beady little eyes penetrating through me as if I was dirt, I just smiled back at him, "Yes Sir! Mr. Graham, you have the pleasure of my company for the next eight months" sarcasm oozing out in my tone. "Just sit-down Brown" he replied turning his back on the class as he made his way to his desk.

Sitting down he took out a cigarette, lit it and began to smoke, ignoring the fact he had a class to teach.

Not one pupil in his class had a good word to say about him. He was a rude, unpleasant man, and everyone loathed him, especially the other tutors.

The sound of the bell, school was finished for the day; I met up with Penny to walk her home, Ryan following with Frank some three or four steps behind. Both chatting some harmless banter, and mucking about, pretend fighting and such. Penny amused, turning her head, watching them both clowning about. I just ignored them, leaving them to get on with it. Leaving Penny, after our goodnight kiss was painful, I really wanted to ditch my friends, and spend some time with her. Yes it's true, as spiteful as it seemed my only thoughts were Penny. I think Ryan knew.

Two more weeks till the big summer break and the freedom to roam about. No more teachers like Mr. Graham barking his orders, ruling us like minions, not worthy of his time or efforts.

Holidays abroad were still rare; few families knew what the sea looked like on my estate, having never ventured any further than the town centre.
 The weather was a cool, moderate temperature, not hitting any highs; but enjoyable, the coastline was still packing them in, but too cold to be wearing a bikini.

Back home, Mum was trying to persuade dad to investigate the cost of a holiday to Spain or France. She had her heart set on drinking an exotic drink next to a warm outdoor pool with palm trees surrounding her, dad said we could go to Cornwall, they have palm trees. If looks could kill, then dad would be laying down dead at this very moment. Mum threw her slipper at him in protest, staring disapprovingly, and hurt.

I sat there watching Blue Peter, keeping one ear trained on the conversation in the room, listening as mum continued to plead her case with dad. "Harold, I have been married for god knows how long and you have never taken me away, abroad" mum sat looking at him with her most pretentious sorry looking face. "We went to France as I remember my dear" he replied. Leaning back in his chair smiling at her.

"That was your sixtieth birthday, and as I remember dear, I paid, not you" mum bitterly shouted loudly back at him.

I had never seen mum and dad act like this; it was quite scary, mum was getting distraught now, I think dad realised this, and tried to talk mum down by promising he would see what he could do. He would never intentionally upset mum; she was his world. Mum was weeping now, and Dad looked wounded. Without a word, dad raised himself from his chair and went out of the front door; he just got in the car and drove off, not a word to where he was going.

The room fell silent; mum was worried he was now upset. Now anxious, thinking she had been trivial crying about this holiday, and was now fretting about dad. Thinking the worse, like he may crash the car. You could read mum like a book. "Mum dad's ok, he might just be going for a drive to clear his head, or because he enjoys driving," I said trying to reassure her, mum just shook her head. "Dads changed since the case, he's not as considerate as he used to be" she replied still shaking her head. This wasn't mum? Mum getting upset over what seemed to be nothing. It would appear the tragedy over Janet and Elizabeth had gotten to us all in some way.

She was right about dad, to some point, he had changed, but not against her or me, just others around us. He wasn't as sociable as he used to be, I think he just wanted to keep his distance, without been involved in other people's lives. Not wanting to put his trust in someone who turned out to be a killer, not wanting to make the same mistake, again.

I sat with mum on the settee, arms around each other, mum was worried, it had been an hour since dad walked out, the TV turned down low so she could hear the slightest noise from outside.

The front door opened and in walked dad wearing a beret and a stripy t-shirt with a string of onions around his neck. Mum's jaw nearly hit the floor, in his arms was a box full of the most delicious smelling Chinese takeaway ever, well I've never seen a French takeaway, not saying there isn't one, but I have never seen one.

Dad looked ridiculous in his get up, trying to imitate a French man, his accent was terrible too, the worse Peter Sellers Inspector Clouseau I had ever heard. "Bonjour Madame I have brought you your tea, sorry not French, but I hope a Chinese will do," his voice tapering off to a Benny Hill Chinese accent, a smiling dad bringing in a peace offering to mum, who was now in fits of laughter at him. "You're a silly beggar, you had me worried," she said crying with laughter. Dad just gave his smile. All was calm, and normal once again.

We enjoyed our tea, chicken fried rice for mum, sweet and sour chicken balls for dad and beef chow-mein for me, this followed by a cream soda ice cream floater, perfect end to a perfect supper. Mum got out of her chair, making her way over to dad, hugging dad, followed by a tender kiss, "Sorry for been silly earlier love" she whispered to him, "I love you Margaret Brown and don't you forget that, We will go abroad" he said in a low, gentle voice, they cuddled again before mum took the empty plates into the kitchen leaving dad sitting proudly on his chair, winking at me with his right eye. Everything was back to normal now, mum and dad snuggled up together watching the T.V, as I made my way to my room, bidding them both a good night.

Saturday morning arrived, I had plans to meet Penny today, Ryan and Lisa were joining us. Me and Ryan had decided to call for Frank, and the girls had decided to bring Tracy. A bit of matchmaking was underway.

Frank was surprisingly up, the time was only nine O'clock, He found it hard getting out of bed most days, but there he was, sat there on their sofa, large as life eating a bowl of cornflakes. Mrs. Shackleton was a feeder, the fresh oven baked bread, the smell wafting through the house, with a pot of homemade marmalade on the tray. The table was offered to us, it was hard to resist, and the smell was overwhelming, you just had to taste some; it was the best bread and marmalade I had ever tasted. Ryan had three doorsteps smothered with the preserve. He didn't take long to devour them, bread crumbs covering his polo neck jumper, licking his lips, and thanking Mrs. Shackleton. Little Michael was sat there, gnawing at the oversized cut of bread, his face covered in butter and marmalade.

At the door, Mrs. Shackleton gave Frank the Scarborough warning, "You make sure you behave, lad, I don't want any crap hitting my door" with that she gave him a whack on the head, "What's that for" he screeched, "In lieu of anything happening" she smiled back at him. Mumbling something under his breath Frank stepped out of the house.

Outside, inquisitively, Ryan asked, "Where's your sister, I didn't see her this morning" Frank's gaze was

236

scary, "Why do you need to see my sister?" Ryan gave a mischievous smile, replying "Think she looks great and she makes me smile, let alone give me a hard-on," did the same for me too, and if I had to admit it, I was disappointed she wasn't there too.

"Well the dirty bitch is still in bed, never gets out before ten on the weekend" Frank moaned. We dropped the subject; Frank was getting into his usual hard arsed self. Switching the conversation towards today, and what we were hoping to do, soon had Frank back on track and eager to go.

We set off to meet the girls; cutting through the school grounds towards the pathway to the farmers' field. The problem with this path was the great big bull he kept in it. Nearly caught me the last time, and yes, I almost shit myself, the adrenaline was pumping like crazy, sprinting across the field with this very speedy one tonne of bull bearing down on me.

We finally reached the farmer's field, and yes there stood the bull, he was already snorting, he looked fierce and very bloody dangerous, and yes, I didn't really want to make the sprint. "Come on you two, let's get in, last one stinks like a smelly whores' fanny" shouted Ryan, howling, already racing across the field. I was next over the gate and pelting it across, not daring to look for the bull, I could hear it charging about, but I just ran, blinkered to everything around me. Screams could be heard behind me; it was Frank. "For fuck sake, help, noooooooo" he continued to yell, crying like a girl, travelling as fast as his legs could carry him. I was over the gate on the other side watching in disbelief; the bull was just feet from him, its head down, the horns poised for the attack. Frank made it, literally throwing himself over the gate, rolling across the road before making it back to his feet. The bull hit the gate hard, buckling the metal rungs. Frank cursing, trying to regain his breath.

The bull was ok, he just shook his head and continued his grazing, snorting loudly. We stood watching this magnificent animal. It was as if we had never crossed the field; he just stood there grazing while we were regaining our breath, Frank did his usual cursing as we continued our walk to Roundhay Park.

The day was crisp and fresh with very little wind. This helped us compose ourselves, Ryan was in stitches laughing at our expense, reminiscing the charge of the bull brigade, impersonating Frank. Frank was not amused, I kept quiet, not to antagonise Frank any more than needed. I wouldn't go up against Frank personally, but Ryan, I think he could probably hold his own in that situation, if it ever arose, and truth to be told, Frank knew this too, so held back somewhat.

It seemed like the whole estate had decided to take a walk to Roundhay Park today. Trying to find Penny was impossible; the crowd of people there must have been in the high hundreds. We didn't have mobile phones back then. You couldn't just call someone and say I'm on the north side of the lake and then have them there in minutes. No, you had to physically look for them. We took our chance of walking around the lake to see if we could find them. After some forty minutes hard searching, and a lot of been pushed and shoved, and the odd "Hey mind where you're fucking going, tosser" from the few so-called hard men, trying to impress their girls, and with Frank being Frank, we got into a little scuffle. Frank squaring up to this thirty-something, who thought he was God's gift, showing off his muscles in his undersized T-shirt, crying to be taken off, the embarrassment of this guy's beer belly hanging over his pants. "Anytime cock" came Franks cool response. With little thought on the matter, the man raised his hands, surrendering to Franks treat. Frank was a giant and quite intimidating to look at, and he was quite bad tempered at times, also very easy to wind up.

Frank gave out a massive roar, bellowing "Over there Dave, I can see them" pointing over at the wall. Petrifying half the population at the same time, even made me jump. Ryan was doubled over, gut splitting laughter erupting at the situation. "Get over it Ryan, it weren't that funny" I moaned at him. Well it was really, just it made me jump out of my skin, and a little embarrassed. His hand slapped my back, " David, you should have seen you all jump, yes it was funny" he replied still chortling.

Penny was as beautiful as ever, her long legs covered in blue jeans and her Star Wars short sleeved printed T-shirt. I managed to keep that tingle at bay, but her presence still made me smile. Tracy was there too, her dress sense improving, after the makeover from Lisa and Penny, she too had jeans and a T-shirt on; her design had an equation of E mc2? On it. She was such a geek. And as for Lisa, she had a look of Elizabeth about her, her sassiness, oozed out; she knew how to flaunt it.

Frank nudged me as we edged closer towards them. "Hey David, Tracy has got some tits, and I think they look good, what do you think?" His wide eyes transfixed on her boobs, his childish smirk spreading across his face. Me and Ryan cracked up, but he was right, now Tracy had regular clothes on, you could see her body shape. For a total geek, she was an attractive looking girl, she was a 30b cup and looked good with it. Frank's face was a picture, he just could not stop smiling, and in fact, it was quite scary.

Lisa ran towards Ryan; she jumped up at him as they met; he caught her mid-flight and spun her around. Frank was stood behind me when we approached the two girls sat on the wall. "Hello Penny, Hello Tracy, you been here long," I said reaching for Penny's hand, "Hi David" they both replied. Frank stepped out from behind me (not that he could not be seen) and introduced himself to Tracy; she acknowledged him with a smile. "I see you do have manners? And you know my name, impressive Frank, for a dinosaur" Tracy responded. Franks head lowered, "Sorry about what I called you in school, it's cos I really like you …A lot" he whimpered out. "So, you fancy me? Eh" she asked confidently. Before another word was said, Frank straightened up, holding out his hand for her, saying "You fancy a go in the boats Tracy" pointing over to the wooden jetty, harbouring several rows of boats. "Can you control one, in fact, can you fit in one" spited Tracy, getting her own back, but not feeling too comfortable saying it, apologetic she quickly cried "Sorry Frank that's rude of me, I shouldn't have done that?" looking down ashamed. "Ha, so what I deserved that, picked on you too many times, and it's only cos I was too scared to ask you out, didn't think you would like me, me being big and fat and …well rude" Frank replied, now his hand cupping hers. They looked each other face on, the two girls cooed, batting their eyelids at Frank. Frank turned to jelly; his face could have melted. Tracy saved his blushes, she moves closer, brushing her face next to his cheek, and lightly kisses him. "Come on then, Frank, show me what a man you are," said Tracy, placing her small hand in his giant palm. Penny placed her arms around my neck, kissing me, jolting her head back and forth.

Together we walked to the pier, paid for the tickets, and gingerly managed ourselves into the boats.

Tracy was happy to share the boat with Frank, she liked the idea of his attention towards her, he was looking pleased with himself, he was the perfect gentleman, and he made sure she was comfortable before he started to row out from the jetty, following Ryan further out towards the centre of the lake. I helped Penny into our boat, she screamed as it rocked unevenly on the water, she managed to sit down before I got in; the boat master uncoupled us and pushed us outward from the jetty. Rowing the boat wasn't that comfortable, the undercurrent pulled one way as I tried to get us following the others. Eventually, I got the hang of it, Ryan ribbed me something rotten, "You Ok there David" he said mocking me as he rowed away, "See who can get to that outcrop over there" he continued pointing some three hundred yards out. I got off to a quick start leaving the other two boats well behind; Penny was as giddy as hell, "Come on then Ryan

...Catch up, come on" she screamed at them. It was short-lived, the current had changed direction, fighting the lake was futile as I found myself going the opposite direction, "Who's laughing now" yelled Frank and Ryan as they passed me in their boats, both Lisa and Tracy giggling loudly leaving us stranded, not able to follow.

It would seem that the lake had joined in the mocking; no matter how hard I tried we just spun around and around getting nowhere, the undercurrent latching on to the underside of the boat.

Penny losing interest was getting frantic and wanted to go back to the jetty, she'd had enough of this boat ride of going nowhere fast. I surrendered the cause and the constant bellyaching from Penny, and somehow managed to make the way back to the jetty. Angrily Penny unbalanced, stumbled back on to dry land, the odd curse emitting from her normally sweet lips, I followed. I looked out to where the other two boats were; I gave them a wave, both Frank and Ryan returned my gesture, then rowed off out of sight.

"That was a waste of bloody time" she groaned, her face bitter, "Penny what's the face for ...so I'm not a sailor," I said as I caught up with her.

"So what we gonna do now ...I'm bored with this," she said stood there, hands in her jeans pockets, her face expressionless. "Did you want to come out with me today?" I asked. I was starting to get a little angry myself. I made an effort to meet up and spend what I thought was going to be a beautiful day out with her and the gang, but no, she was wearing her shitty attitude head today it would seem. Someday I was having.

Penny sighed, unexpectedly she began to cry, no reason it would appear? I held her close to me and wiped away her tears with my hand. "Hey what's wrong, we can do whatever you want," I said trying to comfort her. Penny's face had sadness written all over it; I was ready for the sorry, don't want to go out with you speech.

"David, I really like you a lot" more tears rolled from her eyes, "I don't want us to break up, but I'm leaving the country for good next week" came the words from her mouth. I felt as if I had just been shot, my face now blank and the look of a lost child. If this wasn't the breakup speech from hell, then I will never know what is? Penny was besieged with sorrow, crying, her face snuggled into my chest. "I love you David, but dad's got an office in Vancouver, Canada, and his business has really taken off over there" she held me tighter as if she would never let go. "And we have to move there next week" Her tears streamed down her face, I could feel the damp coming through my T-shirt. "I'm so sorry I never knew" her sobbing inconsolably, she was shaking. I felt as if I was going to be physically sick; my stomach knotted, I had just got used to the idea of being able to care for someone again, only to have her snatched away. I wanted to walk away and tell her to just fuck off, bitch, fuck my head up why don't you? But I didn't, I was in love with her, I didn't want her to go, and I don't want to hurt her, any more than she's already hurting.

We sat on the wall, our heads resting on each other's; we never spoke, just sat holding hands. People passing gave us the odd stare, but we never noticed. Oblivious to the world around us.

It must have been about an hour just sitting there before we spoke again. Penny raised her head, she had her smile back, her eyes were still a little swollen from her crying, but her sparkle had reappeared, "David can we make love one day before I leave."

I turned my head in shock, "Do you think that would be right?" I asked. She squeezed my hand tightly in reassurance. "I Want you to be my first David; I want to feel you next to me ...I need to take that away with me, so I will always have that memory ...and it's the right time, you're the right person ...I know it" her smile genuine and compassionate, her hands still holding mine. Our heads met as we kissed a lingering kiss.

"Look at those two ... Always snogging" Frank's voice breaking our bubble, bringing us back to the real world. "Hi, you lot ... Enjoy the boats?" I said as we jumped down off the wall.

The girls linked arms as they walked behind us, giggling loudly. Frank and Ryan were constantly ribbing me on my boatmanship, well the lack of it. We spent the day running up and down the grassy hills surrounding the lake, in and out of the woodland playing a game of kissy catch.

Tracy and Frank linking arms, the odd kiss, then gazing at each other, kissing again, it would seem our plan to get them together had worked. Tracy was not the geeky plain darkly dressed person she was at school;

she had transformed into this lively young adult, tasting life for the first time. Just seeing them together, made us feel good. We knew then Frank had changed from his bullying days to this gentle giant, all considerate and polite. Well, that was the case when he was around Tracy.

The sun was going down, and the sky was turning a dark purple as the moon shone down high in the sky. Lost in time, and with the day hours disappearing into the late evening, we headed for home, walking Penny home first. Mr. Walters came to meet me at their gate. "I guess Penny's told you about the move next Friday?" he said, concern showing through his words, "It wasn't my plan for us to go so quickly, but the business has increased very rapidly over there, I need to be there to take control over it." His eyes and facial expression were that of sorrow. Not for him, but me and Penny "I needed to tell you that David, I think you're a great lad, so please don't believe that it was against you" he continued. With his head down, he turned before I could reply and headed back into his house, closing the door behind him. Penny had already raced up the path without saying goodnight.

Ryan raced up to me, grabbing at my shirt, pulling at me, "What's all that about" he asked, "Penny and her family are immigrating to Canada next Friday" I said casually, as not to show my real feelings. He pulled me closer to him knowing I was hiding it, edging me closer to the others who were waiting further down the garden fence. I never told them.

We raced off towards Tracy's, dropping her off next; we had to drag Frank away, the big soppy git was almost skipping home. "Thanks, you guys, that was amazing, you think she likes me," he said, his face was beaming, all aglow and giddy. "Of course, she loves you a lot Frank, now stop being a fanny and let's get home," Ryan said taunting him, blowing him kisses and mimicking Tracy "I love you big Frank, I love you." I couldn't look at Frank, I knew he was going to beat up on Ryan for taking the piss, Ryan knew this too, so he was off like a shot, Frank in pursuit. Lisa walked with me, watching, shaking our heads, we linked arms and followed the two up the street. Frank puffing, out of breath unable to catch Ryan, who stood there waiting outside Frank's gate.

Frank went in, too annoyed to speak. Without a word, Ryan, Lisa and I made the walked up to our street. I said my good nights to them both, as they stood outside Lisa's gate. Both waved and turned, entering Lisa's house.

I shut the front door as I entered the passageway. I wanted to cry, but stopped myself, the pain in the pit of my stomach ached, I felt lost. "Is that you David love" mum shouted from the kitchen "you want a sandwich ...are you hungry?". Mums voice picked me up; I walked through to the kitchen passing dad as he went for his favourite chair. The TV was on, it was nine in the evening, and the nine O'clock news had just started, I stopped in the kitchen doorway, the news was showing a picture of Harry Green, Elizabeth's killer. Dad rushed off his chair, and turned the large volume knob on the

TV clockwise, turning up the volume so we could hear better.

The report from the broadcaster was saying Harry Greens' body had been found dead, found in the prison grounds earlier this morning; it continued to say he had been murdered.

Two inmates were held, it revealed pictures of the accused, Gary Flanagan and Joe Flanagan, Janet's' cousins. I remembered them from the wedding. The report said there was no motive for the killing, but we knew the reason.

A satisfying look on dad's face as he stared back at the TV, his words were cold and callous, "What goes around, comes around ...You mark my words son". Dad took a swig from his mug of tea, relaxed back in his chair as if he had just closed a book at the end of a chapter, his mouth had broken into a smile, and he looked contented, "Now that's justice" he said taking another sip from his mug.

CHAPTER 20

NEVER EASY TO SAY GOODBYE

Sunday morning, it's the day before the last week of school. The holidays looming, and I won't have Penny to go out with, she leaves this Friday, and I need to spend all the time I can with her, so I decided I would ring her.

Their phone was ringing but no reply came through, just the continuous dialling tone. Obsessed with the idea of seeing her firmly planted in my head, I decided to get dressed and walk over.

Maybe they're not up yet, and it was only ten past nine. The streets were deathly quiet, no traffic or anyone about, it was another bright sunny day, so it made for a pleasant walk, the birds singing in the trees, acknowledging the few dog walkers as they said hello.

Penny was outside when I got there, she ran down the garden path, arms waving, excited to see me, almost knocking me over as she jumped into my arms, "Hey steady ...Almost had me over then" I said steadying myself. "Shut up and kiss me," she said planting her lips on mine. I noticed the for-sale sign stuck firmly in the ground; this brought home the realities of what was yet to come. Her mum nipped out the doorway, "Hello David ...We're just having some breakfast, would you like to join us?" She had a very posh voice and was always dressed up to the nines no matter what time of day it was; she too was gorgeous, it wasn't hard to see where Penny got her looks. We made our way to the door; Penny went in first tugging at my hand, urging me to enter. The room was sparsely furnished; most had been sold on or already freighted over to Canada.

The room was enormous compared to ours, and they had five huge bedrooms, two bathrooms, and a super-sized kitchen.

The rear gardens travelled on for what seemed forever, fruit trees full of young fruit, and a large freshly cut green lawn. A garden Grant would be proud to own. I think Penny was a little embarrassed by her parent's wealth. We sat and ate breakfast in silence. Over the next few hours, we spoke of many things, but never about the move to Canada. Mr. Walters was very careful not to upset anyone, he was a very intelligent man who cared about others feelings, he surprised me, in the fact he didn't boast or brag, and always found others good side and showed an interest in them, He was fascinated about my parents and how we came about. I explained what I knew.

Mr. Walters gave a glance at his watch as if he had somewhere to go. It was 12:30 pm, he gazed across the room fixing his eyes on Mrs. Walters, "Need to go to the warehouse and collect the paperwork from the safe dear, Need to check the freight times for the last shipment" he said to her, getting out of his chair, and walking to the door. Checking his pockets for the car keys, "Do you want to join me, Anita" prompting her to join him "I think the young ones want to spend a little time on their own" he said winking at Penny. Anita got up and kissed Penny, "Now you two behave we won't be too long," She said joining Mr. Walters out of the door.

Penny and I were alone now, the room was quiet, no sound at all apart from the sound of our breathing. Penny shuffled closer to me, reaching out, taking hold of my hands, her hands sat small inside mine, we cuddled up close, she kissed me, then again, the taste of her sending me into ecstasy. Sitting on the oversized sofa holding hands, leaning on each other, "Do you want to go upstairs" She whispered in my ear, squeezing me tightly, nuzzling my left ear. I turned to face her, my smile said it all, we jumped up in sync and raced up the stairs.

Our clothes flew off as we found ourselves embracing and touching each other tenderly in her bed. We made love, spooning as we finished, we laid there for what seemed like an eternity taking comfort from the warmth of our bodies.

Mr. Walters opened the door and entered the lounge, Penny and I were dancing to Roxy Music's Love is the drug, our arms, and bodies swaying in time with the music, her parents took to the floor and joined us. We all danced and laughed for hours. Mr. Walters had brought home six bottles sweet white wine, and a spicy Italian chicken casserole dish from one of the restaurants in the town centre, we drank and ate till we couldn't move. After a lengthy conversation on school and the move to Canada, Mrs. Walters placed her favourite record onto the player, Kate Bushes "The kick inside" admitting she normally had a spliff when dancing to this album. Once again, we all danced, swaying our bodies, freely encouraged to drink. Penny's parents were not as strict as mine, maybe too liberal, passing a rolled up joint to share.

The day soon ended, it was my time to leave for home, partially drunk and high on weed.

We kissed goodnight at her door, she slipped back in as I made my way home, my thoughts took over by the memory of this afternoon, I just couldn't get her out of my head, tears escaped my water glazed eyes, filled with sadness, I thought about her leaving in five days.

With my eyes blurred, I took my time to reach home, wiping my eyes before I entered our house, so mum and dad wouldn't know I'd been crying.

Mum was ironing dads' shirt and trousers for tomorrow, hanging them on the curtain rail, over the bay window. "Was she pleased to see you David?" mum said as she ironed the crease down the sleeve of dads' shirt. Mum could always tell when I was upset, and this was no different, she did not push for an answer, left me to make my way to the kitchen. "There's a ham and cheese sandwich made up for you in there" mum yelled from the living room, knowing I was scouring the fridge, this made me smile, she always had something ready no matter what time it was. I wolfed down the sandwich within seconds followed by a bowl of homemade trifle. Mum made a trifle every Sunday; it was part of why Sundays happened in my world.

Dad was sat watching Sunday night at the Palladium; Des O'Connor was hosting. Norman Wisdom was up to his typical antics leaving Des O'Connor in fits of laughter, unable to control the rest of the show. Dad found this funny, roaring with laughter, giving out great belly laughs. Normally I would join him, but tonight I was tired, so I kissed them both goodnight and made my way to my room. I didn't sleep that well, the thought of Friday playing heavy in my mind.

"David! Ryan's here, you up yet?" mum shouted from the bottom of the stairs, it was only half past seven; school didn't start for another hour. I crawled out of bed and raced down the stairs missing every other step. "Hi, Ryan why you here?" I asked, "School has a burst water main and schools closed for two, maybe three days, the schools flooded" Ryan informed. Mum chirped in "So how did you lot know Ryan?", "There was a bulletin on the radio" came Ryan's instant reply. Shrugging his shoulders, as if to say don't you guys listen to the radio or what?

The sizzling sound of bacon and sausage frying in the pan sending out the most welcome aroma across the room, catching Ryan's interest, lifting his nose in the air, taking in the aroma, the same time wearing a grin that said yes please. Mum takes one look at his face, saying "Ryan want any breakfast," and as usual, he didn't decline.

We had three days off, which was a bit of luck for me; this meant I could spend more time with Penny. The days past quickly, and leaving her was harder every day, I should have just cut my losses earlier, but no we both grasped the minutes, yearning for Friday not to come.

Thursday morning came, I was feeling low.

Like only a mother would know, she could see the pain, and she knew what to do.

Mum allowed me bunk school today, it was Penny's last day in England. Mum contacted the headmaster to explain, fortunately for me he understood, and he told mum to keep me home till after the holidays.

I was off like a shot, straight over to Penny's, there she was waiting sat on her step. She knew I would be there today, no matter what.

Penny and I spent the rest of the day in Leeds city centre. We spent the day doing her last bit of shopping, buying goods that she wouldn't be able to find in Canada, mainly sweets, crisp, T-shirts and shoes. I felt like a mule, carrying her bags. In and out of the small boutiques, breaking off only, for a sandwich and a coke, not leaving out the kissing.

We arrived back at her house about four in the afternoon; the house was packed with their relatives wishing them good luck on their new venture. I decided to give it a miss and not enter. Penny could tell I was feeling uneasy. We moved closer. She held me close, tight towards her body. Penny shuddered, began to cry, sobbing. Feeling the strain, I released myself from her, moving back two paces, I looked her up and down, then face to face, her poor eyes were swollen, and her makeup was running down her face, Penny was as devastated as I was. The world was a cruel place today; we wanted to die, that seemed kinder, who could understand how we were feeling, ripped apart, but not wanting to let go.

253

I moved in close again, we never said a word, we held on to each other tightly, kissing now and then, no words could heal or say how much we were hurting, the pain swept through our bodies, the feeling of two empty shells.

Eventually, Penny took a step backwards, even with the gaiety from the house, our world fell cold, silent, and dark; we just stared at each other, we couldn't even find a smile in ourselves. She grabbed the door handle, turning the doorknob, and walked through the doorway; I took a few steps back down their garden path watching as Penny disappeared behind the closed door. I found myself looking at a closed door; I stood there transfixed for a moment. I turned around with my head lowered, feeling small, all alone. I headed off home.

Penny never slept much that night; she cried with her mum laying by her side. I did much the same. Mum knew my heart had been broken again. She came into my room and lay next to me all night. I couldn't speak, but then I didn't have to, mum did what mums do best, she just cared.

Friday morning and the Walters were on their way to London's Heathrow airport for their flight to Canada.

I felt sick; my body ached, the pain inside my head was spiralling, repetitively thudding, exaggerating every sound. Mum left me in my room; she had gone to help dad with his breakfast and pack him off to work.

I never really got to say goodbye to Penny, and will probably never see Penny again. I couldn't say goodbye yesterday; I don't think either of us could bring ourselves to say the words. There were no words to find, how do you say farewell to the broken hearted.

I stood by the window in silence, looking out into nowhere, the street had vanished, all I saw was an emptiness, a mass of fading colours swirling around inside my head, blind of reality.

The bright sun's rays came flooding through the window, casting my sorry looking shadow across the floor.

CHAPTER 21

Poor Mrs. Connor

It was 08:45 Saturday morning. Dad responding to the loud knock on the door. Lisa stood there. "What's up Lisa love," he said looking down at her, Lisa was distraught and crying, almost screaming at dad, "Is Mrs. Brown available? Mums asking for her, She's fallen off the ladder, cleaning the windows." Dad went into urgency mode, shouting mum from the foot of the stairs, and in no time, the four of us were over the road at the Connors.

We arrived at the Connors; Mrs. Connor was laying there not moving on the front lawn, the ladder slumped against the high privet between the two houses. Their neighbours were already peering over the privet, but none had gone to help, just stood there gorping and babbling amongst themselves. Dad pushed our way in, nudging the two nosey women blocking the gateway with his shoulders, still in their bedclothes with the tatty dressing gown hiding their unkempt state, "Excuse us we need to get in to help her" dad shouted at them. Frowning they moved over to clear our passage into the garden. Dad tutting aloud.

Grant anxious and too upset to speak, laid next to his wife; blood seeping from her head as she laid on the lawn face down in front of their bay window. Her face wan, expressionless and her body motionless. Mum calmly knelt by Mrs. Connor, running her hands over her head and torso. Grant gazed up, helpless. "Can you help?" his face said it all, "Please," he said, almost begging. With a polite smile and a nod, mum cleaned Mrs. Connor up and pressed a clean tea towel against the wound on her forehead. Poor Mrs. Connor was going to have one hell of a bump on her head, but for now was losing consciousness, her colour draining. "Harold call the ambulance now" commanded mum, dad fumbled this way and that way, rushing around like a headless chicken, "For god sake man, the phone is in their living room" screamed mum. Dad, all frustrated, dashed to the room and dialled 999.

The crowd had now made their way into the garden, keeping a clear space for mum to do what she had to. Bent over they scrutinised mums every move. I was going to tell them all to get lost and leave us all alone, but mum intervened, "If you're going to watch, then keep back, this isn't a bloody game show for you all to gorp at" with that, they instantly stepped back two paces, this made mum snigger.

Grant was an old man and resembled one, his face weathered and worn, looking worse from the tears as he observes mum nursing his wife who lays there unconscious.

The ambulance arrived within minutes, mum reported her findings to the medic, removing herself, allowing the medics to carry out their work. "She isn't as bad as she looks, she will be OK …You did an excellent job treating her" said the tall medic, mum acknowledged nodding her head, taking Lisa into her arms. Lisa wrapped her arms around mums' waist, her head on mums' shoulder weeping, mums embrace tightened.

Grant frustrated, was struggling to get into the ambulance; his health had suffered over the years, and movement didn't come easily to him, even with the aid from the medic he couldn't get himself up, and there was no room for his wheelchair. He sat on the kerb shaking his head, mum intervened, said she would go, but keep Grant informed. With his approval, she joined the crew as they drove on, towards St James hospital. The crowd of neighbours dispersed and went back to their homes leaving us in silence.

Dad and I stayed behind with Grant and Lisa.

With both of them distraught, teary-eyed and looking lost, dad took control.

I aided Lisa, placing my arm around her waist, allowing her to lean on me, making our way slowly into the kitchen.

Sitting her down at the table, she looked up with a half-smile. At the sink I filled the kettle, then placing it on the gas ring to boil, the cups placed on the worktop ready to be filled. Dad aided Grant to his seat and wheeled him into the living room. "Would you like me to ring the boys for you Grant?" dad asked curiously, "No need Harold, she will be fine, and I'm sure they'd be too busy" replied Grant, feeling a little better now, knowing she's in the right place and being cared for.

Their boys had moved out years before, Darron had relocated to London, he was working with his partner Grace, in one of Covent garden's quaint cafes, it was said he was doing well for himself, and expecting their first child in the New Year. Cliff had joined the army the same time as Phil and Carl Backhouse, he had become the best marksman in their regiment, enlisted into many competitions and earning promotions along the way, Sargent Cliff Connor, as he was now, and very well respected, and his trophy cabinet full. As for Robert, he had turned out to be a pop star of sorts, working alongside some of the most prodigious names in pop as a support singer. He was living the high life and travelling the world. The Connors were proud of their sons, and was hoping Lisa would be successful too.

Grant had come around somewhat; the thought of Mrs. Connor not been there scared him; ever since his arthritis had kicked in all those years ago, she had made sure he was looked after, she had been his rock, stopped him ending it all in the early days of his illness. Grant was a very proud man, the thought of having someone having to wipe his backside infuriated him, and he felt helpless and useless, but she had none of it, she loved this man, and all that he was. Told him, he was a good man who had done many special things and had medals to prove it.

He often wondered why she had never strayed, he wasn't the man she had married all those years before when they were young and foolish, but still so much in love.

He began to narrate his stories, reminiscing on how they met at a dinner dance sponsored by her employer.

He was a guest of a friend during his leave from the Navy, chuckling away, his whole face lit up as he continued, saying it was love at first sight, she was the sweetest thing he had ever laid eyes on, she'd fallen for him hook, line and sinker. He was the most handsome and physically built man she had seen, his body was lean, and his movements were graceful. They danced most of the night away. He said she adored him in his uniform. She would often call him her very own Cary Grant, (her favourite movie star) oddly enough he did have a resemblance to him.

Grant searched his memory, gulping at his cup of tea, remembering back to the day when he plucked up the courage and met her parents. He had just docked in Portsmouth, got his rail pass to Leeds, and headed straight up North.

The week before, Grants ship had been the protector to some high-ranking official from the Middle East, they had come under a heavy enemy attack when alighting their load. Grant was part of the marine section that had to bodyguard this Official back to his palace. Grant swore, if he got out alive, then the first thing he would do when he got back home, was to marry his sweetheart.

His meeting with Mrs. Connor's father hadn't gone too well, and he had been given a refusal and found he had to fight him in the street if he was to win her hand in marriage.

Her father was a huge monster of a man with his intimidating two hundred and thirty-two-pound frame, and a man who drank heavily and swore like a trooper, he would sooner knock your block off than speak to you.

Grant was told he had to prove himself worthy of looking after and protecting his daughter. Grant sat contentedly in his wheelchair, knowing he had us captivated with this tale, as he continued. At first, he thought her dad was messing with him, until the first punch hit him in the face, rocking him off his feet. The sheer force rattled Grant, within minutes they fought like two wild animals, punching and kicking each other in the back alleys of Armley town street. After a thirty minute battle and a large gathering of locals, Grant squared up to him face to face and gave the final punch, walloping her dad square on the jaw, the huge man toppled over like a sack of spuds, crashing down onto the cobbled road. In the first instance, Mrs. Connor and her mum thought Grant had killed him, as it took him a few minutes to come around. They didn't check, just looked down on his beaten body.

Grant wasn't sure it was relief or disappointment displayed on the women's faces when her dad got back on his feet. He gave out a mighty roar, and a huge belly laugh, placing his hand in Grants, shaking it firmly, giving him his blessing.

He escorted Grant, and Grant only, back into the local boozer, shunning his wife and daughter, ordering them back to the house to have a meal ready for when they decided to get home. It was past midnight when the drunken pair arrived home, singing and praising each other as they stumbled through the door, mother and daughter looking on in disbelief.

Grant had won the full respect from her dad after that; her dad would brag amongst his friends in the local pubs that this man was going to marry his daughter.

Grant was an orphaned child, growing up in various fostercare homes, he was a feral young lad, who rarely took to being told what to do, he had a tough time during his childhood, but fell into service life with no trouble at the age of seventeen and never looked back. On the day of their wedding, the right side of the church was empty, apart from Grant and his best man, while the bride's side was packed, full of her family and friends. The wedding was the start of their new adventure together.

Grant, s mouth turned up at the ends, breaking into a smile. Now with his story ended, he looked out into the distance, daydreaming of a time gone by, we all sat there sipping from our mugs, the biggest smirks across our faces.

Lisa adored listening to her dad's stories; she promised her dad she would become a writer of short tales, when she grew up. She had written many pages of their lives in scrapbooks along with the photos and illustrations. A future best seller in the making.

Grant fed her story after story, some tales of faraway lands and some close to home, mostly about his Dickensian dreadful childhood, scavenging for nibbles of food, and the sweatshops that he had to endure. Grant knew Lisa was destined for better things in her life.

Lisa was proud of her dad; he had given to her, his military medals, awarded for his bravery during his numerous campaigns back in his marine days. Her mum often said she didn't want them or need them; she had him, he was always a hero in her eyes. Oddly enough I had never thought of Mrs. Connor being so sensitive in the early days, but after our ordeal, I could see the woman Grant spoke about so tenderly. She did have a kind empathic way about her; I was happy for Lisa and Grant that people could now see this side of her.

Dad was relieved, Grant had settled down, and Lisa had stopped crying. Dad reassuring us all would be fine, and Mrs. Connor would be back home in no time.

With nothing more for me to do, and the time being only 10 O'clock, I said my goodbyes and headed for Ryan's.

Joyce answered the door, looking radiant and flush, stood in her pyjama pants and a tee shirt, I couldn't help but notice her nipples were erect and she had a lot of colour in her cheeks, her short hair was wild, unkempt, yet sexy. Clive had left the house five minutes since, calling in on dad. "Hello David, how are you ...Come to see Ryan?" she whispered, smiling at me, leaning on the open door allowing me to enter. "No Joyce darling, I thought I would come and see if you fancy a date love" I whispered back, sarcastically.

This earned me a clip around the ear for my troubles "You're a cheeky little sod ...Get in you cheeky little horror" she said laughing, pushing me through the doorway. She closed the door behind me, then headed for the kitchen "you want a bacon sarnie David, I'm making Ryan one, so another won't go amiss" she shouted entering the kitchen. "Thank you; I will if you don't mind" I replied making my way into their living room, only now realising I had missed breakfast, with all the commotion, and hearing my tummy rumble. I was hungry, and the thought of biting into a good bacon sarnie made me smile.

Radio one was playing on the radio; it was DJ Peter Powell's Saturday morning slot. Slade was being played. "Mama we're all crazy now" filling the room, vibrating off the walls, I could hear Joyce screaming the words out while doing a head-banging dance.

Ryan was sat on the three-seater settee in his striped pyjamas. "Hey up Dave mate you ok," he asked scratching his head. "You got nits? Scratching your head like that, not sitting next to you if you have" I said, giving him an I don't want them look. "Get lost you knob ...No, I don't have bloody nits" he cried back, hurt.

I bounced on the settee next to him jabbing him in the arm, "Thought I would come and see yer ... What you were doing today?" I chortled, with a grin on my face. "Hey, your mum looks devilishly hot today," I said thinking he would kick off. But no, it was me who was put out by his hysterical reply.

I didn't know if I should laugh or sit quietly.

"That's cos they have just had sex, and you think that's bad, well I could hear them and that's why I'm up already, not what you want any morning let alone this one." Moments later Joyce walked in, (her hair still a mess), with a large dinner plate, displaying six steaming hot toasted bacon sarnies. We looked at each other, a massive grin hit our faces, must admit, so glad Joyce didn't know why, however, the smell of the bacon took over, we eyed each other, as to say "hey you're not having my share", they were soon devoured, followed by a hot cup of tea. With our bellies swollen from our feast, we couldn't move, we sat there stuffed, listening to the radio. Joyce took comfort, in seeing the plate empty.

After a few moments rest, Ryan's face changed, concerned he turned to face me, "You Ok David? How you feeling?" knowing how I felt about Penny moving away. I looked back at him shrugging my shoulders, exaggerated "Not too bad ... the way I see it, I can moan about it or just get on with it ...I choose to get on with it; it's not like I will ever see her again". My face changed, just in that instants, I looked a little lost. Ryan nodded in agreement, "David if It's any consolation, I think we all miss her", he then leapt up and made his way up the stairs to get dressed, I waited on the settee still listening to the radio, "love is the drug" was playing, the last song I listened to with Penny

"Hello, Mrs. Backhouse" the sound of Lisa's voice breaking me from my thoughts, came through from the kitchen as she let herself in. We very rarely knocked on each other's door; we were always told to just walk in, I found that I couldn't do that, I always knocked first. Just the way I was. This got on Joyce's nerves, always shrieking at me to just walk in.

Lisa plonked herself next to me, half bouncing back off, hitting me in the face as her arms waved about, "Oh sorry David, didn't mean to hit you" she said eagerly brushing her hand over my face as if she could remove the strike. "Get off me," I said brushing her hand away. Leaning over she kissed my head where her hand struck me, then rubbed my head again, "That better now David" she said in a child mocking way as if I was a toddler. Lisa looked a lot happier now, her face was clear from tear stains, and looked fresh. "You Okay now … and your dad Okay" I asked, smiling fondly back at me, Lisa nodded, "Yes we are, your mum rang the house saying mum isn't as bad as she looked, and mums' fallen asleep and is resting now." We talked some more small talk waiting for Ryan to return, which felt like an eternity.

Ryan re-joined us on the settee, some twenty minutes later, bouncing in between us, knocking poor Lisa off the settee "So come on guys what we gonna do today?" he said excitedly, checking us both. Lisa stood in front of Ryan, her arms folded, her face scorned at him. I found this funny, a massive grin stretching across my face. "Sorry Lisa, really" apologised Ryan, and before another word was said, Joyce walked into the room "Hey you lot, couldn't do me a favour, could you?" we looked back at Joyce nodding. "Pick up Clive's morning paper for me and some milk please." Clive was a betting man and always had a flutter every Saturday; he would sit in his armchair checking out the form of the Gee-Gees before heading off to the bookmakers to place his bet. Dad joined him some times.

Within minutes we were gone, out of the house heading for the corner shop.

Mr. Patel had taken over the newsagents some weeks earlier; he had taken a lot of grief from the locals. You

266

see, folk around here were slow at change, and didn't like it much. It wasn't that the Patel's were foreign, it was just Mr, and Mrs. Sweet had owned the shop forever, but had decided the time had come to sell up and retire. They were a lovely Jewish couple; We had grown up with their children, David and Angela. Played games and even fought against them once or twice, we missed the Sweet family.

It was a time of change, a new beginning, a time of upheaval, and chaos.

Most of the Jewish shop owners were selling up and moving away down south, and the Asian communities were moving in, taking them over.

Mr. Patel was a migrant from Pakistan. He was a short man who was balding on top; he was a jolly chap who let the prejudice of others go over his head. It had worked; the locals had started to warm to him and his family. Obviously there was still the minority who just refused to accept anyone who wasn't a white person, didn't matter the world was changing and new ideals were taking over.

Mr. Patel who was often confused, questioned me many times about my ethnicity, and if I could speak Punjabi, or some other Indi dialectal, at first, I found it rude, I only saw myself as a white man. Back home I explained this to dad, who in turn explained to me that people only see the cover first, and judge on what they see, he promised to explain our situation shortly. He did tell me I had parentage from Asia. I began to see the funny side and accepted people don't see much further than the colour of my skin, after all, I had seen that and experience this first hand.

"Hello, Mr. Patel can we have the sun paper please and thirty pence mix," Rayan asked, (a thirty pence mix was a large bag of mixed sweets from the penny counter). Mr. Patel would just smile his normal smile, showing off his toothless top gum, almost spitting as he spoke, and me feeling the elbow in my ribs from Lisa, as I tried to hide my snigger.

On the way home, we tucked into a large bag of sweets, Lisa and I go straight for the dainty toffee chews (which were anything but, large penny chews the size of your thumb and rectangular in shape). Leaving Ryan to have the jelly ones, the toffees held too much sugar, and that wasn't good for his condition, this left more for Lisa and me. The plus side for Ryan was, he rarely got a toothache. This never stopped him moaning, we did ask why he never just got a bag of crisp for himself, and we would just have the change for sweet.

Mum had returned home from the hospital when we made our way back into the street; Mrs. Connor had a slight concussion and was resting in her own bed now. Grant was excessively grateful to mum and wouldn't stop thanking her, in the end, she told him to shut up, but nicely. Mum was happy to be able to help, after all the time and help Mrs. Connor had taken during the trial, looking after dad and me. To mum, this was giving something back, and this wasn't gratification on mums' part, she genuinely wanted to help.

Mum stayed at the Connors most of the day, watching over Mrs. Connor.

The beautiful thing about how we lived? Were the simple things in life, the joys, and pleasures of helping each other.

The calm, peaceful sense of well-being that can be gained from watching the plants and flowers grow, watching in amazement as the bees and butterflies hover over, sending out an array of exotic colours. This is what you could find in Grant's garden.

Grant explained his love of the garden to us, saying "Only a person who has witnessed death and misery, and been helpless to do anything, really appreciates life and how precious life is." In his many war stories, he had told many tales of the helplessness. How, he and his crew had to endure, the famine, and the conflicts across the globe, all of which as a British marine and at being at war with no-one, they were not allowed to intervene.

Grant sat in the garden with us kids. He loved his garden, especially on a good sunny day like today. The sun was scorching, sending heat waves across the ground, scorching Grants lawn to his dismay. Not a single cloud in the sky. You could hear the birds tweeting high in the trees, the odd dog barking at their gate as people passed by, the rush of youths excitingly playing, their laughter ringing out for all to hear. Just the sounds of everyday life, in an ordinary everyday street.

Grant did what he was able, but couldn't always manage to do too much, his condition holding him back. Grant's arthritis had spread through his legs, arms, and back, making movement difficult for him, his condition worsening year by year. Still, his garden was the best by far. He never got frustrated when the task seemed a little tiresome than normal; he just completed it a little at a time. He felt useless most of the time, but in his garden, he felt like a king. This was his domain, always keeping on top of it, with minimal help from his friends.

We helped in whatever way we could.

Grant sat on the bench next to the flower bed wall acting out like a sergeant major, barking out his orders. "Lisa pick that crap up and put it in the compost bin." Then turning to me and Ryan "Davie lad pull that half-chewed fruit off the tree, where the birds have gotten to it and place it in the compost, and Ryan fetch me a can of Worthies lad, it's bloody hot out here." It was hot; the sweat was rolling off us, his garden was in full bloom, his assortment of flowers and plant spraying out an abundance of colour, glowing in the sunshine. His own garden of Eden.

Laughing we jumped to attention and carried out his orders without question, Grant was the most respected man in the street, especially to us kids.

I remember him sneaking sweets to me behind Mrs. Connors back and winking. He had taken a shine to me all those years before we moved here, he had seen something in me no other had. Back when we live in the old back to back houses, I regularly found myself sat on the doorstep playing with my Winnie the Poo bear; Grant would push himself over in his wheelchair and talk with me. Mum would watch out of the window. My parents weren't overly keen on the Connors but always saw the good in Grant.

Grant would say I would be a world changer, someone to look out for, he often spoke to mum when he was free from his own wife, mum never questioned him, she knew he meant no harm towards me, and never did. All through the years, he had been my friend, he would give good advice, if you had the ear to listen, and I did. For weeks after Elizabeth's death, I would find myself sat in this garden talking with Grant, he would tell his stories of lost love and the good men who had lost their lives in conflicts from around the world, but he would always re-enforce this with how he managed to go on. His beliefs, carrying his hopes and dreams, and how he got stronger from every tragedy he faced.

Now it was my turn to be the one who gave the time, the one to lend the shoulder, not that he needed one, he was my biggest hero, he had done things most people could only dream of, including my parents. But Grant being Grant, played it down.

The fruit trees harvested a good crop year after year, his Peartree, the dozen or so plump juicy pears, and his rows of vegetables, producing a crop year after year, also gave a good harvest. Grants generosity flowed, giving away his surplus of carrots, onions, peas, and tomatoes to anyone who wanted them, and never asking for anything in return. His reward was the number of free pints from the punters in the local workingman's club on the weekend. Very rarely did the Connors pay for a drink, he had fed the many on these streets when they had nothing. This was the only way they could pay him back; he refused money and gifts, would say "It'll only go to waste if someone doesn't eat it." A gratifying warmth would grip him, knowing he had done his good deed.

Grant sent me over to the dozen or so sticks of rhubarb growing wild in the corner of the yard; they were over two-foot-tall and about 2 inches thick. "Snap one off David" Grant shouted across the garden. With an enthusiastic tug, the stick snapped from the root, leaving me with a two-foot stick in my hand. I raced down towards the rest, and passed it on to Lisa, who instantly ran into the kitchen, washing off any parasites, cutting it into two-inch pieces, plating them and offering them out. We sat on the brick wall and tucked in, the bittersweet sending shivers around our jawlines, so opting to dip them in sugar to help take away the tartness. Grant sat, gut splitting laughter at our facial expressions, almost falling off the bench.

Later that evening mum cooked tea at the Connors house. We joined them at their table; it was a simple meal, a shepherd's pie. Poor Mrs. Connor missing out, too ill, she had slept most of the day with mum awaking her for a sip of water every now and again, to stop the dehydration setting in.

The room fell silent; we watched as Grant held mums' hands, cupping them in his. Grants sorrowful eyes looking up at mums, tears slowly flowing down his face, "Thank you, Maggi, don't know what we would have done without you, bless you darling" his tone despondent and shaky. Mum kissed Grant on his right cheek, "It's a pleasure Grant, and I will be back tomorrow, You two looked after my boys in my time of need, I am going home now, but if you need me just send Lisa and I will be straight over." With that said, we left Grant and Lisa to take care of Mrs. Connor and headed home. Mum felt guilty leaving them.

CHAPTER 22

Best OF Friends Forever.

Dad and Clive had become the best of friends and today they were having a buddy day together.

Gone to the bookmakers to place their bets. Dad would bet every now and then, wasn't an avid gambler, just fancied a flutter every now and then. Clive loved this, an excuse to stay as long as he wanted, not that he needed one, Joyce very rarely ear bashed him. The pair of them were having an afternoon away from it all today, calling at the local pub for a few pints, this, to mums' dismay turned into a day at the bookies and most of the evening at the pub.

Mum said, "This is dad having a blowout, letting off steam." He rarely did this. Mum knew the stress of the last few months had caught up with him, and this would do him more good than harm.

We sat watching the evening movie on the TV. Warren Beatty and Faye Dunaway in the starring roles. Bonnie and Clyde, a couple of notorious gangsters, robbing banks and going on a killing spree in the 1930's.

I loved it, but mum thought it was too violent, she still cooed at Warren Beatty. "Now there's an attractive man," mum said, her head slightly tilted. I snuggled up to mum, and we sat huddled up close, my right arm reaching around mums' shoulders.

The TV continued to flicker in the dark room, no need for the light to be turned on, it was our own little cinema, nothing else to disturb us from our viewing, it was bliss.

To say Dad was drunk when he turned in, was an understatement, staggering all over, I had to leave the room before I burst into laughter. Mum gave him that look, you know the one, where the eyes narrow and the mouth turns upside down, only to be reversed when he gave her the dozen red roses and the big kiss on her cheek, swaying on his feet, losing his balance.

Dad had won big today; an absolute outsider had romped home giving him sixty quid in winnings. Clive hadn't been as lucky, but had won, took home some fish and chips out of his winnings. Dad said Clive was jealous and he didn't want to talk to dad anymore, his speech slurred as he told his tale. Mum and I wanted to laugh, but daren't, never knew how a drunken dad would react.

Dad being so drunk, took himself off to bed leaving mum and me to watch the television. We burst into laughter the moment he walked out of the room, then talked for about an hour, discussing what I might want to do when I leave school next year; I had mentioned joining the army, (Grants influence), getting away from here, try to make my mark in this world. Mum was happy to see me join, but said I had more to me than that and maybe I should sleep on it and see where we are in the morning.

Two days later and the first official day of the school summer holidays, and what were we to do? I found myself pottering around the house, I even tidied up my bedroom, not that it was untidy, just dirty clothes left in a pile, mum generally picked them up every Monday. Mum's wash day.

Dad was at work and mum had gone to the shop for Mrs. Connor, she needed her weekly groceries, Lisa had gone with her to help carry the bags home.

Poor Mrs. Connor was still bedridden after her fall; she was getting dizzy spells when she stood up, so mum called the doctor for a home visit. Grant was told she had to stay in bed for a few days, so he asked mum if she could help him around the house with the chores, mum agreed without any hesitation.

I decided to help mum with our house, mainly because I was bored, and she was busy with the Connors.

The kitchen was spotless, so I had nothing to do there, the living room needed the carpet vacuumed, a few spots of fluff showing, so off I went and picked up the vacuum cleaner. Bemused, and not having a clue how to get it going, I put it back and got the broom instead and started sweeping. The carpet wasn't that bad; I thought I would have had a cloud of dust looming, but not in our house; mum had it practically spotless.

Ryan entered the house, without knocking as usual. "Hello David, you up to much?" he shouted slamming the door shut behind him. "What you doing that for? Your mum does that" he said, looking offended, watching me sweep. "It's Mrs. Connor, she's still not well, so mums helping Grant look after her" I explained.

Ryan made his way into the kitchen to see what was ready to eat in the fridge. "You fancy a cuppa and some trifle David" he bellowed, the trifle was last night's leftovers. "Yeah go for it" I shouted back. We sat on the sofa, both eating a larger than the average sizable portion of trifle, the slurping sound on each spoonful causing us to giggle.

Somehow, we got onto the conversation topic of sex. I was shocked to find Ryan was still a virgin, he could have any girl he wanted, he had the pick from any class in school. Ryan was fast becoming a very attractive young man, we nicknamed him the Saint, his facial features resembling a young Roger Moore, even some of the female teachers would flirt with him, and he was a decent height now, towering a good five-feet eleven. Ryan sat there looking uncomfortable, shifting his position right then left then repeating it over. "Sit still you mingmong," I said getting irritated. It was then the bombshell hit me. He looked at me, and at the same time, blurted out in tears. Talk about being confused, I was gob smacked, watching as irrepressible tears rolled down his face. "You Ok," I asked, bewildered, not knowing what to say.

"David, I don't know if you will still be my friend" sobbing through his words, "What's wrong Ryan? you done something you shouldn't have? I said putting my hand on his shoulder; he shrugged me off shaking his torso rapidly, "Hey come on Ryan what you done?" Me annoyed again, and my voice raised, my patience wearing thin.

Ryan wiped the tears away and began to speak. Blurting out, "David, I'm gay Ok ...and I think I've known this for a long time, Lisa knows, and if you don't like it, then just fuck off" wiping his nose on his sleeve at the same time. "Ryan don't raise your voice like that at me" I said, my eyes narrowing, fixed on him. Lowering his voice to an almost whisper he continued to speak, "She has kept to this going out thing out of kindness, for my sake, to keep my family from knowing, sorry I didn't tell you before. If you don't want to be my friend, I understand." his head lowered to his chest, feeling the strain from telling me, I could see it was cutting him up. "Stop being an arsehole" was the best I could come up with, I looked at him, his head still stooped "Course I'll be your friend, you're my oldest mate. You think because you're a fairy I don't want you to be my friend?." We both gave a little smirk at my words. "What kind of best mate would think like that" I answered punching him in the arm, he followed up by hitting me back. To go punch for punch with him would be a mistake, and a punching competition I would never win, pity the man who calls him a poof to his face. We began to man hug, pulling away fast, and realising how daft we were, we burst into howling fits laughter. We would be the best friends all our lives; nothing could change that.

Seriously I had to ask the question "So, you got a boyfriend." "No" came the sharp reply, "So how do you know you're gay?" I had to ask. "You already know who I fancy," he said giving me his don't ask stupid questions glare. "Don't worry David; it's not like I'm gonna jump on you and .... Well you know what?" he continued. "I understand you're not like that, and anyway I'm not into sex at this time, I will find out when I meet the right guy" he continued. I was taken

277

aback by his words, but he was Ryan and my best mate, also one of the toughest kids I knew.

I was getting confused because when we got back from Butlins, he seemed devastated leaving Kathy and never seeing her again. "So, what about Butlins? What was all that about?" I asked,

Ryan looked wounded again; he slumped down into the sofa as if trying to hide and evade the questions. "It was different, I can't explain, I think I was just experimenting with her," he paused, his eyes firmly set on me, his bottom lip started to quiver as he began to cry again, I put my arms around him and hugged him tightly. "I'm sorry David, I'm not sure what to do now" he continued, sobbing heavily. "It's Ok buddy, I know you will be fine, you still have me, best friends forever," I said wanting to make him see I was alright with it. I felt helpless, unable to get him out of this mood; the sadness he emitted was starting to drain on me too.

The day dragged on, we sat there mostly in silence, Ryan feeling sorry for himself, and me not knowing what to say, mostly meaningless crap came out of my mouth, "So what to do now?" I said falling back into the settee, as far as I could. "Shut up David, if you have nothing to say and I don't know? So, what now?" sobbed Ryan, his face still tormented. He made no sense. I got two more bowls of trifle; this helped cheer him up.

Over the next couple of days, Ryan was on edge. The street got to hear about him. His parents were great with him, and as for his brothers, they just said they had always known, and he was too beautiful to be a real man. Ryan was a lot more comfortable now his family had embraced his sexuality. He felt comfortable in his own home.

However, it was the kids on the street who were cruel and called him names saying they would catch horrible diseases from him if he touched them. His fight tally had risen with some of the older boys in the street and some a lot older than him, but Ryan held his own and beat them down; eventually the street gave him back his street cred. Not many called him anymore. Joyce fretted, she had worried for his safety over the last week, Clive, on the other hand, was Ok with it, he knew his son and knew him well, but he always stood in the shadows waiting to assist Ryan, if he needed it, but he didn't. Clive was proud of his son, more now, he was becoming a man, and with it, more responsible.

Lisa still hung around Ryan as if they were in a relationship, going out together, they both enjoyed each other's company and were inseparable. No matter where me and Ryan went Lisa was always there; I didn't mind, she always fussed over us and was very protective, not that we needed it. I think I fancied her, but I was too scared to tell her.

CHAPTER 23

A Picture of My Parents

Three weeks into the school holidays and mum was fed up, all she wanted was me out of the house from under her feet. I was there most days, bored out of my mind. "Go on, go see what Ryan's doing" she would say, almost kicking me out. I would call for him, and we would get kicked out of his, so we would call on Frank.

Mrs. Shackleton answered the door as usual and as always had to shout Frank out of bed.

He would stumble down the stairs and crash through the living room door, followed by his mum shouting at him, followed by a swipe around the head. His mum had quite a clout, and you could almost feel the impact as she hit him. He would just smile and kiss his mum on the cheek. She just shook her head and walk into the kitchen. Loading us up with biscuits, and filling our pockets, Mrs. Shackleton then pushed us out the door. "Go on boys, go have a good day, and Frank" exaggerating his name, "Keep out of trouble," again not wanting us hanging around her door.

We met up with Tracy; she was looking hot these days, her hair was longer, now passing her shoulders and her dress sense had gone into overdrive, gone had the dull oversized bland clothes, in came the ankle boots, coloured tights, short skirts, and tight t-shirts. Her body was wow! What a shape, it was as if she had transformed over the last four weeks since I last saw her. Frank was well in there; I don't think they came up for air during their five-minute snog.

Ryan burst into laughter at my face; I think I was a bit jealous. He knew just what I was thinking. Frank didn't have the great looks; he was quite an oaf, saying all that, his personality had changed over the last month, also lost about a stone in weight, manners had replaced his hard arse attitude. He was actually a nice guy, Tracy had an influence over him, and Mrs. Shackleton welcomed the change.

With nothing much doing we decided to take a trip into town, jumping on the next bus to the Leeds city centre. We hung around the shops. I still got the odd look by strangers, one even asked what I was doing with these nice white kids, Ryan told them where to go, but not in a polite way, this seemed to have shocked them, and they left rapidly, they didn't dare look back.

Boredom set in quickly, running around the superstores and getting into bother with some of the shop assistants, was becoming mundane, not that we were carrying on, mainly just because we weren't buying, just looking. The day was long, and time seemed to drag, we found ourselves sat outside the chip shop eating a large portion of chips with scraps between us. There wasn't much to do for a fifteen-year-old. You were too old or just too young.

I asked them if they fancied a walk down to the Wellington street army careers office, after all, we weren't doing anything, shrugging their shoulders, they all agreed and followed me.

Inside the three-story town building sat two duty sergeants, both looked up from behind their desk as we entered through the glass door. The place was empty apart from the two of them. Both immaculately dressed in their uniforms. "How can we help you," said the sergeant by the window, he stood up and looked us all up and down. Nervously I approached the desk, "I'm interested in joining up, after leaving school next year" I said just short of stuttering. His hand out, pointing to the chair opposite his, he offered me a seat and got down to the questions, "How old are you and when are you sixteen and why do I want to join." I answered his questions, gaining confidence as I went on. He was a mild-mannered man, about thirty-four, thirty-five? He was probably in the latter part of his contracted service. "Well son" as he offered his hand. "Next time bring your parents, and we can go through the application and don't forget to bring a report on your estimated exam outcome, also you can do our test, so we can get an idea of where you should go." His tone strong almost a command, placing his shovel-sized hand in mine, giving a hearty handshake. "I will," I said feeling pleased with myself. Yeah, I had just got through my first interview.

The rest just looked on; it was as if I had just lost my mind and thrown away my life to them. The other sergeant stood up from his chair, looking straight at Frank and Ryan, "So what about you two strapping lads ...interested?" "NO!" they both shouted retreating through the door, tripping over each other. Tracy just shook her head; the two sergeants gave out a chortle.

Outside the building and with nothing else to do, we decided to catch the next bus back home.

I informed mum and dad that night, told them I had been to the Army careers; they said it was my choice and would help in any way they could. Dad wasn't too pleased; he seemed to be upset.

Mum asked me to join her in the kitchen, while dad sat watching Benny Hill on the TV. We could hear him laughing on the settee. Guess I'm gonna get a lecture from mum on why I should not join the forces.

I followed mum and sat at the table waiting for the lecture to start.

Mum spoke about my arrival into this world and how they had come adopted me. I always knew I was adopted; anyone could see this.

Mum had mentioned this before, but at that time it made no sense. I was happy with mum and dad and told her this, she had no worries on those grounds, I loved her and dad, and they could never be replaced. Not by anyone.

Mum's eyes began to water, but she was fine, it was the memory of my birth that brought on these sad feelings, she was there, the time of my birth and the tragedy the day I lost of my parents. Midwife Pearce had passed me over to mum minutes after I was born. It was mum who cleaned me up and gave me my first feed. Mum had connected with me at that moment, the first time she saw me, looking at this newborn little boy in her arms.

I had never seen a picture of my birth parents; I couldn't say what they looked like or if I resembled either of them? Mum opened the bottom cupboard and pulled out an old biscuit tin box, she passed it over the table, edging it towards me. "Open it David" she paused a while taking in a deep breath, "We have been waiting for the right time to give you this my darling ...It's things that belonged to your mum and dad" the tears were flowing now, her nose running too, she picked up a tissue and wiped her eyes followed by blowing her nose. Mum put the kettle on and prepared three mugs; she needed to distract herself.

I slowly removed the lid from the tin box; apprehension taking hold of me, it was full of paper documents and photos.

Mum sat on the wooden kitchen chair next to me, placing the hot mug of Ovaltine next to the box. Sipping on hers, she spoke softly, "You need to look at these, this is your mum and dad" showing me a photo of a happy young couple, a tall Asian looking man, and a beautiful young white woman, they were finely dressed. The picture was of their wedding day, stood outside the LEEDS registrars building. You could see they were in love; they were holding hands smiling at the camera. He was tall but muscular; she was attractive and reasonably tall too, my mum had been a stunning looking woman.

A sickening ache hit me hard in my stomach, almost causing me to vomit. Holding it back I began to cry, the tears streaming down my face, but I didn't really know why? I didn't know them; I had no real connection with them. Sniffling I went through the papers. I had been left an inheritance of six thousand pounds in an account with my name on it. Mum and dad set this up after the adoption. I would receive this on my eighteenth birthday. The little Lloyds bank booklet had all the transactions written inside. The solicitors had handed the book over to mum as she was my ward of court up to my eighteenth birthday. I put the book back into the box, buried it under the pile of paperwork. Rummaging through the box I found a letter from my dad to my mum, I handed it to mum, and mum read it out loud to me. Mum had read this letter many times, she could almost recite it.

Dear Jane

I am writing to you today to let you know I will be home soon.

I have two more weeks to serve, and then I can re-join you in our home.

The immigration committee said I have won my case and I have the right as an ex-serving officer member of the merchant navy, shipping and supplying the army during the last campaign, I now have free passage in this country. I was proud to serve alongside the British Army in the Pacific. My delay is the paperwork. Also, I have been living here paying taxman for this country for some 9 years now.

I miss you too much, how is your pregnancy doing, I trust you doing well. The food here is terrible, I should cook the food, and it would taste much better. My heart is waiting to see you; I miss you so much and love you so much.

Your husband
Khalil
Xx

"He must have loved your mum so much, I believe your mum was twenty-nine and your dad was forty-one when you were born, we have the marriage license in the box" mum said folding the letter and placing it back in the box.

Their home had been demolished a year or so before our old house in Armley. The money awarded from the house had been placed into a trust fund for me along with any savings they had. He had married mum in June 1957; his occupation was that of a carpenter and mum was a seamstress. I wondered how they met.

There was a letter from the local MP of that time who had written to my mother stating he was fighting for the release of her husband; he said he was not an illegal immigrant and had the right to live here. Mum looked up at me; melancholy filled the room. Tears still flowed from our eyes, we both sat there in silence for a few minutes. "I remember Dr. Jones talking about how your father discarded his injuries for the sake of his wife, your mother was called Jane, and your dad was called Khalil" mum continued to tell me.

I was proud of them, but again I had no idea why, it was like an automatic built-in feeling, it just couldn't be explained, how you can love someone you have never met or known, this reminded me of mum the day Elvis had died and how she was.

I was grieving for two unknown parents. I actually felt a real loss, a sinking feeling grabbed me, weighing me down, I felt sickened for my loss.

Dad stood there in the kitchen doorway; he had been watching and listening to us for the last hour. We hadn't noticed.

It was strange to know who I was and who my parents were. I wasn't confused, but for that short time, in that moment, I felt like, like I was alone, not belonging.

Mum hugged me "You are always going to be our boy David, we love you so much," she said teary-eyed, I smiled "You are my mum and dad, and you will be forever," I declared, tears rolling down my face. We all knew how lucky we were to have each other as we hugged tightly, all three of us. We never spoke much about my birth parents after that day. The tin stayed in the kitchen cupboard.

The following morning, the sky was a bright clear blue, silver slivers of clouds breaking up the blue, like flashes of lightning, the sun on full show, today was the hottest day of the year. Dad had left early for work, leaving me and mum sat at the table eating our breakfast, mum had done us proud, full English, the aroma filled the kitchen, the smell of bacon, the best smell in the universe. "You Okay David" mum asked looking across the table, "I had a bad nights sleep, if that's what you mean mum" I replied. The sound of the front door opening made me and mum laugh; it was Ryan as usual, I'm sure he could smell the breakfast. Mum was smart; she had a meal plated up ready.

"Hello Mrs. Brown, Ooh that smells good," he said with a broad grin running across his face, he knew the reply before mum said it. "Sit down Ryan, got yours ready, and a nice mug of tea" giggling as she set the table. Ryan looked over at me, nodding as if to say, yes this is why I'm here.

Ryan took his time over breakfast; he loved a full English and relished every mouthful. To him, that plate was a piece of art.

We left mum doing her daily chores. We walked over the road to see if Grant needed any help today, well mum sent us, so we just did it. Lisa greeted us at the door, stood in her pyjamas; she looked scorching, we just stood there staring, impure thoughts racing through my head. She was developed well for a fourteen-year-old, and with make up on, you would certainly think she could be mistaken for seventeen. "Come in then," she said oblivious to our thoughts, still holding the door open; we entered the house and made our way to the living room.

Mrs. Connor was sat on their sofa drinking a cup of tea. "Hello boys how are you and thank you for helping out the last few days," she said looking up at us, she still looked pale and weak sat there in her nightie and dressing gown. She was looking older than my mum, who was now fifty-eight, and for a woman, ten years younger, the injury had cost her a price.

Lisa said she was going to do the laundry for her mum, and asked if we would help her with the bags. After some ten minutes of Lisa putting the dirty washing together and getting dressed, we set off on our way to the launderette; I had the large box of soap powder while Ryan carried the full basket of laundry; Lisa just skipped empty-handed, smiling at us. I was amazed at how grown up she had become; she was going to make some bloke proud someday. Lisa knew she was becoming a looker and played on it. Teased me like crazy, she knew deep down I fancied her, and as for Ryan, she knew he was in love with her, but not in a love relation, he loved her like a brother, sister relationship. He cared for her more than anyone else I knew.

It wasn't long before Lisa had the machine going leaving Ryan and me sat outside on the pavement, our backs against the shop wall, watching some young kids playing football across the road, kicking it against the corner shop wall. It wasn't long before Mr. Harris came running out, his face all flushed, waving his fist at the boys as he chased them off, we sat there shaking our heads at him. "You'll kill yourself one day if you keep doing that" I shouted, His health was poor, stood five feet three inches tall and weighed some nineteen stones. "I know, maybe I'll get a dog," he said puffing and panting. "You've already got one; you married her" shouted Ryan spitefully, laughing at him.

"You two can get lost too," he said shaking his fist as he retreated back into his shop, disgust written all over his face.

I agreed with Mr. Harris; this was uncalled for. "What you say that for?" I asked,

"No reason, just thought it was funny" he replied shrugging his shoulders "Just a joke didn't mean anything." I looked at him blankly, why would he be so cruel, and he fought his way to gain his street cred back. I wouldn't mind, but he knew what it was like to be on the receiving end of bullying.

Ryan had changed and not for the better; now he had told the world he was gay, he took it upon himself to be aggressive towards people, maybe this was his inner protective shield, and not seeming to care what anyone thought of him made him feel more secure.

Returning home, I carried the washing, leaving Ryan and Lisa to talk. Ryan had other plans; he rushed over to a group of kids playing a football game on the field. The ball was loose, rolling across the grass, Ryan raced over, lobbing their football yards down the street. Lisa and I weren't impressed, and he knew it too; his body language changed, he went from the boisterous rebel to an inverted shy little boy, he said he would see us later and ran off down the grassy hill towards home. I thought I saw him crying?

"Is he Ok David?" asked Lisa worried, "I guess not" I replied shaking my head. We were both concerned about him; he's all we spoke about on the way home.

It had taken another ten minutes before we got to hers, I dropped off the washing and went home to mum, Lisa followed, jumped up at me from behind, throwing her arms around my neck, leaving me almost giving her a piggyback ride to my door.

Mum was sleeping in her chair, the radio was playing an oldie from the sixties, summer in the city by the lovin' spoonful, and if mum had been awake, she would have been jiving away on her own.

We walked back out, quietly closing the door behind us as not to disturb her.

Lisa linked arms, as we made our way to Ryan's, Joyce answered the door, she stood there looking glum,

"Sorry David, Ryan doesn't want to see anyone today" braving a smile she continued "Try tomorrow love, I'm sure he will be feeling much better then?", "Ok Joyce, tell him we came," I said looking a bit down, "Of course I will David, look you two go enjoy today, he's ok, just a bit sorry for himself at the moment." Joyce closed the door behind her.

Lisa tugged at my shirt, "Come on David …Let's go cause havoc in the shopping centre."

On the way I told Lisa about my family, she kissed me on the cheek saying "David you still have the best parents ever, and the best friends". I knew this and nodded my head.

The day was wasted, we were just hanging around the Seacroft Centre, the awful looking grey concrete two-tiered square block, housing various stores and cafes. Most of the kids on the estate hung about there. We spent time with them for the rest of the afternoon, running around and shouting like loons. The odd shopkeeper taking offence, spouting their mouths off back at us for no reason, just because we were in a pack, and loud.

I got home just after six that evening; the sun was still burning down, there wasn't much movement in the streets, I guess it was just too hot. Lisa kissed me on the cheek then ran off, waving as she entered her garden. Don't ask me why but I think I blushed, what the heck, it was a kiss from Lisa, not like we were going out with each other. However, I was a bit smitten with her.

Dad was sat in his chair and mum opposite in hers. "Sit down David; I've got something to tell you," dad said excitedly, I sat on the settee, nearest corner to them. Mum couldn't help herself and blurted out "We're going to Cornwall," "On Friday for ten days" interrupting dad. Dad didn't make a fuss over mum's outburst, he just nodded.

I looked over at mum saying: "Thought you didn't want to go to Cornwall mum, thought you wanted to go to Spain or France?"

Mum was beaming. "David the summer here is as hot as over there. Your dads got a deal from Mr. Turner at his work. Mr. Turner owns a large converted barn that sleeps up to eight people" mum spoke excitedly, quickly and never took a breath. She had a giddy tone in her voice "And it's only a mile from the beach, so I asked Grant and Doreen (Mrs. Connors Name) if they would like to come, and Lisa of course and that leaves two spaces for your friends ... Who would you like to come?" mum said gazing at me. Before I had the chance to speak dad took his turn in butting in "Ryan of course, who else would he want ...You know they're joined at the hip", I had to admit dad was right. "could I ask Frank as well, If he's allowed to come, and see if he wants to come? I asked, a massive grin across my face.

The three of us just sat there smiling at each other. That night I slept well, no troubles praying on my mind, I knew Ryan would be okay eventually, so I had no worries about him, and he was the primary person on my thoughts of late.

I was at that age when my dreams started becoming exotic, tonight I dreamt of Lisa, funny enough, not in a sexual way but we were walking together holding hands. Then as dreams do, the image faded away.

CHAPTER 24

CORNWALL

Frank was busy helping his dad carry his parent's old double bed over the road to Mrs. Gilbert's house, her daughter had married two days earlier, and her husband was moving in with them.

Mr. Gilbert was happy to receive the bed for his daughter Christine, they couldn't afford the luxury of new furniture, and money was tight in their home, seven kids to feed and only Mr. Gilbert working.

Things would change now Paul was moving in; he worked at the metalworks on Kirkstall road along with Mr. Gilbert, working long hours on the burning furnaces, producing machine parts for various industries. It was Mr. Gilbert who had introduced the two to each other, at their last works Christmas party. The whirlwind romance, followed by making Christine pregnant, and he soon had them married.

Mr. Gilbert wasn't a big man, but his fiery temper could get the better of him. He had his belt out to Christine, the day she told her parents, Mrs. Gilbert stood in-between them, protecting her daughter, "You just touch one hair on her head, and you can get out and leave us forever" she screamed at him, her little frame pushing him to one side. His alternative was making Paul take up on his responsibilities for getting his daughter pregnant in the first place.

Paul was now accountable for both him and Christine. Mr. Gilbert making sure, and not spending another penny towards her keep.

Furniture changed hands many times on these streets. Families couldn't afford new all the time, so hand me down furniture came up trumps for most. One man's trash became another man's riches; we lived simple lives and openly accepted help from our neighbours.

Everyone had something, someone needed.

The large grey delivery van parked outside the Shackleton's. The two men jumping out, both dressed in their green overcoats and leather gloves, taking charge of the new bed, following Mrs. Shackleton to the master bedroom, Mrs. Shackleton directing them to where she wanted it placed, followed by the mattress.

I stood there watching the hype as the new bed was delivered. Frank made his way over from the Gilberts after dropping off the old bed. "Hi Dave, what brings you here?" he said. His dad behind him, interrupting before I had a chance to reply, "Hello young Brown, you all Ok up the street, how're your parents" his voice loud, Detective Shackleton never spoke to anyone, he always bellowed his words, it was a bit like the actor Brian Blessed talking. I nodded in response. I never felt comfortable around him, always made me feel as if I was doing something wrong.

He left Frank and me to talk, heading into the house, Mrs. Shackleton was waiting in the doorway.

"Well go see if you like it, go on ...Go bounce on it"
she said tapping his bottom lightly, you could feel the
embarrassment on his face, his expression was priceless,
it was as if he wanted the ground to open and suck him
in. Everyone in the street creased up laughing. Mrs.
Shackleton gave a curtsy just as she closed their front
door. The delivery van drove off, out of sight down the
road, about half a dozen screeching topless eight to ten
year old's chasing after it.

It was another sweltering day, temperatures soaring
to the highs; most of the kids were topless, running
around playing games, most barefooted. The older kids
were in jeans and t-shirts, which was pretty much the
fashion of the day, gone had the days of short back and
sides, in came the long-haired hippy types, boys with
shoulder plus length hair, from behind it was hard to tell
which sex was which? Frank had a loose perm, to me he
looked odd, his big rounded face housing a loose perm
down to his shoulders. He looked like a hairy raspberry.

"You fancy going to Cornwall this Friday?" I asked
pulling on his shirt. It came out like it was just a hop,
skip and a jump on the number 15 bus route and not the
three hundred and sixty or so miles journey. Franks
face lit up; he couldn't get his words out quick enough,
stuttering "Yes, if I can, if dad lets me."

Mr. Shackleton was very protective of his family;
this could be to do with his job. I spoke to Franks
parents selling them the idea as if it was theirs; they
were happy for him to go as long as he was safe. It
didn't take long to convince them; they said the break

would do him good anyway, with that sorted we made our way back up the street to Ryan's.

Ryan answered the door; he looked exhausted, kind of drained, maybe admitting his sexuality wasn't a bright idea after all. "You Ok Ryan," I asked. "I don't know any more David, I'm confused," he said ruffling his hair and yawning at the same time.

I stepped passed him, making my way to the living room, followed closely by Frank, leaving Ryan stood in the doorway. The room was vacant; no other members of his family were there. The room was spotless apart from the half-eaten bacon butty left on the settee arm.

"What's up?" said Frank shrugging his shoulders.

"I just seem to be fed up. Lately, everybody treats me different now everyone knows I'm gay" came Ryan's dejected reply, "You eating this butty Ryan," Frank asking, already placing it in his mouth, "Guess not" grinned Ryan, watching Frank devour his sandwich.

"Well if it makes you feel any better, you're still the best-looking guy on the estate, and most of the girls would still want you to, well you know what" I chirped in, trying to cheer him up. Ryan smiled back declaring "You know what David Brown, I bloody well am!". Throwing off his top, revealing his six-pack, he raced upstairs and changed out of his panamas. Frank raised his top over his oversized stomach, more of a barrel shape than any six-pack.

"I hate you two, no matter what I do I can never get rid of this fat belly of mine," he said, prodding his stomach, finishing his sandwich at the same time. I gave a little sneer peering at his stomach outstretched over his belt line.

Ryan was back down again fully dressed, ready to meet the day with whatever it could throw at him. The instant change was incredible. Confidence appeared to be oozing out, knowing Ryan this was bravado, a protective front.

Outdoors, the kids in the street were having a water fight, using used washing up bottles to spray each other. Three of the brats attacked us, soaking my shirt through, laughing as they continued to spray us, dancing around chanting at the same time. Four more joined in, soon we were surrounded, unable to escape, ducking and diving we managed to get into my house for salvation, soaked from head to foot.

In the bathroom, Frank grabbed the first towel, throwing the next one to me, Ryan waited until I finished drying off before I passed him mine.

Joyce and Clive were sat there in the living room discussing the holiday with my parents. Ryan was keen to get out of Seacroft, away from the jibes and sniggers from the kids on the estate.

Joyce and Clive were more than happy for him to go, a change would be good for him, may even settle the ill feeling in the streets towards him. Joyce grabbed me and hugged me; I was surprised she had such strength, squeezing the breath out of me.

"Thank you," then thanking mum and dad too, "Just what Ryan needs right now" tears rolled down her face. Joyce was worried for her boy, he had been reduced to a recluse the last few weeks, not wanting to venture out, and spend time with his friends. His playful, happy go lucky approach disappearing.

Ryan was sent off with enough money to last him the week.

Joyce, double checked he had enough underwear too, commenting "Don't you dare get knocked down in dirty underwear, you make sure your clean ...Not having any doctors say my kids wear dirty underpants and socks," her face as serious as a face could be. I was smirking the whole time while Ryan turned red with embarrassment, just wanting to escape.

Packing for the trip to Cornwall was complete, mum had two suitcases, dad and I had one, mums' defence was a lady has to have enough clothes to change into, dad just agreed.

We were to drive down with Frank and Ryan, while the Connors would use the train, Dad had arranged he would collect them from the station.

Mum was getting excited, ten days away from Seacroft. We hadn't been on many holidays, mainly because dad was always working. We didn't go without either; in fact, quite the opposite, many families were quite envious of us. We owned our home and had a decent car, always neatly dressed and had all the mod cons for the house, along with the latest T.V, and kitchen appliances, yes, I guess we had a lot to be thankful for.

It was the night before our holidays; dad ordered us a takeaway, both Frank and Ryan were staying, we were to be leaving early the next morning.

Dad said we need to set off about eight in the morning; the journey was going to take us at least nine hours.

The Chinese takeaway arrived, dad paid, and the delivery man was swiftly on his way. You could smell the food, wafting it's way to our nostrils.

"Ho my God that smells bloody great" yelled Frank, all eyes turning towards him as he shrunk deep into the settee embarrassed. Mum, as usual, plated us up. Frank had never tasted Chinese food before; he was lost in taste bud heaven, having a taste of all the dishes. The four of us looked on amused, munching away.

Mum had opted for the radiogram tonight rather than watch the TV, playing her favourite LP, the Osmond's greatest hits, it had gotten to the third song "let me in", when me and Ryan had to leave, mum and dad beginning their rendition of the songs, well if that's what you would call it. I hurriedly ate my food, kissed mum good night, and gave dad a hug. I speedily retreated to my room, Ryan followed, but Frank stayed and joined in the singing. It became a dreadful pain on the ear, as they all sang paper roses.

Ryan was doubled up in fits of laughter rolling around on my bedroom floor. Thankfully it wasn't too long before everyone was sleeping, apart from Frank, who was as giddy as hell, nudging Ryan and me most of the night. "Ooo, I can't wait till tomorrow" he kept on saying, with his big Cheshire cat smile painted on his face.

"Get to bloody sleep" boomed mums voice across the landing. It wasn't long before the sound of snoring filled the house.

Commotion from dad awoken us all, followed by his constant running up and down the stairs, double checking the windows and rechecking he had not forgotten anything, this was a reminder we had to be out of bed and in the car, ready for him to drive off. To say dad was a manager at his work, he was definitely displaying a lack of control; mum stopped him in his tracks with the bacon butty and hot mug of steaming tea, she finally had him seated and calm. We joined them, the three of us enticed by the smell from the butties. It was only seven O'clock. As always Ryan had to have the lion's share. Frank watching feeling a bit out of sorts, yearning for that last butty, he had no chance, Ryan was already halfway through it.

The car was packed, and we were seated, heading towards the motorway. Mum sat in front next to dad, us three lads in the back, I sat behind dad, Frank in the middle and Ryan behind mum. The sand and sea of Cornwall calling.

We thought it was going to be a long journey for us in the car; the Connors, however, had set off at five this morning to catch the early train and wouldn't be in Cornwall till six this evening, then another hour for dad to pick them up. Even with today's modern transport system, it still took over twelve hours to get from Leeds to Cornwall, a whole day taken up in travel. They were definitely going to be tired by the time they reach the cottage.

Even at sixty-two, dad never faltered while driving. His love of driving had made him relaxed, the tailbacks, with the odd spell of heavy traffic, the heat from the sun and us snoring in the rear seat didn't faze him, he just coolly went about his business on the motorway, mum feeding him humbugs every now and again.

We made one stop at a motorway cafe outside Bristol for a toilet break; now this did upset dad, the ten-minute break became twenty minutes, it would seem Frank needed the toilet more than most. He joined us back in the car, with a massive grin on his face.

The smile on his face was soon removed as dad scolded him for being too long. Frank never utter a word for the rest of the journey, "Harold you didn't need to do that" mum said, disappointed in dad, dad nodded and turned to Frank, "Sorry son, didn't mean anything by it," Frank nodded back in reply. We were soon back on our way heading along the motorway.

Turning off the motorway, dad took the narrow road leading up to the single dirt path road to the converted barn. Dad was finding these tracks hard to negotiate, climbing up slopes and back down again, the twisting hedgerows overhanging scratching the side of dads' car. Dad churned out a few choice words which I found amusing, not ever hearing dad swear as profoundly as this; this came as a bit of a shock for both me and mum. "David shut up ...It's hard enough for your dad, without you laughing" mum scolded at me, I went quite very quickly. Out of the corner of my eye, I could see Ryan shaking his head at me.

Dad applied the brakes, the car came to a halt, dirt from the dry track kicking up in a cloud of dust, leaving the engine idling over. His head turned to us in the rear seat, dad looked tired but sprightly ordered "Frank go open the gate in front of us, and close it when we get passed, there's a good lad" pointing to a large heavy looking gate in between a thicket of privet, blocking the entrance to the dust path leading up to a long one-story stone building. Frank responding, did as dad asked and walked up behind the car as dad drove up the dirt track.

The building was old, built with large stones topped with a slate tiled roof, the window frames were small, ten each side of the building, the large wooden door was situated smack in the middle of the building.

Dad removed the small tree from the green plant pot, revealing a set of keys in the compost. Within seconds' dad had the door opened. In single file we entered. Mum gave a great gasp of delight, the interior was impressive, to the right was the lounge area, a large open log fireplace set up ready for use. Three rooms ran off it, two bedrooms and a bathroom. The left side housed an open plan modern kitchen, again three rooms, two bedrooms, and another bathroom; the one thing I did notice was that there was no TV in the lounge. How would we survive?

Frank appeared in the doorway; he was covered from head to foot in the dust, the colour of grey, he looked like a statue. "What have you been up to?" mum screamed at him, dad just started howling, "It's the dirt

303

from the track, Maggie ...He's followed the car up the track" dad said still laughing. Frank stood there, feeling dejected. Ryan pushed him back out the doorway, myself and Ryan took pleasure on dusting Frank down, intensely slapping his body with force, this was the only time we would get away with this. Didn't stop Frank from cursing, to his peril, Mum scorned at his use of bad language, he fell silent once again.

Mum had fallen in love with the place. It was idyllic, it stood in the middle of a field, bordered by a thicket of privet; the only exit was down the dirt track out through the gate. As you looked down the hill, you could see the small village in front of the beach, and a beautiful calm blue sea, it was picture postcard perfect. This was mums piece of heaven for the next ten days.

It was getting late, and dad had to journey on. He set off to collect the Connors from the Truro train station, Ryan had volunteered to go with him, which left Frank and me to help mum prep dinner and sort out our sleeping arrangements.

Mum started on the dinner, Mr. Turner had his caretaker stock the cupboards, fridge, and pantry with every kind of food you could think of. There was milk, bread, cheese, pork, lamb, and a beef joint and an untold amount of vegetables in the pantry.

There on the top shelve of the fridge was our usual Sunday treat, a cherry trifle. Made me smile, I knew Ryan would be pleased too.

Mr. Turner had thought of everything to make our stay as memorable and comfortable as he possibly could. This must have cost Dad a least a month's wage.

The interior was amazing; it looked like something out of a James Bond's villain's lair, the furniture was white with sharp lines and crisp finishing's. The lighting was small round spots embedded into the walls and ceiling; the floor was highly polished stone tiles throughout. The rear wall in the lounge housed a wooden shelf unit covering the whole wall; it contained a vast library covering all kinds of literature from factual to fiction for all ages.

Mum explored the fridge and pantry seeing what she could throw together for the evening meal; it looks like a shepherd's pie tonight. Mum struggled at first to ignite the cooker, Frank took one look at the stove and got it lit, "Thank you, Frank, I was struggling then" said mum collecting her ingredients, Frank waddled his head, with his shoulders back he swaggered over to me. "You're mum's great; I'm like her little hero" sounding louder than a whisper as he thought. "Yes, you are my little hero Frank and thank you" mum's mocking tone giving an unwanted reply. Frank was flush red with embarrassment.

Within minutes' mum had the minced meat browning and the pot of potatoes and vegetables boiling.

Frank and I left mum busy in the kitchen area, accompanied by the radio, blaring out her favourite radio 2.

It was time to explore our surroundings; the house was situated in the middle of a field covering a vast area, at least two football pitches size, either side of the building, at the far right end of the building was a small tree line, extending out further to the privet hedge. We raced to the far end, past the trees to the privet. A large hole at the bottom of the privet exposed a dirt track on the opposite side. I got down to the ground and crawled through, Frank followed, struggling a little, due to his sheer size.

I stood there laughing as he struggled through, cursing all the way; to make matters worse, he snagged his shirt on a thorny outcrop of the privet and ripped it down the sleeve seam. "For Christ's sake look at this, my bloody shirts ruined" cried Frank as he got to his feet. I was still laughing, so he punched me in the left arm, it hurt, and I soon stopped laughing, which in turn made him laugh.

On examining the area, we found ourselves just feet away from a steep slope travelling the full length of the pathway down towards a river; the slope must be at least twenty meters down, meeting up with a gravelly river bank. Like the fools we were, we started down the embankment. Soon losing our footing, getting faster almost sprinting, we both stumbled and found ourselves rolling down towards the river at speed, unable to control our fall, screaming in-between our laughing as we bounce from one small ridge to another, finally reaching the riverbed. Me hitting my head on a stone sticking out of the grass, lucky for me not too hard, but enough to leave a bruise, poor Frank ended up in the drink, his body weight aiding to the speed and momentum. He sat there waist deep, splashing the water as he waved his arms about.

"This just sucks, now I'm bloody soaked" moaned Frank, not looking too pleased. I offered him my hand to help him out. Instead, he pulled me in, and that was it, we started to pretend fight, dunking each other under, playing around like two wild bear cubs.

"What the bloody hell have you two been up to?" yelled mum as we walked in dripping wet, leaving small puddles on the shiny floor. "get out of those clothes now" she ordered, red-faced with anger at the sight of us. Frank was all apologetic; almost falling over himself, I just went and got cleaned up, placing my wet clothes in the wash basket. Not like she could send me home, my spoilt arrogance showing.

The pie was cooked and resting on the table when dad and his passengers arrived, they all looked worn out, Ryan rushed with their luggage putting it in their rooms. If looks could kill, me and Frank would be dead; Mum sneered at us, "Lazy brats, you could help Ryan" Standing there we both looked shameful, but still didn't move. The smirk on Ryan's face said it all.

Lisa danced around the floor like a giddy school girl, and just like mum had, she adored the decor and the house itself. "How beautiful is this place," she shouted to anyone who was listening, "It's very nice" repeated Mrs. Connor as she helped Grant to one of the large white wooden framed easy chairs. Grant nodded in reply, too tired to speak, the long journey taking it out of him.

We hardly spoke through dinner; we sat quietly eating mums fare. Meal finished, me and Frank were ordered to do the clean-up.

With everyone else tired and exhausted, they all retired as the days' travel had gotten the better of them.

Mum couldn't just leave the washing up to us, she had to intervene, "Ok lads leave the rest to me, go to bed now, you two must be tired so leave it to me" Mum kissed me goodnight and finished up in the kitchen. Glancing back, I could see the happiness shining through. Mum felt my gaze and blew me a kiss, I smiled back, leaving her alone with her chores.

The Connors took to the left side, and we took the right, me, Ryan, and Frank sharing the large bedroom, it had two single beds, and a single spare mattress from Lisa's room made up on the floor. Ryan chooses to use the single mattress for his bed, thus eliminating any conflict on where we were going to sleep.

The house fell quiet, everybody sleeping within minutes..

The next couple of days were fantastic. The weather sustaining a constant high, a pleasant freshness in the air, hitting out all around. The salty sea air, a welcome change from the built-up urban streets that we were used to, and the different sounds, the sea rushing in crashing against the rocks or sweeping across the sand, the sounds of people laughing and singing, the lack of police sirens and the constant shouting from our neighbours battling each other. This was bliss.

The days were still, the sun blazed down, scorching the sands, as we played tippy-toe across to the warm clear sea, trying not to burn the underside of our feet.

T-shirts and shorts were pretty much the order of the day. The carnival sounds from the arcades, inviting mum and dad over, playing the penny slot machines, Grant and Doreen basking in the sun, ice-cream cornets in hand, enjoying the clean open air.

Us kids, we ventured through the local village, investigating the sights, sounds, and smells. Mum purchased quite a lot of brick a brac from the market stalls for our home in Leeds. We experimented with the local food types, the main ingredient being fish. My first and last oyster, yuk it felt disgusting sliding down my throat, the taste wasn't much better, had the rest of them in stitches.

None of us escaped the sunburn. Mum continually complaining it's too hot, Frank in his own world; he was never out of the sea, I took to it also, as did Lisa, we had one problem, Ryan wasn't that good a swimmer and hated the sea.

"It's the movement under your feet, makes me weary of it, I don't like it," said Ryan, looking an unusual pale in this heat. "So, don't come in" I replied sarcastically, a bit disappointed in Ryan, the all-rounder sportsman scared of a bit of water.

Lisa could see this hurt him and gave me a great big shove on my back, laughing as I fell face first into the water, losing my balance.

I clobbered my head hard on the seabed, my head ricocheting, sending the sands into a swirling a mist in front of me. The undercurrent twisting my body further away from the shore. Panicking I thrashed about till managing to find my feet, Lisa was still laughing, I couldn't get annoyed at her, she was like a new bloom, yet innocent and kind, I liked her too much to hurt her feelings and anyway it served me right for being harsh on Ryan. After about sixty seconds I had retrieved my composure, back to normal breathing.

"Sorry David, but you deserved that, you Ok though, I did push you a little too hard" apologised Lisa, looking a bit embarrassed, standing with her hands on her hips. "Yes, Lisa I'm Ok, like you said, too harsh on him." Ryan shrugged his shoulders and made his way to the stone breaker and sat watching, Lisa followed him, to comfort him. I joined Frank; we swam as far out as we could before turning back.

Surprisingly, Grant was a strong swimmer, even though his arthritis slowed him down; he was genuinely enjoying the freedom of movement, He was at home in the sea.

He raced Frank and me to the buoys and back, he was no Olympic swimmer but gave us a run for our money. Doreen looks on from the edge of the sea, a little concerned, the surf eddying, lapping at her feet. Tears of joy rolled down her face, she quickly wiped her face, leaving no trace of her tears as Lisa disturbed her, breaking her concentration from Grant. "Wow mum, look at dad, he's…" Lisa paused, she too was welling up, "He's looks so free mum, and dad's really having fun out there" Lisa continued, pointing out in his direction. Doreen, too taken aback, wept, unable to speak, her hand found Lisa's, and they stood watching, so happy to see Grant finally after many years bound in his wheelchair, moving about unaided.

The day was closing in, and our parents opted to explore the village for its liquid refreshment establishments, finding seven taverns, relishing the taste of Cornwall.

We, on the other hand, were left to fend for ourselves, enjoying the time on our own, time to explore, which is what we wanted, to be on our own.

Lisa was attracting attention from the locals, as was I but for the wrong reasons. It was as if no one had ever seen a coloured person before down here. The girls liked it, but the boys got a little aggressive. One asked Ryan where do you buy one from, referring to the TV program Roots. The lad showing his ignorance. Ryan hated this sick humour, and been total ignorance, he just found it offensive.

Ryan replied in his usual way, punching him hard on the nose. Needless to say, that wasn't welcomed, and we soon found ourselves being chased out of the village, that was until Frank ran out of breath unable to run any further, so decided to take them all on. First one, followed by the second and third, all found themselves lying on the ground nursing their faces, punch after punch from Frank, who now stood with his hands on hips, head held high, with the biggest I fucking showed you lot smile on his face.

The remainder stopped in their tracks, after watching Frank plough through them. Ryan raced back up the street and took his place next to Frank, I followed with Lisa behind.

The tall kid on the ground pulled himself back to his feet, shaken and a little startled, he put out his arm and offers his hand to Frank, Frank took it, keeping at arm's length. "Ok mate, but don't pick on my pal Dave Ok," Frank said, his voice, like his fathers, a strong Yorkshire accent, commanding and intimidating. The tall kid replied, warily "Sure thing, sorry fella" his hand now extending to mine, I smiled at Frank and took the lad's hand. This was the start of a week-long friendship that got us to see places we would never have known about. In fact, had this not happened, I dare say for us kids, boredom would have raised its ugly head, and we could have been squabbling, if not fighting each other.

Outside the beach café, we sat in conversation, introducing ourselves to each other. The tall one, like Ryan, was a sportsman, the two immersed themselves in discussion about the state of football and who they supported. Ryan was a patriotic soul, and only Leeds United could be his team, Kieran the tall kid followed Southampton, they jibed each other for hours. Two of the girls asked how I got my tan so natural and golden. Lisa stepped in (very protective). "He's a natural tan cos he's a darkie, and yes he has sunburn too, just before you ask." Her face was screwed up, offended anyone would even question my skin colour, "Didn't mean anything nasty, I like it, he's quite cute for a northerner" the red-headed girl replied protectively. Lisa found her reply amusing, bursting in to laughter as did the two girls. I was enjoying it, three good looking lasses debating me, couldn't get any better than that.

Nine in the evening, time soon crept up, the sun was dropping into the sea, with the moon rising ready to replace it. The gang of youths left us at the village edge, pointing out the way back to our holiday home.

Mum and dad were drinking the local wine with Doreen and Grant; they were sat outside on the wooden bench, when we arrived back. Both sets of parents looked worse for wear.

Someone was going to be suffering in the morning with a hangover?

The holiday had reached the mid-period point. Grant and Doreen had decided to stay behind.

"We will make a meal for you this evening," said Grant, Doreen holding his hand in agreement. "Ok Doreen, Grant, hope it's going to be nice," came mum's reply, as she was leaving the room to join dad in the car.

Grant shifted in his chair, "I will be making one of my special curries Margaret," mum smiled back at him, closing the door behind her.

Grant had travelled the world during his time as a Marine. He had learned how to cook many exotic foods during his campaigns around the globe; we were in for a pleasant treat this evening.

Doreen set him up at the table, gathering his ingredients. She didn't mind, Doreen was pleased to be helping him, watchful, and caring. To Doreen, this was Grant on a great day, full of life and a willingness to please others. She had seen the bad days, the day when Grant couldn't move, the pain being too much for him to bare, Yet he fought it, as he did any attack on him and his loved ones.

The last few days had tired him out. He wasn't moaning, quite the opposite, he had enjoyed every minute of it. "So glad we came Doreen, happy to see you smile again love," he said glancing up, Doreen had recouped her youthful looks, her hair appeared to have more life and colour, her eyes brighter and her complexion fair. The fresh outdoors agreeing with her. She leant over and kissed him.

Dad drove through the narrow streets and country lanes leading us to the animal reserve. Dad's camera never stopped clicking. Mum posed with the local ranger holding a young red fox, and yes dad was there click, click, the sound of the camera clicking into infinity.

Frank and Lisa went off on their own, looking around the domestic pen, looking at the cats and dogs. Cooing and aweing at all the kittens and pups.

As for Ryan and I, we were bored stupid, not wanting to be there, we made our way around the complex, people spotting, there wasn't much to do for Ryan and me. We were fifteen-year-old boys looking for adventure, not walking around nature reserves. Mum was a bit fed up with us, trying to find something to please us, I had told mum I wanted to meet up with the locals again, but she told me I had to stay, and meant it. If there was the one thing I did, it was never upset mum intentionally and to do as I was asked. Mum knew I was a good kid, so without any fuss allowed us to explore on our own. Mum knew we were up to no good of sorts, nothing malicious, but we did annoy quite a few visitors. All dad said was "Boys will be boys."

We got home late evening, Frank waking us from our sleep, Ryan laying in the floor well between the front and back seats.

Dad opened the house door, and smack; we soon awoken, alertness hitting us as we entered into a room full of exotic flavours, it smelt divine, the aromas filled the room, tickling our nostrils. We fought to get to the sink to wash our hands, and darted towards the seats.

Sitting down to dinner was a culinary delight. The fresh ginger, garlic, coconut, and coriander. The flavours danced on your tongue, sending pleasure signals to the brain, we had never tasted food like it, the sensation was unbelievable. It was like having a sugar rush; my head was exploding, my tongue was dancing, It was food sex! My whole body felt alive, WOW, what an experience.

The spices weren't hot but flavorous, the chunks of lamb tender, almost melting in the mouth. Lisa couldn't contain herself; she had had this food many times before, so found us amusing, every bite gave a different taste. Mum was in food heaven as was I. Ryan and dad helped themselves to seconds, and as for Frank, well he was on to his third dish full. Mum was stunned, she had never seen anyone eat so much.

Grant was beaming; he so was happy to see us all enjoying our food. We never spoke all the way through dinner.

Doreen made her way to Grant and kissed him on his cheek, he responded by kissing her on her lips tenderly.

We lifted our glasses in a toast to Grant and Doreen for the special meal, the rosé wine finished the dinner off, complementing the food.

We kids cleared away and washed up giving our parents a break, allowing them to sit back and relax. The four sat there, pint glass in hand, sampling the local cider, deep in conversation.

Once again Grant surprised us; Doreen had gone into their bedroom and returned with a guitar which she handed to Grant. "Does anyone know about a guy called Duane Eddy?" Grant asked. Mum, and dad obviously said yes, and Lisa nodded her head too, we boys just looked at each other blankly. Grant began to pluck at the guitar, and soon a tune was playing, mum, Doreen and dad were tapping their feet in time to the music. "For all you young ones, this is called rebel rouser, this was a smash hit back in the fifties," said Grant taking in the plaudits. Soon after we were all singing summer holiday as Grant played his guitar.

I wanted Grant to know how much I looked up to him, how much of a hero he was to me. If I grow up showing the same strengths and aspirations, I think I will grow up to be a good man. I sat there watching him, then looking around the room. Grant had his audience fixed, he controlled this small but precious time.

Doreen noticed mums concern, watching Grant playing, she knew Grant was in pain, but she also knew this was something he had to do, after all this was his holiday too, and this was his way of giving her and Lisa a memory to share.

As the night played out, the sky filled with a million stars, mum, dad, and I lay on a blanket outside on the grass, looking up into the night sky. The night was warm, and you could feel the heat on your body as the soft breeze passed over, mum brought me in closer, same with dad, "Look up there David, could be a star that has never been seen before, out there and we could be seeing it for the first time" mum said softly whispering as if not offend them, pointing out, arm fully stretched. This made me smile, the thought that out there, there are still many things to explore and find.

Lisa placed a blanket next to me and joined us. The stars floodlit brightly against the black of night, they seemed to go for an eternity, lost in space. We laid there for about an hour, trying to make out the shapes of all the constellations. We eventually joined the others inside. Yawning as we entered.

Enveloped in peaceful silence, we slept on full stomachs and contentment. Safe under the heavens of a million shining stars, the night passed peaceably.

Mum was startled, almost choking on her own spittle, the loud rap at the door, had mum rushing out of the bedroom to answer the door. We were all still in bed, unstirred to all the commotion. To mum's disappointment, stood six local lads and eight girls. Mum looked like she wanted blood, who would be waking a group of holidaymakers up at this time, and why? "How can I help you?" she said giving them an odd look, "Hi I'm Kieran Thomas from the village, is Frank and David about," he said, "There in bed, why? What do you want with them, it's only six O'clock, you mad or what?" hollered mum, looking anxious and cross, the group looked at each other confused, "We're going down to Fisherman's Cove, just off the harbour road turn off" blabbed the short spotty kid. Mum a little disorientated and very cross told them to wait there while she checked this out with us.

"David there's a group of kids at the door asking for you and Frank, what you been up to?" mum said raising her voice, waking me up. Mum practically shaking me out of my bed. After a few grunts, I came around and went to the door dressed only in my pyjama bottoms. Mum made her way back to bed.

Rubbing my eyes, I saw the gang of kids stood there, all hyper, wide awake and ready for the world, crazy bastards I thought, my mind trying to register the image. "Hi guys," I said as I reached the doorway, the picture becomes clearer. "Hello David," said one of the girls. I had never seen her before, but I had to say she was a good-looking lass, tall and slender, probably my age too. Wow was the first thing ringing in my head; I could feel the smile stretching across my face, her flame red hair was wild, twisting in all directions from her head down below her shoulders, "Hello" I said surprised. "We're off to fisherman's cove, David you coming?" said the short spotty kid, almost jumping on the spot. I stood talking to them for about another five minutes, Frank joined me, hearing the commotion, mum was back up, not able to get back to sleep, pottering about, chuntering to herself in the background.

We decided to meet in ten minutes by the gate. I got Ryan up then entered Lisa's room, to wake her, she was sprawled out on the bed wearing just her knickers, at almost fifteen her body resembled that of a young

318

woman. I could see Lizzy laying there. I yearned to join her and hold her; the image disappeared after a few seconds. Lisa shuffled in her bed showing off her perfect breast, momentarily I found myself standing there, the teenage tingle working its magic, all of a sudden I felt guilty, embarrassment filled my emotions, my tingle subsided super quick. I walked back out quietly as not to disturb her further.

Embarrassed, I explained to mum I needed her to wake Lisa, mum kissed me on the cheek and said she was proud of me for respecting my friend. It wasn't easy for me; I saw Lisa in a whole new light. She wasn't just the girl next door anymore.

At the gate, the gang waited. "Hey, here they come" shouted the short spotty kid, they all turned to face the house; we all were walking down towards them, every one of us chewing on a jam butty.

We left the field closing the gate behind us, trailing off down the hill following the winding road. We travelled for hours by the cliff edge; we had passed the village over an hour ago, we were now walking down the beach to the craggy rock formations in the distance. The beach was pebbly and uneven underfoot.

The tall kid explained the reason for the early call; it was that when you take the beach route, it takes up to three hours, and that allowing the tide to be out by then. The sea became more aggressive the closer we got to the cliffs on the knoll side, sticking out from the lower grassed sandy dunes, as a prominent land feature. The calm sea was left behind with the peaceful white sandy beaches; the waves now threw themselves at the rock formations thrusting out of the sea joining the pebbled, uneven rocky beach. Flocks of seagulls perched, darting into the sea every now and then, claiming their prey. It was fascinating to watch as they dived, almost disappearing into the waves, then reappearing with a fish hanging from the beaks. We stood there in awe.

Kieran stopped, placing his hand above his eyes shielding himself from the sun, scanning the cliff side, "It's over there" he said pointing out at a rock face some twenty meters away, the face looked to have a hollow, a dark shadow seemed to show itself, running halfway up the rock face. The closer we got, the more noticeable the opening was, "Wow what's this then?" Lisa said, amazement showing on her face. We all took a few more steps closer to the entrance of what seemed to be a gigantic and incredibly deep cavern. "This my friends are the old smugglers access to fisherman's cove, a lot of ships went down in this area," Kieran said, the rest of his friends nodding in agreement.

A slightly small framed girl pointed out to what looked like a rock sticking out of the pebbled beach just short of the water's edge. "You see that there, it's a ship, got grounded back in eighteen hundred and somat, it's been mentioned, the locals did it by not lighting the fires to guide it in," she said enthusiastically, jumping and pointing at the stated rock. Ryan was like me, loved history, "Is it ok to check it out?" he said looking at the girl, she responded by nodding eagerly, already darting for the outcrop. We all followed, towards the jutted outcrop of rock, it was unbelievable, the shape of the ship could still be recognised, the port bow was missing, the rest seemed to be there, granted covered in barnacles and rocks formed from the sand and sea over the years.

I was wishing I had dad's camera now, these would have made great pictures. Ryan was finding it hard to take in, the full length of the merchant ship was still visible, well the deck height. The decking was again rocks, but you could make out the shape, the main mast had been removed along with the smaller pole, probably days after it had met its demise. "Why didn't they use the ship as scrap?" Ryan quizzed the girl, "They will have taken what they could carry before the insurance companies, and ship owners could investigate" she replied smiling at him. "She's a boffin about local history," said the short lad scratching his head and pulling a nonsensical face at the girl, she replied with a two-fingered salute, we all erupted into a burst of laughter as the short kid grunted, scurrying off towards the cave.

The Ship shimmered in the sunlight and the dampness of the sea, reflecting a kaleidoscope of colours. "It's said when two lovers kiss for the first time on these decks, they will love each other till their dying day," said the flamed red-haired girl pointing down to the deck, I jumped into the centre and closed my eyes waiting for her to kiss me. Lisa leapt onto the rocky deck and lunged towards me, kissing me hard on the lips, I responded by kissing back, the taste was good, the feeling stimulating my senses, A little taste of heaven. I opened my eyes. Surprised, but not in a bad way, I saw Lisa standing there and not the redhead; I kissed her again. To my surprise she didn't pull away, this pleased me. Lisa leant forward and whispered in my ear "you like me don't you" then walked away back to where Ryan stood. I did like her, I liked her a lot, but this time I had to wait, couldn't do the falling in love thing again. I made my way to Ryan, passing the red-haired girl. "You're a lucky guy to have someone feel that way for you," she whispered as I passed her, I nodded. Ryan and Frank teased me for most of the day about Lisa; I didn't care, I was secretly admitting to myself I had a real fondness for her. Lisa took it all in her stride; she purposely clung to my arm to fuel their taunting.

Spotty kid tugged at Frank, " You hungry big lad" he said tugging harder, It was just short off midday. "Yeah, bloody am at that" replied Frank rubbing his belly. We sat at the entrance eating the home made Cornish pasties the girls gave us. "You like our pasties?" asked the flame headed beauty, looking directly at me, Lisa moved a little closer, almost rubbing shoulders with me, this made the girl smile. "Do you have a boyfriend?" Lisa asked the girl, "No, but I've kissed most of the good looking guys" replied the flamed headed beauty, Lisa shook her head, a, I respect you girl grin across her face.

With our lunch break completed, Kieran marched us deeper into the cave, leading us through the narrow, twisted chambers, the dampness of the walls lent to a smooth finish. Silt gathered on our fingers as we ran our hands across the cave walls, silky smooth to the touch. Taking in the stalagmites and stalactites formations, twisting upward and downward, tapered ends meeting, the sight was beautiful, the anaemic colourless shapes, shining like polished ivory pillars. Frank tried to pull one off, without hesitation, one of the boys pushed him hard on the back, hollering "Hey Numbnuts you know it takes a hundred years or so for these to form like that, don't need some big oaf like you destroying them" total disgust displayed across his face. Frank apologised, patting the lad on his back, at the same time warning if he shoves him like that again he will pulverise him, the boy didn't flinch. This impressed Frank, who kindly apologised this time. Ryan asked what were the stalactite coloured objects littering the floor; The young smart girl stepped in. "These are old pot wine or rum flask taken from the ships, like the stalagmites over the years have formed into these" Ryan squatted down rubbing his hand over one, "Wow how smooth are these." "They would be perfect if you took one and stripped off the built-up silt from them" replied the girl. Ryan was impressed; he joined arms with the girl, they walked on, discussing the cave.

The climb was arduous, the steeper the cave became, leading to the opening. Eventually we found some steps carved out underfoot leading to a thick wooden door that had seen better days, the warped shape no longer fitting the frame. Sunlight shimmering through the gaps, giving a glimmer of life to this lifeless hole, the moss growing up the sides of the walls diminishing to nothing as the light rays disappeared.

The bright light of the sun played havoc with our eyes as we struggled to focus, giggling like school kids as we bumped into each other, blinded from the contrast of daylight against the dimness of the cave, slowly we refocused, planting our backsides down, so not to fall.

It was hard to believe we had made our way back to the top of the cliffs just yards from the path leading to the village below to the right of us. I thought to myself why didn't we just go down and back up the cave, would have saved about half a day.

The Stoney dirt path, leading down some two hundred meters to the village was empty, a clear road, we started to race down the track, yelling loudly, screaming, and laughing, mocking the slower behind us.

Ryan was meters ahead of the rest, followed by the short kid, who was really fast for his size, the rest followed tapering off to three of the local girls lagging behind. At the foot of the village, we waited for the three girls to catch up, one was hobbling, you could see why; she was wearing her platform boots. They caught up moaning and chuntering amongst themselves, Kieran told them to stop bickering and headed off towards the village centre, we followed chatting idly amongst each other.

As the day passed, the crowd of local kids got less till only Kieran and the flame-haired beauty was left, they escorted us back up the road to the farmhouse, we all shook hands, Kieran smiled, moving closer to Lisa and pecked her on the side of her face. With a tilt of her head and a wink of her eye, she thanked him. The Red-headed girl grabbed me and planted her lips on mine, she knew she was fuelling the fire for Lisa, but didn't care. Wow, it was good to come up for some air, but she was good, and she knew it. She gave me a dirty grin, followed by a naughty kiss on the cheek. Lisa was watching; you could tell she was put out but tried to hide it.

Saying our goodbyes, we watched as the two slowly walk out of sight. I put my arms around Ryan and Lisa as Frank linked up with Ryan, we strolled towards the house exhausted from our day with Kieran and his friends. We had run riot in the village centre, causing mayhem for the local shop's owners and shoppers alike, just pranking about.

"Hi, you kids have a good day," asked Grant shuffling about in his wheelchair trying to get comfy. "Yes, was great dad," Lisa replied "We went into this long cavern that led from the beach to the top of the cliff just meters away from the village" she turned to us for confirmation, "Was used for smuggling" Frank butted in excitedly. Grant smiled at us, he pushed himself closer towards the settee where we were all seated, then he began to tell his story, from back in time, during his marine days, a time when he and his buddies were protecting a strip of the river along the Nile, and how he could tell them, describing everything to the last detail, they had clashed with the river pirates.

We loved to listen to his stories even though they were stretched a bit. He always had a medal to show at the end of his stories to make them more authentic. His medals were for marksmanship, sports tournaments, but most were for genuine bravery, there was one time when he had swum out to sea to help passengers on a capsized yacht, that had hit a rock smashing the hull of the vessel. He had saved four people's lives that day. Grant was a genuine hero. Not that he mentioned it much. But we loved him all the same.

As the final days of the holiday came to a close, we spent the days on the beach. Playing football with the locals, while our parents sunbathed. Mum had a fantastic time; she got her chance to drink an exotic cocktail under a palm tree.

Dad had done his David Bailey impression, taking many photos, camera always in hand. We did all we could to avoid him. Click, click is all we got from morning until night, and he was eager to have them developed, couldn't wait to be home and get his slide show revealed.

Doreen and Grant were splashing about by the sea edge, Doreen giving the odd shrill as the water hit above waist height. Lisa, Frank, Ryan and I would keep running in and out of the water, Ryan stopping just short of shoulder high, which had been a vast improvement on his first day here, the rest of us swam out as far as we were allowed. It was great to have Kieran and his gang joining us. Lisa noticed I was watching the flamed hair beauty, as she danced in and out of the surf in her two piece bikini. She was a beauty, her body was all girl, and Lisa knew it. "David, stop looking at her" Lisa said prodding my side, I turned and winked back at her, "You can't be jealous, were friends, but best friends, and that's all we are" I said, giving another wink. Lisa just shook her head, left me standing there, I watched her disappear in to the sea, swimming out as far as she could, joining Frank.

I knew I had hurt her feelings, but I couldn't hurt her, and not wanting to hurt myself too. We were too young, maybe in a couple of years if we still have the same feelings, this cut me up, because I really had fallen for her, but I'm not doing the love thing now, I know all too well how it feels, when it all goes wrong.

We found it all quite emotional, saying our goodbyes to our new-found friends.

Kieran and the hot redhead, hugged us, saying they would miss us all. Lisa and Frank left the group, heading back to the lodge, I shook Kieran's hand for the last time and pecked the girl on the cheek, she smiled "Take care guys, been fun" Ryan and I nodded in agreement and headed back too. That evening we all mucked in cleaning the converted barn, it was spotless. The night passed in silence, each keeping our thoughts to ourselves.

The next morning dad had to travel over to Truro, delivering the Connors to the rail station for their return train journey back home, then drive back to pick us up for our trip home.

The drive home was long and tiresome, hot too, the sun never letting up, dad was tired and found it hard going.

We got back home sometime after seven that evening, Frank kissed mum and shook dad's hand, thanking them for a great holiday, saying he'd had an excellent time, wishing Ryan and me a good night before heading down the street. Ryan stayed at ours that night. Dad finished sipping from his favourite mug, kissed mum, "Won't be too long love, just going to pick up the Connors from the station" he said receiving a return kiss from mum.

CHAPTER 25

FAREWELL MR CONNOR

Leeds city centre train station was bustling as usual; the dense crowds of commuter's toing and throwing from one platform to the next, the mixed smell of diesel and fresh coffee irritating the nose, and the constant, muffled messages over the loud speakers.

On this occasion, a little more hectic, the police and paramedics were racing from platform B2 to the emergency station, where the ambulance was waiting. Mrs. Connor almost sprinting, to keep up, her body showing signs of strain and fatigue as they placed the stretcher inside the ambulance.

The ambulance sped off at high speed, no hesitation, the siren sounding over every other sound.

Dad confused places the Connors baggage into the car. Lisa lost for words, too upset to speak, sits in the front passenger seat, reaching out and closing the door behind her. Dad says nothing, he too in shock, he chooses to drive home in this unnatural cold sad atmosphere.

Mum was shocked to see Lisa with dad; mum had dads fish supper plated out on the table ready. Not that he had an appetite now. Not knowing the reason, mum began to set out another plate.

Lisa's face was pallid, rimmed with dark circles around her eyes, the watermarks running down her face, the tell-tale signs of her sobbing. Mum placed the plate on the table, then stopped, realising this was so odd, she turned to look at Lisa, "Hello Lisa, you all right darling" mum said placing her arms around her, seeing she was more than upset, Lisa was heartbroken, sobbing on mum's cardigan. Mum ushered Lisa to the sofa. Ryan took over from mum, he supported Lisa on his shoulder, through sheer exhaustion, she fell asleep, still, a whimper now and then. Ryan sat there, not daring to move, he didn't want to disturb her, he didn't want to see her hurt anymore. Tears ebbed from his eyes as he listened to dads tale. Dad explained that Grant had passed away on his journey home. Mum held back her emotions; her thoughts were with Lisa, she saw that Lisa was to be taken care of first, making her a priority and getting her as comfortable as she could.

I sat there in a daze; the unthinkable had happened, my friend had passed away, in an instant, like a flash of lightning, I was only saying see you back home to him twelve hours earlier. How? The questions running, racing around my head, poor Mrs. Connor, poor Lisa, not the way you end a holiday, you should be still excited, shouting and reminiscing of the time spent, not grieving.

Lisa now laid on the settee, sleeping, still whimpering like a puppy in its sleep.

Dad decided to contact their boys; he was on the phone to Germany speaking to Cliff; dad couldn't hold back his tears any longer as he explained about his father passing away during his journey home from Cornwall. Grant had suffered a heart attack. Dad got through to Darron in Covent Gardens in London and told him the same tale. Unfortunately, he was unable to contact Robert who was somewhere in America.

With Lisa now having to stay, I made up the spare room, Ryan carried her to bed aided by mum.

Mrs. Connor spent the night in the hospital chapel praying and speaking with the priest.

As morning broke the night sky, the early birds seemed to have come out to sing their song of sorrow, for the loss of Grant. The sound was eerily, haunting, yet right, unusually right. Ryan and I entered Grant's garden; the trees were full of birds, all varieties, they perched there, continuing this haunting sound, it made me feel uneasy, this was very spooky, nothing like this seemed normal. When you normally enter a garden, the birds would take flight to the next yard, but not today, it was as if they were paying homage to Grant.

The garden would be empty now without Grant tending to the fruit trees and plants, sitting amongst the bushes telling us his stories, sharing out his bounty from his fruit trees and shrubs.

Dad arranged to pick up Doreen from the hospital. It was early but Dad didn't care, he still owed her for looking after him all those moths before.

Mum welcomed her in with a cup of hot tea, "would you like any breakfast Doreen?" mum asked, "yes please" said Doreen, her tears had passed with the comfort from the priest's words last night. Been a religious woman she believed Grant was now going to a better place with no more pain to suffer. Dad made the breakfast, leaving the women to talk.

Mum explained, Lisa was sleeping upstairs, Mrs. Connor asked if we would leave her to come around on her own, mum agreed without question.

Both sat on the sofa eating rounds of toast and sipping on their hot tea, the two of them lost in conversation.

"How did it all happen," mum asked giving her a heartening look, not wanting to upset Doreen further. Adjusting her posture Mrs. Connor made herself comfortable, then began her tale. "We were just getting passed Sheffield, that's when Grant squeezed my hand, so I asked him what he wanted? if he was Ok ...Grant turned and smiled at me, I could see then something wasn't right. He told me I had been a good wife to him, and that he never strayed and he had always loved me" tears started to cascade from her eyes, but still she smiled, mum passed her a clean cotton hanky. The room was silent, gloomy, Yet Mrs. Connor wasn't unhappy, yes she was sad for the loss of Grant, her face even though was crying had an half smile, Doreen wiped her eyes and cleared her throat before she continued "Grant kissed me and told me not to worry, the boys would see him right, at first I didn't understand, but I do now ...Lisa saw the whole thing and was crying by then, noticing he wasn't looking right. Grant kissed her and told her to keep up the good work at school, telling her she would go far," mum joined her in the crying now, both women sat there sniffling into their cotton hankies. The two women sat in silence. Dad stood in the kitchen doorway silent releasing tears of his own.

Mrs. Connors hand clutched mums firmly. "Grant ask me to thank you and Harold for a lovely holiday" looking up at Harold, her face still smiling. Harold nodded too upset to speak. "said he knew it was his last. He told me I should carry the memories fondly and not grieve too much, but celebrate his life and live a strong life for the both of us" the tears were like flowing rivers as the two sobbing women consoled each other. Now the hurt was ebbing it's way in, an emptiness growing inside her. "I miss him, Margaret ...He smiled at us both, He had that sparkle in his eyes, the one when he tells you he loves you, you know it's true cos the sparkle makes you feel good, ...then he just closed his eyes and passed away. He never showed any pain he may have suffered" sniffed Doreen. "That's the way he was Doreen," mum said embracing her tight "He was a Marine through and through, always taking any problem in his stride" mum continued. "That was the problem; he never saw one, even the day he was told he would have to use a wheelchair for the rest of his life, all he did was thank the doctors for their help and just got on with it, me? Well, I was crying like a little girl the day they gave us that news" came the words from Doreen, now resting on mums shoulder.

The two women sat there for hours talking about better days and shared their memories. "Do you know Maggie, Grant blasted me the day I ranted at you and Harold bringing your newborn home, he told me I was wrong back then, and what you two were doing for this child was wonderous, I know now how wrong I was, and how much my family owe you. over the years with your handouts and help." Doreen's sincere look made mum cry even more. "Doreen Connor you owe me nothing and what you said or didn't say, is well buried in the past, how do you think I managed during the trail and how we got through poor Elizabeth's death, It was you who helped me through, and don't you forget that, you owe me nothing" replied mum sternly yet meaningful. The two women embraced tearful, shaking as they sobbed.

Lisa enters my room. Stood in the doorway She can see instantly I'd been crying, she shuffles in closer and sits on the edge of the bed with me.

Lisa had done most of her crying last night, the truth of Mr. Connor's death had just clicked into place for me, returning from his garden.

Ryan left the garden returning home heartbroken and teary-eyed, telling his parents of what had happened. Clive and Joyce were over in a flash on hearing the news, to offer their condolences to Doreen and Lisa.

Dad met them at the door, Clive flung his arms around him, blurting out tearful "What the fuck Harold, how?" Harold just shook his head "I don't know Clive, I just don't know" they stood embraced in the doorway crying like two lost boys.

Joyce made her way to join the women sat in the room. Wasn't long before Doreen's tale was retold.

Lisa held my hand and placed her head on my shoulder. "It's Ok David ... I don't think dad suffered much; he said a lot of beautiful things before he passed away ...He knew he was dying," the tears getting the better of her now, "I don't want to cry anymore, David ...I do miss him, but he was brave, right up to him closing his eyes" the tears and sadness chipping away at her words. "It's Ok to cry Lisa ...look at me? I can't stop now ...I'm gonna miss Grant and his stories" I said to her, we both gave a little grin at the thought of Grant telling one more of his war stories. Our head collided as we rested on each other, sobbing, hurting, and yearning for it to stop.

The funeral took place three days later; it was a small gathering, the Connors, Backhouses, a few neighbours and us. Dad and Clive held one of the ropes as they lowered the coffin into the earth. The day was peaceful, serene and calm, even the birds were silent above in the trees. The sun was high, sending out a mellow warmth. Grant was now at peace, no more pain, and if I know Grant, he's sat on his cloud smiling down at us.

We toasted Grants memory in the Melbourne pub, The snug room full, most of our neighbours each taking solace from the next. Doreen was overwhelmed and thanked us all for coming. The coins filled the jukebox. Dwayne Eddies Rebel Rouser filled the room, we all smiled at the memory of him playing his guitar, Dad swore he could taste the curry from that night, mum held him close telling him it was because we all missed him. We all could feel something or hear something that reminded us of him. I could have sworn I saw him standing proudly in the doorway saluting us, wearing his Marine uniform, then realising I was stood there saluting back at the doorway. Needless to say, I got a few odd looks, yet no one questioned my actions. Doreen said, "She could smell lavender everywhere she went," it grew under their bay window in pots on the pavement.

The only one of their children missing, was Robert, no one was able to contact him.

The rest of us drank late into the night, reminiscing our favourite times spent with Grant.

It took another four days before Robert finally got the news, Poor man, he was devastated, he was the apple of his dad's eye, Doreen was happy to see him back home, Doreen and her children sat for hours recollecting about their childhood and how their father had influenced them.

Doreen's only wish, was for Grant to have seen his boys one last time, before he had passed away.

CHAPTER 26

THE TRUANT OFFICER

No one was ready for the last year of school, not even the teachers. All we got from them was "You need to start thinking about what you will be doing when you leave school next year. Don't forget, it's your exam results that make or breaks you, do well, and you could be looking at college or for some of you, university?". All the teachers now singing from the same hymnbook. It really wasn't the best of times.

The atmosphere in school was tense; the pupils were panicking a bit too much. The stress levels elevated, bringing down the moral and the enjoyment that school has to offer, friends bickering over little unimportant issues, this kept the teachers happy, mainly because they could control us better, as our thoughts were about our grades and not the playful school pranking and getting each other into trouble.

I missed not having Penny around. I yearned for her beautiful face to be looking back at me, teasing me with her big eyes and wide-mouthed smile as she flaunted herself. Her gentle prods in my side, when I would pretend to ignore her, life at school was quiet for me, now that she lived in Canada, it seemed a lifetime away. I took my consolation from my close friends Ryan and Frank.

Ryan was having a tougher time of it; now the schoolyard banter had gone full circle condemning him as a leper, now they knew he was gay. Mr. Graham had taken it upon himself to persecute Ryan. This did not bode well for anyone. Ryan was not going to take this lightly and found himself expelled from school for punching the living daylights out of Mr. Graham for his constant barrage of homophobic gestures towards him.

The local authorities left the complaint well alone, not wanting to get involved with any of these issues, mainly because the topic of homosexuality had become big news over the last year or so. The school didn't need that kind of publicity to drag it down.

Mr. Graham was fortunate that Ryan and his family didn't take it further; this was mainly because Ryan didn't want his parents to get involved and dragged through the mire. He knew he would be Ok, and that he could handle it.

Mr. Grahams job was safe, but only after he had been given the Scarborough warning from the Headmaster, that if any more of this comes to light, his head would roll. Mr. Graham was more tolerant after that, he looked wounded and was extremely wary of Ryan, and Ryan knew this.

Every morning was the same, a bit of a groundhog syndrome. I would meet up with Ryan at my gate, call in at Franks, this was always fun. He was never up and always got scolded by his mum, "I swear Frankie boy, one day ...Yes, one day" pointing her finger at him "I'll .... well just one day Frank," she said to him, making no sense at all. Frank just looked blankly at her, collected his coat and a couple of rounds of toast from the toast rack on the table, and we would be off, making our way to school.

Frank's face would light up instantly he clapped his eyes on Tracy in the schoolyard. He had become quite smitten and a softie when he was around her, but don't let that fool you, if you got on the wrong side of him, then woe betide you. Old Badass Frank turned up.

Something amazing happened, changed the outlook in school and everywhere around us, you couldn't go anywhere without this burst of euphoria hitting out.

The school was in Grease mania. The hit movie was the talk of the town, all the girls swooning over every picture of John Travolta, all the lads drooling at pictures of Olivia Newton-John in her leathers. It was a crazy end to September, the harsh realities of the last year of schools carefully studying diminishing, taken over by song and dance. The schoolyard replicating the hit songs from the movie. The teachers were great; most of them would be singing a tune of sorts from the film. The Grease mania had impacted on morale, giving what seemed, the whole of the UK a lift. It was daft, unreal, people sang and danced around, whiles doing their usual chores, even my mum and dad pulled off their rendition of summer nights, must admit, always had me in stitches, watching my parents carrying on like this most mornings.

Frank and Tracy had a movie date together. They had watched Grease, you guessed it, all they did from morning till night was act out the two main characters, this drove Ryan and me mad.

I wouldn't mind, but Frank had no singing voice at all, Tracy, on the other hand, could actually sing, which again surprised us all. She was a smart, attractive, talented girl; the future held high prospects for her. Frank was right to brag about Tracy, at first, we all thought he was mad, Tracy was dowdy and drab when I first met her, however since Tracy met up with Penny and Lisa, her outlook changed, and now bright and colourful, and full of life, able to express herself freely. She had positively transformed from an ugly duckling into a beautiful swan. She was good to be around; her positivity absorbed freely. Tracy had become one of those individuals everyone enjoyed being around.

Autumn weather was now setting in and over the next few months leading to Christmas, the cold rainy wet days had taken its toll on the absent reports. The majority of pupils and teachers alike had gone down with the flu over the October and November months. The torrential rains and high winds causing more of a chill than normal. The flu epidemic had spread through the nation like a wildfire.

This was a busy time for the truant officer, always making it, its business to visit our homes.

"Hello Mrs. Brown, I am calling to see why David has not been at school over the last two weeks," said the thin man (resembling the child catcher out of the Chitty Chitty bang bang movie). Mum looked at him; dressed in his unpressed blue suit, and wet through dirty white over coat, her anger displayed freely on her face "Are you all stupid ... You are aware of the flu epidemic that's doing its rounds" mum responded, now even more furious. After all, she had contacted school making them aware I was ill.

"Mrs. Brown please let me assure you," looking down at his leather clipboard, with the see though paper bag over it, protecting it from the rain. "They are many pupils who use this to their own advantage, so please excuse me if I am a sceptic," he said smugly. Mum turned and faced the living room door "please come in and see for yourself, sir ...I sure David will be happy, not to try and sneeze on you" mum replying sarcastically. "No, it's no bother Mrs. Brown, just how long do you see David being away from school ...Will save me returning if I know" he said trying to keep the upper hand. "Well, sir I believe the DOCTOR said he should be able to be back to school in another six days ...So next Monday" smiled mum. The thin wet blue-suited man scribbled a few notes on his leather clipboard, then turned and headed up towards Ryan's house; he didn't even say goodbye, he knew he wasn't welcome, like most families on this estate, we found him a hindrance on society, and thought the council could have put the money to better use.

Mum closed the door behind her still shaking her head in annoyance.

The hot Beecham's powder drink mum made tasted revolting, as a young kid mum would add one spoon of sugar to mellow the taste, but now as a young adult, mum said I should grin and bear it. My poor nose was red raw, my nostrils were scabby and the cold sores around my mouth added to the pain of being unwell, feeling miserable, and to top it all off, I had been cocooned in my bedroom for the last two weeks unable to see any of my friends. This was a real manflu, hitting young and old alike.

Trouble was most of my friends were in the same predicament; Dad had fallen too to the dreaded lurgies; he had to take a week off work. Mum's hands were full looking after two sick men.

Mum being fed up with this virus controlling the house, took time to visit Doreen and Lisa, mainly due to me and dad sleeping off our illnesses, and the craving of some good company, and a room full of clean air, and not contaminated by the dreaded manflu.

Doreen was always pleased to see mum. Armed with a bottle of Liebfraumilch in hand, Joyce would join them, and the three of them would submerge into gossip, all subjects covered from me, not at school to who was seeing who, and what was happening around the local area. Lisa found it comical listening to the three of them putting the world to rights. She had often told me how much the three of them carried on, they could run Parliament she would say to me, your mum and mine could be the bloody prime minister, what they don't know between them, seriously our mums even argue with the television. I guess we weren't that different from our parents.

I finally got back to school the following week, the flu epidemic ebbing out of the country, setting normality back into our worlds. I couldn't wait, I was fed up of being cooped up at home bored out of my mind.

It was good to be back with my friends. Frank, the oversized Wally, flung himself at me, almost taking me out. He had me in a bear hug; I could hardly breathe from the pressure. Ryan yelled "Hey Frank, I think you're killing him?" Frank let go instantly, looking me up and down, my face was drained of colour as I tried to control my breathing, "Shit man, really sorry David ...Was only trying to give you a hug" Frank's voice shaky as he thought he had hurt me. "You big buffoon, do you cuddle Tracy like this" I shouted back at him overly aggressively.

A little shaken from my outburst, Frank replied: "No David, I was just glad to see you, I miss you guys you know, and you're my best mates." Both me and Ryan grinned at each other, almost laughing, "You two are a set of twats, so you are ...I care about you, and you two just poke fun at me ...Well, thanks" sulked Frank. "Hey, big guy ...Thanks for being concerned and yeah you're a mate too" I replied, the three of us threw up our arms till each hand touched, raising our arms we shouted, "all for one and one for all" laughing as our arms dropped back to our sides. Just like the three Musketeers did, from the novel by Alexander Dumas.

The school corridors booming from the footsteps and shouting from the pupils' toing and froing from one lesson to the next, the crying from bullied kids and the raised voices from teachers trying to control the situations, this was a welcome sign that things were getting back to normal. Ryan and I were well and truly back in the real world.

Mrs. Cunningham's class had taken on a sizeable mathematical project towards their A grades, for their future exams, something to do with atmospheric pressure and gravity, keeping them there, after school hours. With Tracy being part of that class Frank decided to walk home with us most days.

We stopped at his house. With the winter cold drawing in, the frost had taken over from the green of summer. Our eyes preyed on his sister who stood in the doorway, the tight jumper clinging to her, showing off her shapely body, her full rounded shaped boobs exaggerated by the stretch of the tight woolly jumper. Her long legs covered by her jeans, wearing her high length black boots, she was sexy, and she knew it, tall, curvy, and very attractive, I could feel the tingling starting, my thoughts were impure and not to be said aloud. Ryan stood next to me transfixed, "Thought you were gay?" I said reading the signs on his face.

"I am David" he replied, his eyes not moving from her,

"So why do you have a stiffy on?" I questioned, pointing down at his manhood.

"I don't know; it's her, she's just so hot ...Don't you think Dave?" mumbled Ryan, shifting his privates, trying to hide the bulge.

"Yes, I do Ryan," came my reply, the biggest smile on my face. The bulge in my pants also displayed.

She stood there wafting her long hair with her hand at the same time smiling back at us. "Get in you tart" shouted Frank to his older sister. "You two don't look at my sister like that" he barked, almost stamping his feet in protest. "Sorry Frank but your sis is scorching, and I would like her to teach me a thing or two," I said without realising it was Frank I was talking to.

The pain at the side of my head reminded me; the swift punch I received soon had the tingling subsiding. His sister blew us a kiss, and then went indoors leaving us to fight. Frank scolded off calling us names and his sister even worse. Ryan was still smiling, "So come on Ryan how is it she can do this for you?" I said. The pain at the side of my face subsiding. "Well it's a bit like this David, I think I can get this feeling from girls, but when it comes down to it I don't like the touching bit," Ryan said looking puzzled. Shaking his man bits inside his pants to get comfortable, before we headed off up the street towards our homes, both grinning at the thought of Mary. Within seconds Frank was back out of the door shouting "David I'm sorry, it's just she's my big sis and all." Shouting back, I replied "Frank It's ok mate, see you tomorrow and tell your sister she's got great tits" I just couldn't help myself, I had to reply with something, Frank just gave me the two-fingered salute and went back in smiling.

If I had, to be honest, I couldn't wait to call for Frank in the morning, who knows? Maybe even get a glimpse of his sister. "Ryan, would you, you know, with Mary?" I said knowing how his body reacted to her. "I would like to think I could, but no, she doesn't make me feel like I want to, what about you?" he replied checking his tackle, fumbling inside his pants, still trying to hide his erection, making himself more comfortable. "Too right mate, if she grabbed me, I would be like a lamb to the slaughter," I said laughing,

"You're a dirty little bastard, Mr. Brown," Ryan laughed, prodding my arm.

"Do you touch yourself, thinking about her?" Ryan asked smiling at me, "No I don't" (I protested too much) "Well I hope you don't feel yourself, thinking of me," a look of disgust written over my face. Ryan fell about laughing, "Of course I do" he replied joking, howling at me. "Now who's the dirty bastard," I said, venom in my voice, the mood was jovial, Ryan was in stitches, he found it hard to control his laughter, and at my expense.

We continued the walk to my house. Mum was sat in the living room gossiping with his mum when we entered. "There's a couple of pork pies in the fridge, to get you by till supper time David" mum yelled, hearing me rummaging in the refrigerator. With a glass of dandelion and a pork pie each, we sat quietly at the table, enjoying our tuck.

CHAPTER 27

FRANKS SISTER

Our school was finally winding down for the Christmas break, concentrating on the festive season, a break from the exam swatting school days. Only two weeks left, and then a three-week break. I was looking forward to the break; school lessons had been intense, mock exam after mock exam, taking so much out of us, the stress levels catapulting far beyond breaking point. Watching kids at each other's throats over the slightest little thing. The head teacher was double checking everything. Our school was going to be ready for the summer examinations; he wanted a high pass rate for the GCSG results. His task for our final year was to make sure every pupil had a fair chance of passing. He knew his stuff, and he cared enough to take the time to talk to those behind in their work, offering evening classes after school.

However, for the next two weeks, it was all about being creative, and the rehearsals for the seasonal Christmas pantomime.

As always, it was the last year students who had the pleasure to perform it, so this year it was our year's turn.

The performing arts teacher had us doing puss in boots, in a grease-like scenario, Tracy had landed the lead female role, not for her looks but her singing voice, she gave the best audition our school had seen in years, singing her version of Dolly Pardon's "I will always love you." It was amazing, filling the hall with her haunted style, she had the whole room mesmerized. Frank and I were told not to try; they said we had no hope. The talented Nancy boys got the parts anyway, and anyhow who wants to be prancing around like a twat, having everyone taking the piss out of you, not me and most definitely not Frank.

We didn't mind, meant we had less to do for two weeks. Still found time for detention though, mainly because we were bored and had too much time on our hands. This gave us time to pick on the younger kids, like make them do dares, or play Scabby Queen. This game was great, using a pack of cards and wrapping the knuckles of your opponent, and a free shot if they moved. Most of the kids would cry and run off to blab to the teachers. Still, we didn't learn. Truth to be told I should have known better than to bully the younger kids, in fact, any kid. I didn't like it when it happened to me; Frank had this mischievous way of getting you to do bad things and feeling good doing it.

The follow-up visit to the army careers soon came, Mum chaperoned me to the army careers office after school, for the follow-up visit. The bus was full of school kids. Luckily for us, we managed to find seats on the lower deck of the bus, smoke and school kid free. The kids, they always preferred upstairs where they would curse, smoke and just cause havoc. Most of the other commuters would try to keep off the top deck at this time of day.

We entered the building, the army careers sergeant was pleased to see me return, and had me sat isolated in a windowless room.

I had three exams to complete, one was written, another maths and the last was general knowledge. I sat in this tiny room with no windows, just me sat there, a single table with one chair either side. I briskly worked the papers, hardly pausing for breath, completing the test with time to spare; I found myself staring at the four grey walls, for which seemed like an eternity before the desk Sergeant entered.

He looked me up and down, smiled and beckoned me to follow him into the main reception area. Mum was sat opposite the other Sergeant; their conversation must have been interesting as both mum and the Sergeant went on forever.

I was asked to sit near the Sergeant who had collected me, he browsed through my test papers, sometimes nodding, and occasionally shaking his head but all the time he had this smirk on his face as if he knew the outcome. "Well young lad ...I can say this much, you have passed with high scores so you could join any service you would like to," at the same time still looking over my papers. He stood up quickly and offered me his hand to shake, I placed my hand out, and his vice-like grip almost crushed my fingers. I could feel my fingers going numb; then he shook it again, vigorously, it felt like he was going to dislodge it.

Mum joined us looking very pleased. "What now," said mum looking up at the tall Sergeant. "Now he needs to decide where he wants to go, and I think he should join the junior leader's Regiment of the Royal Artillery, as I did some nineteen years ago" replied the

Sergeant. We sat for another thirty minutes discussing the types of units and what role they played. I had decided there and then that I would join the Artillery, this pleased the two Sergeants, who then told me they would send a date for me to be sworn in, if that is what I still wanted to do, as long as I passed my medical. Once again, we shook hands, and then we left for home.

Dad wasn't overjoyed when he received the news, but accepted it was my choice to join the army when I finish school. He said it was a shame because there was more to me than army life. I folded my arms around his neck and hugged him, "Dad there's always life after the military, I just want to see more of the world and be part of something bigger than …Well this" I told him pointing out of the window. "Ok David, I understand, I think you will make a good soldier no matter where you end up" he replied, hugging me back.

We sat watching the television, for most of the evening, Dad loved it when we watched the old westerns, it was our time together, our bonding time, our cheeky beer time, when he allowed me a few cans. Dad having a rare moment with his boy. He often teased me on who was the best cowboy? "So come on David, John Wayne or Robert Mitchum or maybe Richard Widmark? Which one?" my reply was always the same "John Wayne of course," this would always have dad laughing saying "Right you are son".

Mrs. Connor was a regular visitor now, Mum and Doreen had become excellent friends, and anywhere they were Joyce was never far away. Dad had to escape by going to the pub with Clive. I would go to my room and play my vinyl's before falling into a deep sleep. Mum would always turn the record player off as she passed my room, throwing the bed cover over me, as I slept fully clothed.

Mrs. Connor had mellowed with the loss of Grant. She was full of life, vibrant, hadn't given up. Unlike Mr. Carrol, after his wife passed away all those years ago, at number four. He became miserable and callous and wished ill of everyone, till the day he died, two years after. Most of the gossips said he had died of a broken heart, for us kids we didn't realise he had a heart.

Mrs. Connor never forgot Grant, she just had more time on her hands now, and got to do the things she wanted to do, without any burden, (not that Grant ever was to her).

The next morning Ryan and Frank were sat in my living room when I entered. Total shock ran through me; it was seven O'clock Friday morning, a school day, when had Frank ever been up in time for school before, NEVER! "What you two doing ...It's only seven" I said, still in my pyjama bottoms, rubbing my hair dry with the towel. "It's the last day" yelped Frank like an excited puppy dog. Mum's voice carried from the kitchen "Any of you boys want a bacon sarnie?" In unison, we all shouted, "Yes Please" then broke into fits of laughter almost rolling on the carpet. I left them in the room, making my way back upstairs, and dressed ready for school, swiftly returning to join them, the taste of the bacon sarnie sending pleasure waves, catapulting around my tongue. I gave mum a kiss on her cheek and left for school, Ryan, and Frank in tow. We all wore our parkers. Outside the weather was terrible, the winds were blowing hard and cold, with the snow settling, already about six inches thick and looked like getting deeper by the minute.

We made Frank take the lead, following his size twelves, stepping into his footsteps, he was moaning good, but thankfully we couldn't hear him over the wind. He cursed well; with the effing this and blinding that, you would never tell he kissed his mum with those lips.

Today was the day that the assembly awards were given out to the best pupils of the year.

Our Headteacher Mr. Harrison stood on the stage looking very pleased with himself. He offered his hand to all the pupils as we applauded watching them received their prize.

Mr. Harrison looked out towards the full assembly hall, shouting out "Ryan Backhouse, for outstanding sportsmanship this year, Captaining the football team, and also, let's congratulate him on his personal score tally of thirty goals for this season, his contribution helping win us the championship." The room filled with whistles and applause. Ryan, bashfully made his way to collect his prize. Mr. Harrison lifted the championship school cup above his head, the assembly went wild, cheering, and stamping their feet, he then handed it to Ryan who repeated the gesture. Again, the room filled with applause, the sound deafening, the cheers growing louder. Ryan was beaming; you could see the elation on his face. He had become a legend and would be in the school's sports history for all time. Ryan received his prize then left the stage to the left, the row of teachers all took a turn to shake his hand, giving him praise. His demeanour reverting back to his humble self.

Frank was the loudest to cheer for the next person. "Tracy Clarke for outstanding attendance and grade A work in science and math's" the voice of Mrs. Cunningham came traveling down the hall. Tracy stood tall; she was the second proudest person there, second only to Frank who was crying, watching his sweetheart receive her prize. I nudged him and told him to stop the crying, the school could see him, and he could be in danger of losing his reputation of being the hardest kid in the school. Frank turned and responded, "Hey you're right, but if anyone tries I'll knock their block off"; this made me smile, I knew he meant it.

The morning break was a welcomed sight, a break from all the shouting and cheering, the noise had given me a headache. Frank and Tracy were celebrating in their usual snogging way. Colin Parker made his way towards Frank. Made the mistake of ribbing him for crying earlier in the hall when Tracy received her award. Frank let out a right hook catching young Parker square on the jaw; the ferocity knocking him promptly to the ground. Colin hit the ground, walloping the cold concrete yard, snow wisping around him "You will get it one day" cried Colin as he wiped the tears and blood from his face, the swelling up, under his left eye, almost closing it. "So, who's crying now" Frank said mocking him, beckoning him to stand, just so he could throw another punch, none of us dare intervene, this was old style Frank on display. Tracy yanked at Frank's parker, "Hey, let's just not get involved with this crap; you just concentrate on us," she ordered, still pulling on Franks parker. Frank smiled placing his hand in hers, nodding, "Sorry Tracy, he's a dickhead, sorry for losing it." Instantly he calms down, Tracy clutching his hand hard, almost in tears herself, Frank apologises once more, wiping her tears from her face. Tracy being a saving grace for Colin who was now back on his feet, shaking.

Tracy led Frank towards the school doors and re-entered, disappearing behind the closed door.

Colin stood looking at me, almost taunting me, his vicious tongue spouting. "You lot think you're the fucking best in school don't yer," his hands straightening his jumper. "I believe you should be careful who you go against Colin, Franks twice the size of you, and that makes you probably the dumbest person in the school?" I replied. His fixed gaze on me not moving, snarling at me like a wild dog, exposing his crooked teeth. With his feeble threat coming to nothing, he turns away, heading back to the school entrance. Ryan looks on as Colin enteres the building, "He's a recipe for jail in later life if anyone is" he says, shaking his head, in agreement we both man slap each other on the back, and head towards the school entrance. The schoolyard now deserted.

The day ended in celebration; we watched the school panto, a cross between Cinderella and Puss in boots.

Tracy played the princess, she was great, her voice carried across the hall. Her Dick Whittington was equally as good, Graham Turner, a posh kid from Shadwell, played the part. I did chuckle when they kissed on stage, it was a passionate kiss, lingering, looked like he enjoyed it too much. Franks' face was a picture; I thought his head may explode, he was going to get up and hit him, but thought better of it, How would Tracy feel if he had? Then the finale, the full cast doing a rendition of a Grease Mega mix, the hall erupted into applause. The euphoria exploded, multicoloured strands flickered down from the ceiling. The walls vibrated from the applause. Every single person, pupil, and Teacher alike, all dancing and singing along with the performers. Yes even me and Frank.

The final school bell sounded for the last time this year, ringing out to the welcome start of the Christmas holidays. The chaos and jubilation as we ran, well mainly slid through the main gates, the ground had frozen over and slippery, the soft powdered snow covering the deadly ice underneath.

My stomach ached from laughing at the number of pupils falling on the ice, it was so comical, and Frank went down like a sack of potatoes, cursing away as usual, threatening us. We stood laughing at him; we had so much fun running from him while he chased us through the streets, towards home. He was never going to catch us; he just was never going to be fast enough, and probably would never be. We waited for him to arrive at his gate, appearing some six minutes after, red-faced and out of breath, "I hate you two, you know how many times I've fallen chasing you" he said still puffing and panting, me and Ryan continually laughing at him now, unable to control ourselves. Frank's idle threats came to nothing, he could all but stand up.

Frank invited us into his house; we were met with fresh tea and biscuits. Mrs. Shackleton was fantastic, always had a smile and refreshments on the go. She was also a tough cookie, had to be with the men in her life, the detective and Frank were quite a hand full, but she knew how to manage them.

Ryan stood there, gorping, he just could not stop staring at her. Frank's sister Mary had him spellbound. She stood up and swanked over, hips swivelling as she made her way towards Ryan, placing her hand in his mullet. Mary began to tease him, ruffled his hair, her full pouted lips whispered in his ear, "hear you're a bit of a celebrity in school" followed by a wink and a kiss on his cheek, his face instantly flushed as red as a beetroot. I thought he would explode any minute. "As for you," she said, turning to me "I hear you're the resident sex machine" followed by kissing my cheek. I gave a nervous laugh saying "I don't know about that, but I bet you could teach us a thing or two." Mary didn't blush or falter, she just smiled and replied whispering in my ear, "keep that thought" she kissed me again and walked out of the room, lucky for us Frank was on the toilet and hadn't witnessed this.

We didn't wait for him to return, we were out the door, and halfway up to the of the street when he appeared at his gate. "See you guys tomorrow" he shouted, we turned and replied back "Okay see you" waving at the same time.

"Jesus David, his sister is hot," Ryan said, wafting his face with his hand. All I could do was agree. Fantasies danced around inside my head, along with the usual tingle in my nether region.

CHAPTER 28

THE SNOWBALL FIGHT

The lead up to Christmas was hectic, mum dragging me shopping, traipsing me through town like a pack horse, bag after bag, mum loved to shop, Lisa too. Mum asked her to join us. Lisa and mum would talk and search for hours looking and trying on makeup and dresses. I was feeling a bit out of place.

One male vendor shouted at mum, from behind his fruit shop counter, "Could he have a man Friday like me when she had finished with me." Mum exploded into a fury, the likes of I had never seen before, she went total frenzy on him, the crowd of shoppers encouraging her as she clobbered the vendor for his racist remark. Maybe next time he will think before he speaks, we left the vendor, who was now under a hurl of verbal as a group of shoppers continued to mock him.

Thanks to his remark, mum retrieved the bags from me. Lisa and mum carried them instead, leaving me free, hand in pockets following behind. Mum didn't take me shopping again that week, instead mum, Doreen, Lisa and Joyce did it all.

This year we were all invited to Clive and Joyce's home for Christmas dinner, Doreen and Lisa were too. The Connor boys were out of the country, the last time Mrs. Connor had seen them was at Grant's funeral.

Phil and Carl Backhouse would not be there either; their leave was starting in the new year. Phil was bringing his family over this time, his wife had given birth to a baby boy last August, they had named him Clive after Phil's dad. Phil's wife Melanie and daughter Petra were looking forward to visiting Leeds to meet his parents; Petra was only two years old the last time she had seen them.

Christmas dinner was great; the Backhouses had done us proud, Joyce had been going to cookery lessons over the last four weeks, and helped mum on a few occasions making the Sunday roast. She had definitely learnt a lot. We sat there stuffed to the brim, all unable to move, contented.

Clive gave a big sigh, lifting himself from his chair, deciding to bring out the ale.

He punctured the party seven barrel of Watneys, with a whoosh of ale spurting out at speed. Joyce screaming at the mess it made on the floor, throwing a tea towel down to mop it up.

Mum had cleared it earlier with dad, that I could join in and have a pint or two.

We sat there acting all man like, Clive teased Ryan and me, dad laughing in agreement with Clive, mocking our masculinity, I wouldn't mind, but both me and Ryan were well buff compared to our parents. We removed our shirts, displaying our firm trim bodies, dad and Clive joined in. "Put it away" screamed Joyce "You'll scare Lisa, she doesn't need to see your old flabby bodies" she continued pointing at our dads. Mum found this amusing and chuckled somewhat. Lisa said we were all immature and should grow up, shaking her head in disapproval. Mum, Doreen, and Joyce were on the cherry B's and because we were allowed to drink, Joyce allowed Lisa one or two glasses. Now Lisa started to act all grown up, and making a fool of herself.

Mrs. Connor surprised us; she took centre stage, stood there in the middle of the room and began to sing. We had never heard her sing like this before, or for that matter knew that she could. Yes we all sang back in Cornwall, but no one was singled out. She sang beautifully, her voice was terrific, very Barbra Streisand. Doreen sang on through the evening and into the early hours, we joined in every now and then. The night was fantastic; we drank and sang until the early hours of Boxing Day.

The grownups were enjoying themselves so much they forgot to monitor us kids, as we helped ourselves to a lot more alcohol.

Boxing Day came and went, other than the odd visit to the bathroom to be sick down the toilet, nothing much happened, it wasn't just us kids who were suffering, but our parents, they too had over indulged. I don't think anyone of us had escaped a hangover that day.

The 27th saw Frank stood outside Tracy's house, wrapped up in his parker, the cold biting at his face, the snow had ceased falling, but swirled around high from the ground, the winds blowing a gale. Lightly he knocked on their door. Moments later her mum answered. A short, slender-framed woman, her face small and thin, but kind, like Tracy she had high cheekbones and a little nose, her lips were thin, but wide, which portrayed a pleasant smile along with her long shiny brown hair cascading over her shoulders. "Hello, Frank ...Sorry but Tracy has gone with her dad today, to visit her Nana in Wakefield, should be back tomorrow morning".

Frank disappointed, smiled back at her "It's Ok Mrs. Clarke ...Just wanted to invite her to our New Year's Eve party, if that would be Ok with you and her dad, she could stay the night" his face going red, flushed with embarrassment, Mrs. Clarke look up at him with a naughty grin. "No," he said holding up his hands defensively "Tracy will be staying in my sister's room" he continued, breathing heavily, the chill hitting the back of his throat. Mrs. Clarke stood there, her hands in her piny pockets, "Frank dear I'm sure she will love it, and I'm sure you will be the complete gentleman ...so if Tracy wants to go, she can". Frank thanked her and headed back towards our street, a new skip in his step, forgetting how cold it was.

Snowballs were flying in all directions; the younger kids were busy building a snow wall across the road, causing havoc with the car drivers, the road across the street was almost completely blocked off. Drivers diverting back up the street, swerving as they reversed, one vehicle hit the lamp post, cursing and swearing the driver got out, then thinking better of it, looking around, feeling the kids parents eyes praying on him. He slipped back into his car and slowly drove away, followed by a volley of snowballs.

Snow had laid thickly over the last couple of days, must have been some sixteen inches in parts.

Mr. Phillips from number eleven, was in a conflab, complaining at their parents, getting nowhere. Little Johnny Collins dad flings a volley of snowballs at the group of men. The first hitting Mr. Phillips followed by three or four more times on his back, Phillips now raging races over, cursing as he goes, within minutes the two men are fighting. These are not just slaps and fairy punches but real slogging, knocking the hell out of each other. Ryan and I watch as a few more dads get involved, each blaming the next, within minutes seven men were kicking the hell out of each other, no reason other than the alcohol intake and Mr. Phillips constant moaning. The kids jumping and running around like crazy, shouting "Fight, fight, fight" and throwing more snowballs there way, the noise elevating as the fight continued. Mrs. Phillips panicking, distressed and worried for her husband's safety races back into her house and dials 999 for the police.

Within minutes, three Black Mariah's sped into the street breaking through the snow wall, splitting the wall into slabs of snow walling, sending them out, hurtling through the air hitting everything in its wake. One piece missing me by inches. The twelve policemen soon dispatched from their vehicles, settling the chaos, throwing the men into the back of the vans, both sides throwing the odd punch or kick as they did.

Now, most of the families had gathered, most of the wives screeching at the policemen.

Without any notice, another police van enters the street, from the back emerge two Alsatian dogs with their handlers. With their teeth bared, snarls and aggressive barking, the road empties rapidly; no one was going to mess with a police dog.

Within minutes the street is quiet again, the police officers secure their vans and drive off towards the Gipton police station.

Ryan and I find ourselves standing alone, the street empty, just the sound of the wind, blowing a mist of snow. Silence is soon broken.

"Hi, guys you alright" bellows Frank as he makes his way towards us, excitedly running up the street.

"You missed it all Frank ...police with dogs," Ryan said excitedly pointing around the street. "Mr. Phillips and Johnny's dad were slogging it, fist for fist, then skinny Chris Thomas joined in and four others ...it was great" Ryan continued his face beaming, even more excited. I just nodded in agreement. "Why were they fighting" asked Frank looking disappointed because he had missed it. "Little Johnny Collins and skinny Thomas's three scrawny kids built a snow wall across the street blocking off the road," I said pointing to the debris left at either side of the road. The remaining snow towers still standing three feet tall on the pavements as a reminder.

With the streets bare and leaving us with nothing else to do or watch, we retreated back to mine.

Frank throws himself on the sofa, eagerly he shouted out to my parents, the news about the planned party at his house for the New Year, mum was pleased to accept the invite, and said she would call in later to see if his mum needed any help with the organising of it. Clive and Joyce had already been invited.

Mum had spoken to Mrs. Shackleton and extended the invite to Mrs. Connor and Lisa, who eagerly

362

accepted. I was pleased to hear Lisa was going to be there.

Lisa and I spoke about Elizabeth, and how much we both missed her. Her face, smile, well everything about her. Lisa placed her arms around my shoulders, pulling me close. I always felt lost, more than just sad when I spoke about Elizabeth, I don't think I will ever feel anything different. She was my first love and would have been my only love, had her terrible end never happened.

We took comfort from each other, spending hours working on her dads' garden. The melancholy found us some days, not looking for it but the small reminders of our lost loved ones took us there. Small things like the bucket and trowel Grant used when he deweeded his flower beds.

Ryan was a keen gardener now; he took pride in keeping Grants plants alive and reproducing the fruit, keeping up with the housekeeping, cleaning the greenhouse, tending the paths for weeds, not that much grew in this weather, all the same, Doreen was grateful to us all.

We took time for each other, listening to stories, encouraging each other to be happier. As the time passed, we became very fond of each other, but never said. I knew I was falling for Lisa, Ryan knew this too. As for Lisa, she loved hanging around with us both; she loved joining in the boy stuff, getting her face dirty, getting told off by her mum, yes, she was pretty much one of the lads, but better looking.

CHAPTER 29

NEW YEARS PARTY

The 30th December was another quiet day, the weather keeping us in. The snow falling heavily, covering everything in sight, even the fence had a two-inch drift built upon it. Mum and dad braved it and went to see a movie to break up the monotony of their day. I just laid on my bed eating crisp, sweets, and drinking fizzy pop, while listening to music on my record player. Ryan was doing pretty much the same in his home. On hearing the one knock on the door, followed by the door opening, I knew it had to be Ryan or Lisa. We met in the living room. "Hello David, was bored at home" followed by a surprised full on mouth kiss. I think I went to jelly, my legs gave away in shock. Lisa kissed harder, inviting me in. "Thank you Lisa, that was good" I said looking through her eyes, her eyes sparkled, saying that you're welcome look. I took her by the hands, Lisa swayed her body in time with the music, we began to dance in the living room, mum's vinyl's on the radiogram. A bit of David Cassidy followed by Wizard vibrating the internal speakers. Having turned fifteen, she was developing into a great looking young lass. She was five feet six, towering her mum, she got her height from Grant. Her dyed blonde shoulder length hair waved about. We jumped and shouted, as the music pumped out from the speakers. Lisa leaned in, her lips touched mine, we kissed again, a light kiss pulling away fast, we stood there just looking face to face at each other, music

364

played, but I don't think we could hear it. It was the ring from the telephone that broke us away from our trance. Frank was ringing confirm we were still going. I could have killed him, I was ready to pop the will you go out with me question, but now, the moment had passed. Franks' mum was fussing over what to serve and constantly cleaning her house. Frank said, his mum had cleaned the loo four times today, she's not having anyone say she doesn't keep a clean house, he was laughing down the phone, then a painful moan came over the line as his mum hit him across the head as she passed, catching him mocking her. The call ended with Frank saying he was bored and asked if he could come to mine, of course, he could, and he didn't have to ask.

It wasn't long before both he and Ryan had joined us, a little disappointing for Lisa and me, we wanted to know if that kiss was the start of something amazing, maybe we'll never know?

The evening closed in, leaving us watching the movie Calamity Jane, with Howard Keel and Doris Day on the TV. Mum and dad returned home, catching us all singing the "deadwood stage" along with the movie cast. Dad's face, watching us from behind the door was in hysterics. We were making that much noise we never heard them enter. Mum did what mum always did, got the treats out, along with a special alcoholic treat. Ryan asked to stay over, there was nothing unusual about that, he always got a yes, and don't forget to tell Clive or Joyce. Frank had his treats then left with a high five. The movie finished, with the time now nine in the evening, Lisa promised to see us tomorrow as she left for home. I walked her to the door, we never spoke, just smiled, I took her hand, allowing it to slip out as she passed through the door. I yearned to kiss her goodnight, but was afraid I got it all wrong. I stood and watched her home, closing my door as she disappeared through hers. I had butterflies dancing inside me, the truth to be told, I couldn't believe my luck, but I didn't say anything to Ryan, I wanted to but I couldn't. Needed confirmation Lisa felt the same.

Sunday the 31st of December 1978, the day was met with high winds and heavy snow. The streets bare, deserted, everyone staying indoors. Most still asleep, tucked up in bed.

Not Mrs. Shackleton, she was up and about early, she had a side of beef prepped and roasting in the oven, and a ham joint boiling away on the hob, the kitchen heat was unbearable, all this activity and before six.

Mr. Shackleton was making himself scarce, keeping out of the way of his wife, he knew better than to get in her way when she was stressed, and doing one of her parties. He made his way to the Gipton police station, would rather catch up on paperwork than getting scolded by his wife. The night duty sergeant giving him an odd look as he entered the station. "Bloody hell Shacks, Missus finally kicked you out?". "No Roger, she's up getting ready for tonight, already got the oven on, You and the missus still coming?" chortled Shackleton, the desk sergeant nodded.

Frank wasn't mum smart like his dad and got in her way. Unusual for him to be up at seven, Frank loved his lay-ins, but the noise from his mum's chores had him out of bed early.

Mrs Shackleton read him the riot act and warned him he would be one ugly kid if he got under her feet again, Frank got the message clearly this time, he grabbed his coat and made his way to mine.

The knock on the door awoke dad, who scurried down the stairs to answer the door.

"Frank, what do you want? It's only seven thirty in the morning and a Sunday morning at that" dad yelled, looking frayed and annoyed, his face screwed up as he tapped his watchless wrist. Frank looked at dad with sorrowful eyes "Sorry Mr. Brown but mums kicked me out for the day while she gets the house ready for tonight and I don't fancy getting a kick in for being in her way" he replied looking even more sorry for himself. "You had better come in then lad," dad said opening the door further.

Frank slouching walked into the living room and dropped on the settee; dad awoke me, shaking me quite vigorously, still annoyed at being awakened. "David Frank's downstairs." Dad didn't say much else, went back to his bed leaving me to get up and see why he was here?

I found it amusing when Frank told me his story; Frank said I was a bully, and was always poking fun at him. I don't think anyone could intimidate Frank, he would rip you apart with his bare hands, and he resembled a giant grizzly bear.

Mum was down thirty minutes later, her regular routine of bacon sarnies on the go, the kettle filled and boiled and the tea brewed up within fifteen minutes.

Frank and I sat there on the settee eating through the mountain of bacon sandwiches, washing them down with the hot mug of tea. Frank sat there resting his hands on his swollen belly, "Dave I think I'm gonna burst," I turned to look at him half lying there, his stomach did look like it would erupt, I was stuffed with the three I had eaten. "How many did you eat," I questioned Frank, unable to take my eyes off his stomach. "Just seven," he said smiling. "Jesus Frank! I'm not surprised; you're gonna explode, where do you put it?" I said, my eyes wide open in disbelief. Frank just sunk even further into the settee and smiled.

The smell of the bacon aroused Ryan, he was up, and down the stairs in record time. "Sorry Ryan, Franks ate all the bacon sarnies, I could do you a sausage sandwich? There's one going begging if you want it?" mum shouted from behind the kitchen door, knowing Ryan had gotten up for his sandwich and a hot mug of tea, this had become a ritual for mum over the years, most weekends. "Yes, please Mrs. Brown" Ryan shouted back, then spinning his head towards Frank "You're a greedy fat git Frank, you know I come here for my sarnie," Ryan said frowning at Frank. Frank didn't say anything; his big broad smile said it all. It wasn't long before Ryan was munching on his sandwich and slurping his hot mug of tea.

The three of us sat there on the settee, quiet and contented; then without warning, Frank gave the noisiest, smelliest fart ever, we almost choked as the fumes hit the back of our throats. Mum raced into the room, "Frank Shackleton,I think you may need to go home and change darling," she said in a fit of giggles. "I could hear that in the kitchen" she stated, the three of us burst into hysterical laughter whiles wafting our hand to aid us from the stench, then he followed with another, jumping off the sofa Ryan and I darted off upstairs to get dressed, leaving Frank in his own smell. Mum had both the back and front doors open, even the bitter cold was more bearable than the stench from Franks backside.

The day had seemed to have passed quickly; it was seven o'clock in the evening already, time just flew by, and I hadn't had the chance to speak to Lisa, not seen her yet.

With the Shackleton's party looming, Ryan and I made our way over to Lisa's house, to see if she was ready to go. She wasn't, she had just got out of the bath and was still drying her hair. Mrs. Connor said she would be about an hour because she had to do her face and pick an outfit. Men were never that much trouble; we found clean jeans and a jumper and that was it, well not quite Ryan always took about thirty minutes just to get his hair right, he still donned his mullet.

It was about eight-thirty before we set off to the party; I was dressed in my jeans and paisley shirt, with my shiny Chelsea boots, well-polished. Lisa was wearing a body clinging jersey, low cut revealing her back, her tight jeans showing off her long legs complemented by her two-inched black high heels. Ryan was dressed the same as me, we were often called twins, the only difference being he was dirty white, and I was coffee coloured, not that many people noticed, only outsiders.

Mrs. Connor had met up with mum and dad an hour earlier, making their way to the Shackleton's, Clive and Joyce had arrived ten minutes after mum. Everyone complimented Mrs. Shackleton on her beautiful house and how clean it was; they also made a fuss over the spread Mrs. Shackleton had put on. It was incredible; it ranged from cocktail sticks with melon balls and cheese to roast beef sandwiches, boiled ham sandwiches, fish sticks and dips. The six-foot table was covered in various food types. Doreen had supplied the homemade spicy plum chutney, made by Grant, earlier in the summer this year. This brought on a small conversation to the memory of Grant and how much he had loved his garden. Doreen enjoyed the chat, she didn't show any sad emotions, quite the opposite, she was pleased to see people spoke about Grant in a good light, after all, he had been a good man. Mum was the one to shed a tear, "Maggie stop that now, Grant had only good things to say about you, and you should not get upset about his passing now" said Doreen, her arms wrapped around mums' shoulders, "Sorry Doreen, just being silly" mum smiled reassuringly.

Clive and Joyce brought their contribution, four bottles of wine, two red and two sparkling white. The drinks table was overflowing, the variety, ranging from the wines, whisky, port, and beers. More than enough to serve the guest. Mums contribution was the lavishly decorated Dundee cake.

Mr. Shackleton was a proud man tonight; his wife had done a spectacular job in getting the house ready for their guest. It wasn't long before they all had a drink in their hands.

By the time we got there, the party was in full swing; the radiogram was tuning out a bit of Des O'Connor, our parents were singing along. Frank met us at the door, Tracy by his side, she wore an all in one red catsuit, her hair tied back, this exaggerating her black eyeliner eyes. She was glowing, her smiling face leaning on Frank's shoulder. He looked well pleased with himself. "Hi guys," Frank said ushering us in passed the front door, we huddled in, Lisa was the first to compliment Frank on his dress sense and how dapper he looked in his stay-pressed trousers and plain blue shirt, his hair combed to the side. Frank's sister Mary had cut his hair earlier that day, his long locks all gone, now a tidy short back and sides. It suited him, made his face a little slender looking.

Ryan's eyes met with Mary's, he turned red almost instantly, and her goddess of a body walked over deliberately and kissed him on the mouth. His face was flushed, he blushed, not knowing where to put his face. Mrs. Shackleton told Mary to stop teasing him, "Mary leave him alone, you know he gets all coy in front of you" then they both gave out a little giggle, allowing Ryan to escape in the crowd of people. Mr. and Mrs. Gilbert were there too, with their daughter Christine and her husband, Paul. They must have been about forty plus in the house; I was introduced to various relatives of the Shackleton's, all shapes, and sizes, none of which I could remember the names of.

Mary was beginning to tease Ryan again, Ryan had found his confidence, he knew what she was doing, today he was able to control his nether regions, not allowing himself to blush this time. Mary enjoyed teasing Ryan, if I didn't know better, I would say she had a thing for him.

The room was filled with laughter; there was a good humorous atmosphere flowing in the room, everyone was enjoying themselves, eating, drinking, and singing the night away.

Mr. Shackleton stood in the bay window with Doreen Connor; the room fell silent, Mr. Shackleton introduces himself and Doreen. "Ladies and Gents, I have the pleasure to introduce you to Miss Barbra Streisand" pointing to Doreen, who gave a curtsy, "And to Mr. Neil Diamond" taking a bow himself. Both inhaled a deep breath and turned inwards to each other as they began to sing a duet, "You don't bring me flowers." They were fantastic, they really complimented each other, Frank stood quiet, absorbed in the song, Tracy watched him adoringly, Mrs. Shackleton swayed with my mum to the rhythm. The whole room was spellbound, all eyes wide, taking in the beautiful sound, their voices were like velvet, crisp and clear.

An eruption of cheers filled the room when they took their final bow.

Mum wondered and asked Doreen why she had never taken it up seriously.

Doreen told mum, she felt she could only sing for Grant and her children, but now he was gone, she said singing kept him alive inside. Made her feel good about herself, like she had an identity of her own.

Barry Thomas had made his way to Lisa, he was a fifteen-year-old lad, built like Ryan, tall and athletic, and he was a handsome lad, he smiled at her as he introduced himself. The green-eyed monster was brewing inside me; I had feelings for her, strong feelings.

I knew I shouldn't feel like this; it was hard, I drew back on my emotions, knowing, if I was to go out with her, I should have asked her before now. The kiss, that bloody kiss, I should have blurted out then, no point wanting to punch this kid in the face, at least he had the balls to speak to her. Lisa looks content and happy to be in Barry's company, and they were getting on so well, so who was I to interfere, I left them to it. Ryan as usual brought me back to reality, wasn't long before we were sipping on the odd brandy, ok choking on the odd brandy would be more descriptive, but it was fun all the same, reminded me of the time dad and Harry, the last Christmas I spent with Elizabeth. This memory was the first one that didn't leave me upset, as bad as Harry was and did what he did, this memory was still a good one.

As the night was drawing to midnight, Mrs. Shackleton passed the small glasses of port to all her guest. " Let's all get ready to toast in the New Year" shouted Det Shackleton. The television presenter was stood outside Trafalgar Square, surrounded by thousands of people ready to cheer. The countdown began, "10,9,8,7,6,5,4,3,2,1" then the mightiest roar from the crowd. Welcome 1979. The Shackleton home ignited in celebration as we yelled and jumped about, kissing, and hugging each other. It was my turn to kiss Mary; she had trapped me in the kitchen, closing the door behind her. Her soft lips touching mine sent me to heaven, pure paradise, as we lingered. She took her time before releasing me from her kiss, grabbing my hand she led me outside the back door and into the garden, back around to the front door, where we re-entered, Mary directed me upstairs to her room and closed the door behind us. I knew why I was there, throwing caution to the wind, not allowing my fear of the consequences to take over, allowing her to take me.

I awoke and looked at the clock on her bedside table, it was twenty past five in the morning. Lying next to this beautiful naked woman, the heat from her soft warm body touching mine. I didn't want to leave, but the thought of her dad catching me here, was something I defiantly didn't want. My clothes laid at the bottom of the bed. My thoughts turned to how I was to get out of here without disturbing her family; they were soon cut short as Mary stirred, she smiled at me, leaning over, exposing her body, she kissed me one last time. Again I wanted to stay, but knew I had to leave, I removed the covers and got dressed, I took one more look at Mary, God she was hot, and she wanted me, Wow my head was spinning, but not in a bad way, I could still feel her touch. I felt great. What a new year.

Sneaking down the stairs, leaving Mary's room, leaving her all curled up cosy and asleep in bed. Just have to be quiet now, not get caught.

To my surprise the party was still going. Mr. Shackleton was thankfully too drunk to realise I had just joined them, placing his arm around me. "Hello young David, hope you are enjoying it," he said in his bellowing voice, if he only knew? He would be killing me now. I looked up at his drunken red-nosed face and smiled back at him.

Ryan was next to me in a flash, a glass of rum and black in hand, "Here David try this, it's great" he said pushing the glass into my hand. I had to admit I enjoyed the taste; we went over to the alcohol table and poured two more. Mum and dad were sat on the sofa with Mrs. Shackleton talking. Doreen occupied the table looking worse for wear, her head slumped on the table, she was funny, made me chuckle, watching her try to lift her head to get a drink from her half pint glass of larger, spilling most of it. The Gilberts had left apart from Paul who was talking to one of the relatives.

Lisa was sleeping on the easy chair alone in the corner; Barry had gone home a few hours earlier. I knocked back my drink in one, coughing after, feeling the burn as it slid down my throat, warming me through.

From the corner of my eye, I noticed Lisa had awoke from her sleep. Drowsy, she started to head for the door, unable to keep her balance, I offered to escort Lisa home, Doreen managed to understand and passed me her door keys, there was no way Doreen was making it home, slumped over the table, she was almost asleep already. Mum kissed me goodnight and said they would be home later. I said my goodbyes to the Shackleton's' and told Ryan I would call for him later that day.

Placing my arm around Lisa's waist, and placing hers around my shoulder, we made our way out of the garden.

She almost fell over again, pushing me away, Lisa stared at me, I wasn't sure she could see who she was with. We finally got passed the gate, the fresh air knocking me for six, instantly feeling drunk, now who was taking who home? We must have looked comical, one step forward two steps back, wobbling all over the place. The frosty air nipping at our bodies joined by the slippery surface making it more of a laborious task.

Lisa stumbling, tripping over her feet, thumping the ground hard. Me almost rolling over the top of her. She curls up and begins to cry. Sobering up somewhat I lean over her, trying to comfort her. Her drunken sobbing transforms into a cry of pain. The sound of Lisa's moans grab the attention of the group of six drunken men stood on the other side of the road; You could have been mistaken into thinking I was assaulting Lisa from where they stood. But looks can be deceiving.

"Hey, you leave her alone" one shouted over waving his fist at me, innocently and without any thought I replied, "It's Ok mate, she's fallen, we've been at the Shackleton's for a drink and were a bit drunk."

The six men were now almost upon us, cursing at me as they did. Not listening to whatever I had to say.

I knew this going to go bad, Lisa was still crying; her jeans had ripped at the knee, and she was bleeding. The pain, more from the biting cold.

"Get away from her you Paki bastard," said the large heavy built rounded drunk, swaying in front of me, showing no willingness to listen to anything I had to say.

"What you are calling me that for, I'm helping her home, she's fallen over that's all," fearful I stuttered out.

Now I was worried, and confused unable to get my head around the abuse I was receiving. After all, I was helping her, surly anyone could see that?

Two others chirped in "Get your fucking black hands off her or we're gonna kick the shite out of you," standing there with their hands curled up in a fist. Now shaking their fist at me once more. Looks like there just looking for a fight, maybe wrong place, wrong time.

I stood up and tried to reason with them telling them they could ask Mr. Shackleton if they didn't believe me. The atmosphere had turned tense; I could sense the warmth of the piss traveling down my leg. I was scared, terrified of what was coming next. I was standing in a living nightmare. I could feel the fear set in.

It was no use, the first volley of punches from three of them hit hard and fast, I never saw them coming, just felt the pain travel around my body, as my head rocked from side to side, without realising it, the damp patch started to show as the steam escaped. laughing they poked and mocked me. "Filthy little nigger, pissboy" the fat round drunk shouted, his companions encouraging him, followed by his large curled up fist impacting on my face. My nose exploding, a sea of red splattered out, hitting my assailants, I was soon on the floor curled up trying to protect my body from the vicious blows. They took turns to kick and stamp on me, enjoying the infliction of pain raining down on me, time and time again, another boot finding its target.

Blood escaping from the cuts forming around my head and hands. The drunks' kicks striking me square in the face, discharging into a sea of claret, as my face becomes unrecognisable with the breaking of my nose. Now coughing and choking on my own blood, I struggled to breathe. The six of them taking it in turns at executing the pain. Unconscious, I lay there unaware of the broken bones and massive swelling to my head. Without any reason, other than an act of yobbishness the group continued.

Lisa had come around some now, and was horrified at what she was now witnessing; the unbelievable scene in front of her, her screams, so loud it was deafening. Hysterically she screams out "Stop it! Stop it! Leave him alone, you fucking stupid, you're killing him" scrambling back to her feet, at the same time.

Pushing at the drunks to get them away from me, trying her hardest to protect me. The fat one pushes her back, spitting in her face. "Let's get the fuck out of here," he laughs to his companions, "She's not worth it, little slag, fucking nigger lover." With that said, they turn away, their footsteps disappearing into the streets.

Lisa stands there, shaking, not daring to move. Nausea sweeping over her as she looks down at my broken body, limbs twisted and swollen, blood casing the whole of my body from the broken flesh wounds. Screaming and stamping, Lisa turns, buckles over, and vomits uncontrollably over the pavement, splashes hitting her shoes. Lisa knows she has to get help; Her world spinning around in her head, confused, should she leave me, not wanting to leave, but she knows what's needed, and slowly she walks back in a daze, fragile, sobbing and shaking, and not from the cold, but the horror of the beating. Screaming out to anyone who may hear. "Why is no-one helping me". The streets are deserted, white desolate streets, stripped of life, the world in an alcoholic comma, after the dawning of the new year.

She finally reaches the Shackleton's to raise the alarm.

Lisa's appearance is enough to raise the alarm, Ryan instinctively knows this is bad.

In disbelief, Ryan is the first out of the door; sprinting up the street, no thought of danger, the cold of the early morning air biting into his lungs.

Breathless, he reaches his destination, he stops dead, motionless, one look is all it takes.

Breaking down instantly; the sight he sees is unimaginable, his best friend lying in a pool of blood not moving. He instinctively starts to check for my breathing; it has stopped. Ryan cries out a primal scream, that of a wounded beast. Sitting next to me, he cradles me in his arms. Tears blinding his eyes, unstoppable racing down his face. Shuddering with cold, he holds my body close, stained from my blood. "David, Please wake up, come on David, it's me, Ryan, please David, please." His head sinks down into my chest. He rocks me back and forth, like the soothing of a child.

Mum and dad in denial, not wanting to believe the horror facing them. Mum throws her body onto mine, almost falling, dragging me away from Ryan, Dad slumps down to his knees next to mum, tears flow overpoweringly, unable to control his body from shaking. He places his head-on mum's shoulder. They don't move, just hold me tightly, squeezing. Ryan rocks himself back and forth behind them; no one could help him, lost in a violent rage he jumps up, heading out, wandering the streets full of anger, looking for my attackers.

Mr. Shackleton had rung the police and ambulance services before leaving his home. Lisa couldn't watch, she couldn't take any more of this, sitting with the policeman on Shackleton's sofa. His questions unanswered, Lisa too distraught to remember anything. Mrs. Connor oblivious, unconscious in her drunken state.

Mr. Shackleton looked down at mum, he gently gets mum and dad to their feet, the police constable helps mum and dad into the patrol car.

His face drained of any emotion he kneels next to me and starts cardiopulmonary resuscitation, blowing into my swollen mouth followed by compressions on my chest till the ambulance arrived. Mum and dad watch from the window, weeping holding each other close unable to help, the medic takes over from a drained exhausted Mr. Shackleton.

CHAPTER 30

THE BOY FROM NOWHERE

Many were left standing at the back, all the seats were taken, Louis Armstrong's "What a wonderful world" is playing. Many of our neighbours enter, taking their place, showing their respects to the memory of a friend they once knew.

The highly polished dark mahogany timber coffin, displaying mums favourite picture of me in a silver frame, surrounded by flowers, "R.I.P ... my beloved son David". The sobbing drains out the sound of the song. Sorrow cloaks over the ceremony, the many heads unable to look forward, peering groundward.

Doreen strolls to the altar, her footsteps echo in the now silent crematorium, she turns to face the grieving mourners, tears fall from her eyes, weeping, she doesn't wail or make a sound, nor does she wipe away her tears. Her face is kind and thoughtful, though her heart is grief-stricken, empty and sad. She glances over at mum. Mum nods in reply.

Mums stood there, holding dad's hand, squeezing it tightly, her body shaking, waning, wanting to collapse. Her inner strength and love for David keeps her upright, too proud, she's not going to fall, she going to stay strong, allowing every ounce of her inner strength to hold her up. Maggie is in pain, a pain that rips through the very heart of you, leaving you feeling empty, a dirty hollow blackness, a void never to be filled.

Today is her day, her testament, to her child.

Music starts to play over the speakers, Doreen stands upright, almost at attention; she inhales a deep breath, looking out at the grieving mourners, all looking back at her. Clearing her throat, with a cough, Doreen begins. The acoustics perfect for her tribute, her pure Streisand style tones capture her audience.

"Somewhere over the rainbow, way up high, and dreams that you dream of, once in a lullaby." The words silence room, Doreen's voice is the only sound to be heard. She sings with pride, her gift to a child she once scorned. Her pure angelic tones capture the building, filling the room with pride. The sniffles start like an epidemic around the room. Doreen struggles with the words briefly, regaining control she continues with her tribute. Doreen had finally fallen in love with David, just like a mother would. Staying strong, ignoring the pain, she gives her all.

Dad takes mum in his arms as she slumps down on into his chest, her legs giving way; her heart heavy, she takes a glance to the right, my coffin laid before all. She coughs, choking back with her sorrow, the feeling enveloping, wrapping its ugly black mist over her. The sound of her cry echoes through the chapel, our friends and neighbours look on, not daring to speak or take their eyes from Doreen.

A sea of tears fill the room.

Doreen lowers her head as the song fades out into the sea of tears, she turns towards the large wooden cross fixed to the wall, bows, crossing her body with her right hand, then slowly makes her way back to mum and dad, standing in the front row. Lisa, Ryan, Frank, and Tracy stood by their side.

Mum thanks Doreen as she re-takes her place, next to mums' side. Ryan turns to his dad, not able to speak, trembling, his face, full of grief, unable to stop his flow of tears. Clive knows his son is distressed and suffering from the loss of his friend. He seizes him close, embracing him in his arms, trying to comfort and give strength in this time of sorrow, but even Clive can't hold back the tears, his feeling of utter uselessness of being unable to save his son from this suffering.

Frank sits back down hurriedly, his legs giving way, lacking the strength to hold him up, the occasion too much to bare. Frank turns his head towards the coffin. "Sorry I couldn't help you David" he whispers to himself. Shame hurting him. (Not having any reason to feel shameful, he was a good friend to me). Tracy hugs him close, teardrops falling from her face, settling on Franks' shoulders. His tearful eyes look up, too helpless, too upset to support his girlfriend, he sobs, pulling close to Tracy's waist.

Courageously, Lisa takes to the podium. She cast her eyes across the room, the many familiar faces, friends, and neighbours of ours, not one head held high does she see, not out of lack of respect, but because today is too sad for words.

Lisa keeps her composure and yells out like a firebrand preacher "I hope you all don't mind, but I would like to say a few words" the mourners look up to see this young, tearful woman looking and reaching out to them. "Mrs. Brown and Mr. Brown, please allow me to say how much we all join you in the loss of our David. Yes, I say our David, because he was our David, my friend, your friend and most of all, your son, I, like all of you here, miss him so much. I think I can speak for Ryan, Tracy, and Frank when I say he was the one special person who brought us all together; he was kind and gentle. He does not deserve to have been taken from us, but he has, so I ask that we all try to smile in his memory, this is what David would have wanted, and I know he will always be in our hearts, ... If there is a heaven, he will surely be looking down on us smiling, thank you" Courageously Lisa steps down, making her way back to join her friends. Ryan holds out his arms, just one look at her face tells him she needs him, unable to escape her tears, she looks wounded. "Thank you Lisa" he hugs her, for a moment she loses her balance, Ryan steadies her, hands clenched they stand side by side, taking solace from each other.

The vicar moves in, takes his place on the podium, his voice loud yet compassionate, he begins to recite my life, and how life was both right and unfair, with his stature sturdy, he continues to say, how much love my parents and friends had shared with me. The laughter and tears, relevant for a young boy growing up in this world.

He reminds them how cruel the world can be, and how the simple-mindedness and an old way of thinking can cause so much harm, causing devastation to an already destructive world. He pauses and watches the faces in front of him, he sees a sadness, loss and an emptiness that needs replenishing. He continues to remind us, this is why we should not judge a book by its cover, installing, that we should be charitable, kind and embrace the unknown or anything we don't understand. He asks that we talk to one another, and work things out. How looks can be deceiving and how we mistake what we see to be wrong, when all along there is a simple explanation.

Softly he asked everyone to lower their heads in prayer.

He prays for forgiveness for all men and women, for the sins they commit and the pain and suffering that should be avoided. He prays that one day my family and friends would see better days and enjoy life, once again.

Everyone recites the Lord's prayer. "Amen."

Mum looks around, her heart overflows with a joyous relief, realising that many of our friends and neighbours have taken their time to show their respects, proud thoughts whisper inside her head. Contented mum holds dad close to her. Her inner strength pulling through.

The music starts again; the mourners begin to leave the room, sobbing as they go. The front row remains to say their last goodbyes.

The coffin travels towards the furnace, and the curtains close behind it, leaving them standing, gazing into emptiness. Mum turns to my friends and hugs them one at a time, thanking them for their support and friendship towards me over the years. Ryan finally finds the strength to say goodbye; he promises the sound of the furnace behind the curtain, he will remember, and love me, never to forget me.

The dulcet tones of Tom Jones ring out through the speakers.

"The nights grow cold, my search for gold
Is leading nowhere
Whichever lonely road I take
It seems to go where
It's a fight to survive just until tomorrow
How can I display what I know I'm worthy of?
When they turn me away?

The doors are closed to such as I
A boy from nowhere
But not to those who merely buy the right
To go where
They'll be met with respect,
not humiliation
A man's place on earth
I have come to realise
Is decided by birth
So, what's the future
No matter where I go, I will still belong…"

As the weeping congregation leaves the chapel, the song continues.

The sun breaks through the clouds, sending a warmth across the streets of Seacroft. Birds fly back and forth from one rooftop to another, the odd stray dog barking, chasing cars along the road. The sound of children playing fills the air.

The everyday folk going about their daily routines, continuing their normal everyday lives.

Life continues.

The End.